YOU ARE WEALTHY
... STARTING NOW!

Free Your Wealthy Mindset - Develop Your Life's Wealth Plan

C. G. Musgrave

YOU ARE WEALTHY… STARTING NOW!

Paperback ISBN-13: 978-1-43824-167-8
Paperback ISBN-10: 1-43824-167-4

Contents

* Companion excel worksheet explained, with illustrations & examples

Mission Statements

❏   To focus and educate on what value and wealth really means, and how anyone can reasonably become wealthy.

❏   To provide effective and simple-to-use excel spreadsheet tools to help you develop, assess and apply your very own detailed wealth plan.

❏   To empower low to average income people to rewire attitudes and behaviour about consumption, debt, savings and investments in order to obtain real wealth and freedom.

❏   To discuss various value perspectives to challenge and expand your understanding of wealth, and to help find the best fit to maximize opportunities while limiting risks.

❏   To prepare youth of the legacy costs they will be forced to deal with individually, and to know that more responsible government is needed to manage our nations future wealth.

In short, to develop and put into action your wealthy mindset!

Dedication & Acknowledgements

To my Dad, who provided the vision of wealth that I needed, and draw on every day!

Many thanks to Barb, Bart, Mabel and Eddie for reviewing and editing this project.

Introduction

You are wealthy… starting now! How can this be? I didn't think I was wealthy a minute ago. My crappy car is the same. My home isn't any bigger or luxurious, or my TV, my watch, my clothes, or anything else for that matter. I just looked and my bank account isn't any bigger, and my credit card balance isn't any smaller. Heck, I'm struggling just to pay the bills. There's a stack of them right in front of me and I'm still waiting for it to disappear. Where's the beef here?

Waiting? What are you waiting for? Do you hope to find a magic lantern, to rub it and suddenly all your bills disappear with a pile of money in its place? Or do you believe everything works out over time in its own way? Not likely! If it did, then you should already be better off today then last month, last year, and 5-years ago. Are you?

If you are that's great! How much better off are you? Can you measure this in dollar terms? If you keep this up will it be enough for later, so that you don't have to work until you die? Do you believe the new things you keep buying means that you must be better off now than before? For a moment perhaps, but are you even buying these things with cash, or with credit?

Have you ever thought, maybe I should just throw in the towel and give up trying? This all seems hopeless. I'm just not lucky. My hands are tied keeping up day by day, month by month and so on. As soon as I get a break somehow, I'll figure this all out later.

Hogwash, wealth doesn't work that way. Later becomes later again, and then never at all! Action must be taken now… right now! The good news is that you already started by opening this book. I'm not even going to wimp out and say that I don't have all the answers. I think I do, from start to finish, the what, the where, the when and the why. The-who is you! And I can show you how to do this within your means today. I'll show you where you are, where you need to be, and how to get there. This is all about your wealth plan, not mine or someone else's. Will you let me show you the way?

Hello! Are you still there? Good! Where's the catch you say? Well, we do need to go over some basic fundamental wealth concepts, which I call The Wealthy Mindset. My dad taught me these concepts when I was 8-years old. I've refined them a bit and added a few of my own, while trying to keep everything within any high-school students grasp. There's some heavier math work later on, plus my own story and future views, to fatten the book up, but you will already have the meat of what you need to know by then.

For this to work, you do need to put these wealth concepts into action, from now on, forever. Before you ask, you do not have to slash and burn your expenses! But you may have to make some adjustments to live within your means and save a little. A little, you say? Yes a little, saving 10% of your net income does the trick for most of us. Maybe less if you are ahead of the game with some savings already, or you don't have much debt. In any event this shouldn't hurt too much, look at it as just what the wealth doctor ordered.

But I wouldn't have the first clue where to put this extra money, to make it grow. Good! Then you don't have any bad investment habits to break. Investing can be as simple or as complex as you want it to be. Simple is always better! People want to make it harder, depending on their personality. Some feel they need to know everything first, or hire the best investment guru, to make their money "work hard". If you can do basic math, or use a calculator, you can do this all yourself, easier, cheaper and with superior results. But only if you focus on real investments, not risky stuff, and turn off any noise that wastes time or distracts you from wealth building routines. How did anyone invest before stock-talk TV, analysts and stockbrokers? I wonder… not! Trust me, all you need, to invest successfully, to even outperform most experts, is found here and between your ears!

But I don't make a lot of money! Well, that could be a problem. You do need to make at least the legal minimum wage per hour, or close to this, to become wealthy. If you don't make at least this much, this book is not going to help you. When you do start earning this, read on. For those still with me, minimum wage or higher, let's keep going.

So you are, making at least the minimum wage per hour. Great! Maybe you are at the other end of the wage scale, earning lots of money, or at least lots compared to someone making only the minimum wage. You think you are doing ok, or not, and you want to do better. The main thing you have in common with the minimum wage earner is that you too can barely keep up with your bills. You make more money each year, but you don't know if you are better off now than a year ago, and you have no idea if you will have enough to retire wealthy someday. Sorry, but you are just as poor as the minimum wage earner, you just have more stuff to pay down each month!

Wealth is not measured in stuff! How many or few, how big or small, your house, your car and personal belongings are, doesn't matter. Not even how much you make really matters. These things only show your bank and the Jones' next door how much stuff you can rent. How much you save is what matters! Those other things don't matter because you will never be wealthy unless you live within your means. If you don't, your employer and your debtors are in control, because they can take your stuff away.

An Eskimo in an igloo with a winter's worth of blubber may be wealthier than someone who could lose everything if they lost their job tomorrow. The Eskimo builds his igloo and catches his own food that is plentiful and close. He controls his livelihood. Farmers should be wealthy too, but the Eskimo has two major advantages. The farmer doesn't control crop prices and has debts to repay! Our modern world measures wealth in money, not blubber. We need enough money to support our lifestyle for the foreseeable future. You may have enough money to keep going a while longer, but to be wealthy you need a plan that saves enough to support your lifestyle forever, including paying off all debts. This is an outdated example as Eskimos are Inuit and most don't live in igloos anymore.

Wealth starts with a wealth plan, knowing where you are and where you are going. This is nothing new. Surely you've heard this before. Imagine showing up at an unknown place, not knowing how you got there, where to go, how to get back, or what to do while you're there.

You might ask someone for direction, but they are not you and don't know what's really going on in your head. Wealth is more than just direction because it's also about freedom, security and control over everything you need for as long as you live. This involves also knowing what's going on in your heart, and everyone is different.

From this book you will at least take away some great wealth building ideas. This is where most personal finance books end, after the author tells you to do it this way or how someone else did it. The difference with this book are the excel tools provided, designed to do it your way, to be updated as often as your situation changes. They were designed to be your personal wealth mirror, with answers that really work, that only seem like magic. There are many examples and scenarios, but the only ones that count are the ones you enter. The results are yours. Reality check first, then answers!

You start by changing blue-cells to your numbers, mostly from memory. This gets you thinking about details. All these ins and outs put together help you visualize where your cash flows are really going. The math is done for you. Then play around with your income, expenses, loan payments and savings, to show where you could be next year. This is simple to do and there are no manuals to read. Everything is color-coded and there are comment help flags. Guide amounts are already filled in, for when you don't know an amount. Once your wealth path is set for next year, the future becomes easy to predict.

The result is your easy-to-build personal wealth plan. This includes 'Your Wealth Now, in a Nutshell', 'Wealth Creation Budget', mortgage 'Amortization Table', plus 'Time and Compounding' savings tables. Everything is factored in, your income, taxes, expenses, debts, savings, investment returns and even inflation. You also have my 'Value Stock Selector', a simple investment model to quickly identify the best value stocks in the Dow Jones Industrial Average and S&P 100. If you need them, you will also find 'Value Calculators' to help you better understand Discounted Cash Flows, compounding methods, annuity payments, how bonds really work, plus the value perspectives of legendary value investors Benjamin Graham, Warren Buffett and Peter Lynch.

A well thought-out plan always works best. A little time invested upfront leads to less stress, less work, less time and less risk later on. Writing this down helps you visualize, focus and stay committed. Results are then not only more predictable, they are better than expected as successes compound to where you start feeling lucky.

Your wealth plan is designed to also help you plan a better lifestyle with more wealth, if needed. The ultimate goal of this book is to help you become independently wealthy, when you can live off of your investments alone. I'm confident in your commitment as soon as you see the effects of small changes planned over time.

This book is all about replacing illusions of wealth with real wealth! Don't worry about terminology; simple analogies and common sense everyday scenarios are used to make everything easy to follow. You are wealthy... starting now, because wealth starts from the moment your wealth plan is set in motion. No more "Buts", let's get started.

Foreword
Summary about each chapter and how to use this book

Wealth experience, philosophy and general information are important, but I also want to offer readers a more tangible take-away – instead of just shelving this book away with other personal finance books. Wisdom and motivation are nice, but I don't believe they really change behaviour meaningfully – long enough to turn your financial situation around. I'm after that sticky factor, to keep you referencing this book often.

All of my companion excel spreadsheets are easy to understand and use. Empower yourself by simply updating a few blue-cells – the result is your complete personal wealth plan. Play with it, save it, print it, reference it, live it! Instead of just reading how-to, you can now apply your wealthy mindset as you advance through each chapter!

Note: This book's publisher does not provide CD's with book orders. Instead email: YourWealthPlan@YouAreWealthyStartingNow.com . Please reference your packing slip or receipt and indicate the order number, date and where purchased, and the price paid. As soon as I confirm this is a new-book purchase, I will email you a free copy of 'Your Wealth Plan' – my 6 spreadsheets referenced throughout this book. If this is a used-book purchase, or you would just like to buy a 'Your Wealth Plan' CD, I can email you where this can be ordered online. Your email address remains confidential and will not be shared.

Chapters 1 & 2
This book starts at the beginning, boiling wealth, in all its forms such as life, happiness, knowledge, money etc., down to managing limited resources well. Fully appreciating these simple but essential concepts are the foundation to get and hold onto real wealth. To be wealthy, you need to think and act wealthy – call it this book's philosophy, if you will.

'The Wealthy Mindset' and 'First Key to Wealth: Savings' dive into these concepts as your future way of thinking wealthy. Topics include: value, needs versus wants, surpluses, luck, working capitals, tangibility and risk.

'Your Wealth Now, in a Nutshell' helps you quickly and easily determine your wealth needs – retirement goals and monthly savings rate, while factoring in taxes, inflation, current savings and investment returns, detailed over the next year and for up to 50-years.

Chapter 3

The 'Wealth Creation Budget' is a detailed yet simple to use Income & Expense Planner, Personal or Family Budget, and Investment Planner, all in one. Start by entering all of your investments, loans & mortgage, and personal assets into the Payments Table and Investment Planner. Then enter your income and expenses – broken down under Mini-Budgets. As yearly income and expenses are entered, you also see these displayed per work: day, week, month and year – to see where your money is spent, as it is earned.

This budget builds in 10% of your net income as a savings rate, as a financial expense – change this to your savings rate determined in chapter 2.1. Complete your budget by applying yearend results as contributions to investments or against loans – even track your RSP & RESP limits and carry forwards, and gauge your Next Home Affordability. This process lays everything out for you, to help you visually discover where better value is needed, and what to tinker with, until your next year's Wealth Creation Budget balances.

The 'Amortization Table' helps you analyze how your long-term loans and mortgage really break down. Quickly and easily setup almost any loan scenario, to then view every payment's details for up to 30-years. Change any payment, at any payment date, to see the short and long-term effects on total interest paid. Structure your upcoming mortgage renewal, in the privacy of your home – to best meet your needs, not your banker's!

Chapter 4

At this point in the book you will have already determined your wealth needs, and how to generate more savings. Now you can project wealth forward with 'Time and Compounding' tables. Four realistic long-term savings plans are explained, with their advantages and disadvantages to each other. The last table shows how to factor-in the negative effects of inflation over time – with education costs examples.

This chapter shows why it's just as important to strategically structure savings, as it is to make the right investments. Everyday time and compounding scenarios are used to help you fully put into perspective the long-term effects of investing: early vs. later in life, increasing vs. set yearly amounts, tax sheltered vs. unsheltered, reinvest tax refunds vs. spending them, tax sheltered educational plans and grants, and nominal returns vs. real returns after inflation. For easy comparison, the first three savings tables are setup to show the same million dollar goal in 50-years, with only the yearly savings amount adjusted. Now you have all the pieces to map out your wealth plan for the rest of your life!

Chapter 5

At this point you will know if your wealth plan is on track or if higher returns are needed. This chapter is all about 'Value Investing' – why and how it is the most reliable way to safely achieve above average long-term returns. Value investing focuses on discovering fundamentally undervalued businesses, both private and publicly traded. Topics include: intrinsic present value, rational value perception, predictable returns vs. speculation, timing, contrarianism, diversification, skilled management, and why mutual funds usually under-perform the market while value investor Warren Buffett consistently out-performs.

The many pros and cons of investing in professionally managed 'Mutual Funds, versus Trading Stocks & Bonds' are explained next. Any questions you had about which way offers you the best value, should be answered after reading this. You will then know how-to deal with: mountains of information, fees, dollar cost averaging, asset allocation, stockbrokers vs. online trading, investment themes and techniques etc.

Next are my top 10 reasons why only 5 to 10 quality stocks are needed. Then my 'Value Stock Selector' is explained as a quick and easy way to identify undervalued stocks within the S&P 100 – including and focusing on the 30 Dow Jones Industrial Average stocks. It only takes you about 15-minutes to update – producing five quick values, added together, and each stock's score and rank. The rationale of why this investment model should outperform the market is fully explained. Learn from it, and if you believe in buy-low sell-high – only the safest, largest, proven, quality companies that continue to pay high dividends and earnings – this might be the investment method for you!

You also need to look behind the numbers, to decide your personal comfort level with each stock. 'Company Value Perspectives' discuss recent events around some of these stocks, with opinions how this may affect future values – and how the Value Stock Selector reacted then. The purpose is to help you really get to know a company – its history, how it compares and its growth outlook – to further develop your understanding and common sense feel about everything that affects a stocks value, before you buy it!

Do you want to know how analysts and professional investors really think? 'Value Calculators' demonstrate various financial concepts that may seem complex at first, until you see them broken down into related parts – revealing most of the mystery of financial analysis. Also learn the simple value formulas and common sense investment principles of legendary value investors Benjamin Graham, Warren Buffett and Peter Lynch.

Chapter 6

'Global Value Perspectives' opine how individual wealth relates to a nations wealth – pointing out likely future consequences unless we better position our wealth resources soon. Many of us are too busy wearing out credit cards to realize that major systemic financial chaos may be on the horizon. You may know that US debt is over $9 trillion, but did you know that total municipal, state and federal debt is around $60 trillion – with social security, Medicare and other under funded liabilities added in? Are you and your kids prepared to pay this growing debt – over half a million dollars per US household?

Governments have no real plan, and baby boomers start retiring en-masse in 2008! Like deer caught in the headlights, unaware of the dangers ahead, we watch ambivalently as the dollar's value continues to fall – and gold values rise. USD standing as the world's reserve currency is now in question – hastened by the prospect of peak oil in just a few years, if not already? Every aspect of our economy depends on energy! Individuals and nations both need to prepare, and find reasonable alternatives fast, as cheap oil will soon be gone forever. Also, global leadership is shifting from the US to China as a result of massive trade and capital imbalances – simply put, a nation of spenders vs. a nation of savers. Once you have a good feel how all these economic pieces trend together, you can strategically position wealth defensively, and even profit from crisis as events unfold.

Chapter 7

'My Value Perspectives' is a revealing portrayal from child to adult, sharing my dad's wealth lessons. I've owned small retail businesses, to fully licensed stockbroker, to director and large stockholder of public companies, to area franchisee of one of the world's largest franchise. I understand wealth concepts, have a strong work ethic, and saved and invested from an early age. In a haphazard way, changing career paths every five years, I achieved wealth in spite of leaving huge amounts on the table and by doing everything the hard way. Nobody is perfect, life is messy at times, and my experiences show how a solid wealth foundation helps you recover and succeed – regardless of the pitches life throws your way.

Chapter 1
The Wealthy Mindset

Do you really want to be wealthy? If so, we should start by defining what Wealth is.

Wealth doesn't have the same meaning to everyone. What is of value to you is a personal decision. For some it is simply an abundance of money, or things that can be acquired with money. For others it represents a carefree lifestyle that includes these things, plus ideals such as good health, happiness, wisdom, faith and family etc.

Whatever your definition of wealth, I suggest we all agree that wealth is a store of Value!

At the top of a blank page you should write down 'Things of Value'. This will serve as a visual aid, to help you stay focused on creating a well thought out and defined plan, the first step to achieving any goal.

We should also agree that a Wealth Plan focuses on Needs before Wants. From now on you should start thinking about needs as all necessary consumption, and wants as unnecessary consumption. The major difference between the two is that needs are limited, whereas wants are unlimited or an insatiable moving target.

As needs are satisfied, any extra income available is a surplus for building wealth or satisfying wants. Planning for wealth comes down to visualizing needs over wants and choosing to prioritize saving over extra spending. Getting started is easier than you think, when you have the tools to properly show the results are worth the effort.

Your first step towards Wealth Creation is simply committing to value and need wealth! In the past you may have said to yourself, "I want wealth". From now on you must say, "I need wealth". Wants are mainly fantasy, whereas needs are planned for and actually get achieved. To be absolutely certain, write it down and say it out loud. This is not psychobabble; do not skim past this. If you don't have a pen, get one. If your throat is sore, just whisper it. Memorize these three empowering words "I need wealth".

The next step is determining your regular Income Surpluses, needed to build Savings and wealth predictably, as discussed in chapters 2 and 3. The other chapters focus mainly on how to efficiently structure wealth and how to enhance investment returns safely.

Everyone has Basic Needs such as food, water, shelter, clothing, transportation etc that cost us value or money. There are also basic needs such as air, sleep, faith, family, happiness and health etc. that may or may not cost us money.

In today's modern civilization, needs are broader than just basic needs and should also include Reasonable Needs such as entertainment, vacations, gifts, fees and service charges etc. at reasonable costs.

When all your basic and reasonable needs are met now and for the foreseeable future, you have achieved wealth! This does not mean you are Rich, which I would argue is simply having a store of value far beyond your needs.

If your first reaction to this is that you instead want to be rich, you must realize that in order to be rich you must first become wealthy! It doesn't really matter whether you are making $25,000 or $250,000 or more a year, as long as you live within your means.

If you consume more than your income and savings then you are not wealthy. If, for the foreseeable future, you will consume equal to or less than your income and savings, you are wealthy!

In other words wealth is having the means to take care of your needs, while being rich is simply having a surplus of wealth. A wealthy mindset prioritizes needs but may later pursue wants after all needs are taken care of, only if wealth surpluses are available.

At the end of each year most people don't know where they are in terms of wealth because they don't have a wealth plan. The single most important way to create wealth is to plan for it. Otherwise you are not creating wealth, losing wealth, or have no idea.

If you don't have a wealth plan to know where you are and where you are going, how will you measure and know if you are wealthy or not? A live only for today attitude, without a wealth plan, invites all kinds of problems we will discuss later.

In order to create and value wealth properly requires a wealth plan and a Wealthy Mindset. It is that simple, the rest is just detail!

To increase your wealth and lifestyle, regular surpluses are needed. Surpluses represent investment capital and deferred consumption for you or your estate. The only way to create a yearly surplus or savings is to add value or increase income, or lower consumption and expenses, or some combination of these.

To otherwise purchase things above your current means on credit, this only defers payment, reducing savings and future consumption. Add on the financing costs associated with borrowing and this type of excess consumption lifestyle pattern should be viewed as Wealth Destruction.

In a way wants represent the opposite of savings and wealth creation, because in order to acquire wants you unnecessarily spend and create a wealth deficit. If you focus on wants as a primary goal, this is contrary to a wealthy mindset and to achieving wealth!

Wants are also a moving target, having nothing to do with needs. Wants tend to increase over time via media exposure and peer pressure, in an endless effort to create and convince you there is a need for new things that may not be needed.

You control your wealth destiny! There will always be a bigger yacht to want, but if you focus primarily on your needs you may actually be able to afford it some day!

Some believe Luck is a major component of wealth. This argument may hold true if you consider lottery winnings or a large inheritance. We should look at this as simply unreasonable odds for momentary good fortune.

Even this type of luck is not real wealth as it is far too common how many supposedly wealthy people lose their fortunes because they don't have a wealthy mindset to guide their consumption decisions.

When referring to family fortunes built and lost, there is a saying that the first generation creates wealth, the second generation enhances wealth, but by the third generation it is lost. In most cases I expect this has more to do with a lack of passing on the meaning of value and wealth, lack of planning and risky decisions, than actual bad luck.

The first generation builds a successful company, operates it within a defined business plan and budget, growing it successfully with a wealthy mindset. The second generation benefits from the first generation's teachings and manages the business well, maintaining growth and generating further surpluses.

However somewhere between the first and third generation something critical is lost. The wealthy mindset of living within ones means is exchanged for living in excess. Lifestyle wants become the focal point, instead of needs.

Hard and smart work within a plan and budget is substituted with impulse and extravagant consumption, reckless financial decisions and speculation, all which more often than not result in wealth destruction. In short the third generation inherited good fortune, but lost it as a result of not having a wealthy mindset.

We started by defining wealth as a store of value. Now we know that it is just as important to appreciate that in order to achieve wealth, or to maintain or grow it, that it is not the monetary value of savings alone that is the primary measure of wealth, but rather a wealthy mindset in action that is of most importance!

If you develop a wealthy mindset you can achieve wealth starting with little or nothing. Even if savings are lost somehow, this is usually only a temporary setback. Without a wealthy mindset, wealth is instead just a mirage or craps shoot at best and you will most likely not be wealthy. A wealthy mindset stacks the odds of success very much in your favour!

Those who are lucky enough to come into good fortune, but do not have a wealthy mindset, most likely will not be wealthy for long. Wealth is a mindset that understands these ideals intimately and practices them everyday with every decision that affects income, savings or consumption!

Wealthy people understand value and live within their means. They see luck as creating the conditions in order to be in position to take advantage of opportunities as they become available, or to solve problems effectively.

The only real luck is the unexpected opportunities or problems that occur. A wealthy mindset understands this and is prepared to act when luck presents itself, good or bad!

Therefore it is true that a wealthy person needs luck, but luck doesn't just happen. Luck is created by discipline, persistence and patience within a wealthy mindset. In other words the harder and smarter you work, save and invest, the luckier you will become!

To complete your first wealth steps, under 'Things of Value' draw a line down the centre of the page and label the left column 'Needs' and the right column 'Wants'. Your needs are your basic and reasonable needs as described above, within your current means. Your wants are everything else you desire, but don't really need.

You should expand and refine this list over time with more detail and actual costs or estimates. Your list of 'Things of Value' forces you to think about the differences between needs and wants to help focus and reinforce your wealthy mindset when creating your Wealth Creation Budget in chapter 3.

Chapter 2
First Key to Wealth: Savings

As stated earlier, savings come from income surpluses. By definition, an income surplus can only result if the inputs of after-tax earned income and net gains on investments are greater than the outputs of all expenses and debt consumption.

In other words we can only generate savings if we live below our means, spending less than we take in. Savings are the First Key to Wealth and should be viewed as Wealth Creation Working Capital.

Working capital includes your money savings, plus all other tangible and intangible stores of value used to create wealth. Tangibility relates to certain value if sold and its collateral loan value if you need to borrow against it.

Tangible stores of value should have a reasonably predictable Market Value. Tangibility increases with more buyers, which increases the ability to sell, making value easier to determine. The most common way to determine relevant tangibility is the stock, bond and real estate markets, and how much your bank will loan against an asset.

A wealthy mindset does not set value at the purchase price. Retail prices are not a relevant gauge of tangibility unless you are a retailer. Tangibility relates to the value received when you sell, or borrow against the value of something.

For example government bonds and T-bills are very tangible as current and future value at maturity is known and the ability to sell is instantaneous. Stock markets are also tangible, as current values are known, however future tangibility is less certain.

Investments with lower perceived Risk are more tangible as collateral, because your bank or broker may loan you a higher percentage of its current market value.

Collectibles such as baseball cards or art for investment purposes may be considered tangible. However they are not tangible unless the eventual value and the buyer are reasonably certain. What happens to value if that one eventual buyer goes broke or dies, or your collectible becomes damaged or proven a fake?

Personal assets such as a car, boat, appliances and electronics etc. may also be tangible assets. Market value can usually be determined easily and accurately with many buyers available. Personal assets may also be considered expenses, as they are replaced often and tend to depreciate in value very quickly from the moment purchased. In other words personal assets are low quality tangible assets because they do not create wealth.

Cash savings, a home and investment real estate, securities such as stocks or bonds and some types of insurance are considered tangibles. Business assets, collectibles, patents, copyrights and even personal assets like cars and appliances may be included, as long as you can reasonably determine market value now and when expected to be sold.

Tangibility has more to do with determining value than risk. However, it does factor into risk decisions as it relates to market value and liquidity. In other words one component of risk is the ability to turn an asset into a predictable amount of cash quickly.

If something can be sold or transferred now or in the future, for money or something of similar predictable value, then it is tangible. Otherwise, for wealth creation purposes it should be considered low quality, risky or an investment speculation.

In order to be considered an investment for wealth creation purposes, your wealth capital must have a reasonable expectation to increase in value and add to savings. The word reasonable relates to the level of risk and tangibility.

A wealthy mindset understands the importance of tangibility and minimizing risk when deploying working capital within a wealth plan!

Intangible stores of value include your physical health and ability to work, education, training, experience and any special talents. They also include your mental, spiritual, marital and family stability. Conceptually they may even include your motivating hopes and dreams, and even your personality.

These human traits should be considered working capital because they affect many of your decisions to earn income, control expenses, and to make reasonable investments.

However, intangible working capital is impossible or at best difficult to value in dollar terms. They are personal assets that can't be sold or transferred, but still important to consider regularly because they contribute or have costs that affect your wealthy mindset and ability to generate and manage wealth.

All working capital is affected by Capital Gains or Losses, and by Debt. Capital gains increase working capital, while capital losses and debt are an offset or drain on working capital. Essentially savings and working capital are synonymous.

The main difference is that savings are liquid or easily and quickly exchangeable into money, whereas working capital tends to change in value over time. Savings have a low risk of loss, while working capital may have a higher risk profile. The important point is that working capital and debt need to be consistently managed properly to create long-term wealth.

It should be obvious by now that you have a wealth surplus when after-tax income, savings and working capital are cumulatively growing faster than the cost of all expenses and debt. These are the main controllable components to drive your wealth plan.

A wealthy mindset also manages well the two expenses that are unavoidable, Taxes and Inflation! You need to value all taxable income in after-tax dollars and all taxable expenses with the sales tax included.

For that matter you need to view the input value received when something is sold, or the output value paid when purchased, with all taxes, fees and service charges etc. factored in. In other words don't just focus on the sticker price, but the total price after all the plus, plus, pluses have been added in.

As for inflation, we mainly need to know that prices tend to go up over time, affecting the value of savings negatively. Even if savings increase in nominal dollar value terms, they also need to maintain their purchasing power, or the real value of goods and services they would have been able to purchase earlier. In other words cash savings are very tangible today but do not have the same future value, as prices tend to inflate over time.

To recap, a Wealthy Mindset understands:

❑   Wealth in terms of needs, rather than wants.

❑   Luck benefits only those in position to take advantage of it.

❑   Regular surplus income and savings are needed to create wealth.

❑   Various types of working capital and appreciates the inherent value of tangibility and minimizing risk.

❑   Only after-tax income offers you value, and when things are purchased and sold, that all sales taxes, fees and service charges must be factored-in.

❑   Today's value is not the same tomorrow because of inflation.

Your wealth plan starts by showing where you are and where you need to be. The next chapter 'Your Wealth Now, in a Nutshell' provides the tools to do this effectively.

Chapter 2.1
Your Wealth Now, in a Nutshell

Your Wealth Now,
A Small Amount Saved Every Month G‹

25.00%	of gross pay,	to pay taxes,	= net income.	Target net inc a
yearly	$ 25,000.00	$ 6,250.00	$ 18,750.00	$ 18,750.00 yr
monthly	$ 2,083.33	$ 520.83	$ 1,562.50	$ 1,562.50 m

A net of $ 39,329.39 after-tax, at a   25.00%   tax rate, equals
To get $ 52,439.19 per year future income, at an   11.00%   R

If you already have savings, enter this amount here: $.
10.00% of net income, to save/invest,   at ROI % of = future value

yearly	$ 18,750.00	$ 1,875.00	11.00%	$ 1,990.56
monthly	$ 1,562.50	$ 156.25	0.92%	after 1-year

Monthly Savings - Month by Month

month	start balance	add monthly	interest added	month end bal
1	$ -	$ 156.25	$ 1.43	$ 157.68
2	$ 157.68	$ 156.25	$ 2.88	$ 316.81
3	$ 316.81	$ 156.25	$ 4.34	$ 477.40
4	$ 477.40	$ 156.25	$ 5.81	$ 639.45
5	$ 639.45	$ 156.25	$ 7.29	$ 803.00
6	$ 803.00	$ 156.25	$ 8.79	$ 968.04
7	$ 968.04	$ 156.25	$ 10.31	$ 1,134.60
8	$ 1,134.60	$ 156.25	$ 11.83	$ 1,302.68
9	$ 1,302.68	$ 156.25	$ 13.37	$ 1,472.30
10	$ 1,472.30	$ 156.25	$ 14.93	$ 1,643.48
11	$ 1,643.48	$ 156.25	$ 16.50	$ 1,816.23
12	$ 1,816.23	$ 156.25	$ 18.08	$ 1,990.56
totals	$ -	$ 1,875.00	$ 115.56	$ 1,990.56

- change dark-blue cells: tax rate, gross pay, target net income,
yrs= to retire, ROI, current savings, % of net income to save/invest.
- if needed, change light-blue cells, but they won't update after this!
- if you see ### in a cell, just left-click the right-edge of that cell's
lettered column above, and pull this to the right to view the number!
- Monthly Savings tables assume tax sheltered investment growth!

in a Nutshell

⟩es A Very Long Way Over Time!

t retirement in,	at inflation of,	is a future value net income of
s = 30	2.50%	$39,329.39 yearly after tax
ths 360	per year	$3,277.45 mthly after tax

pre-tax inc. of $ 52,439.19 as your future target income.
$ 476,719.90

Monthly Savings - Year by Year

assuming net income increases 2.50% every year!

yr	monthly	future value	yr	monthly	future value
1	$ 156.25	$ 1,990.56	26	$ 289.68	$ 336,486.57
2	$ 160.16	$ 4,261.23	27	$ 296.92	$ 379,207.05
3	$ 164.16	$ 6,845.67	28	$ 304.34	$ 426,965.66
4	$ 168.26	$ 9,781.46	29	$ 311.95	$ 480,347.78
5	$ 172.47	$ 13,110.57	30	$ 319.75	$ 540,006.56
6	$ 176.78	$ 16,879.84	31	$ 327.74	$ 606,670.83
7	$ 181.20	$ 21,141.60	32	$ 335.94	$ 681,153.79
8	$ 185.73	$ 25,954.23	33	$ 344.34	$ 764,362.83
9	$ 190.38	$ 31,382.93	34	$ 352.95	$ 857,310.39
10	$ 195.13	$ 37,500.47	35	$ 361.77	$ 961,126.14
11	$ 200.01	$ 44,388.06	36	$ 370.81	$1,077,070.55
12	$ 205.01	$ 52,136.39	37	$ 380.08	$1,206,550.01
13	$ 210.14	$ 60,846.63	38	$ 389.59	$1,351,133.73
14	$ 215.39	$ 70,631.74	39	$ 399.33	$1,512,572.60
15	$ 220.78	$ 81,617.78	40	$ 409.31	$1,692,820.16
16	$ 226.30	$ 93,945.42	41	$ 419.54	$1,894,056.13
17	$ 231.95	$ 107,771.67	42	$ 430.03	$2,118,712.50
18	$ 237.75	$ 123,271.76	43	$ 440.78	$2,369,502.81
19	$ 243.70	$ 140,641.22	44	$ 451.80	$2,649,454.67
20	$ 249.79	$ 160,098.27	45	$ 463.10	$2,961,946.12
21	$ 256.03	$ 181,886.42	46	$ 474.67	$3,310,746.21
22	$ 262.43	$ 206,277.42	47	$ 486.54	$3,700,060.22
23	$ 269.00	$ 233,574.49	48	$ 498.70	$4,134,580.15
24	$ 275.72	$ 264,116.03	49	$ 511.17	$4,619,541.05
25	$ 282.61	$ 298,279.61	50	$ 523.95	$5,160,783.87

Y ou now have the background on why savings matter most in creating, building and determining wealth. It only makes sense to start your wealth plan by putting this into better perspective with your own numbers.

On the CD enclosed, or the .xls file emailed to you (see **Note** on page 11) you will find an excel workbook called 'Wealth Plan'. Save and Open it on your computer. It contains six powerful wealth-planning tools that anyone can master easily. The first spreadsheet you will see is 'Your Wealth Now, in a Nutshell'.

This spreadsheet is designed to better visualize and plan your monthly savings rate going forward. More importantly it shows you if this is enough. Then you will know if and where changes are needed. You simply update the blue-cells, starting with your yearly gross income, to then see the green-cell results automatically update.

There are several blue-cells you may want to update, but you only need to focus on the 7 dark-blue-cells. Amounts are already filled-in as a guideline for when you don't know something. The best way to explain how these tables work is to use the example provided. You need to update this later with your own amounts.

The 'Your Wealth Now, in a Nutshell' table shows how a small amount saved every month goes a very long way over time. See, it even says this at the top of the page. It shows a person making $25,000 yearly, $2,083.33 monthly, at a 25% tax rate paying $6,250 in taxes yearly, $520.83 monthly, with a net income of $18,750 yearly, $1,562.50 monthly.

To the right of this you will see a target net income of $18,750. Roll your mouse pointer over this cell to read the red help flag, "yearly net income that you would like to receive at retirement? Assume you have no mortgage/debts then". Below this cell is another red help flag, "current net income, or adjust to lifestyle desired in today's dollars". In other words your target net income at retirement, ignoring inflation for now, is assumed to be the same as today. Actually you can afford a higher lifestyle, assuming you have no debt payments by then. You may make this higher or lower of course, in today's dollars.

Retirement is far away, so you figure out how much yearly net income is needed in 30-years. To allow for higher prices over time, you build in a 2.50% inflation rate, half way between the government's long-term inflation rate targets of 2% to 3%. This shows a target 30-year future value net income of $39,329.39 yearly, $3,277.45 monthly.

The next table shows that a net of $39,329.39 after-tax, at a 25% tax rate, equals pre-tax income of $52,439.19 as your future target income, yearly after retirement. To get $52,439.19 per year future income, at an 11% ROI, return on investment, you see that you need to target future savings in 30-years of approximately $476,719.90.

If you know you are getting a pension at retirement, you may reduce the $39,329.39 blue-cell amount by your expected net after-tax yearly pension. Another way is to reduce the $52,439.19 blue-cell amount by your gross pre-tax pension. Just don't do it both ways! If your pension is not reliable, leave it out and think of it as a potential wealth bonus.

The next table shows $0 savings, and 10% of net income to save and invest from now on. This does not include equity in your home or personal items that you need to use. 10% of net income works out to $1,875 yearly, and you commit to contributing $156.25 monthly to your tax-sheltered retirement plan, used to buy a mutual fund you did your homework on. In addition to tax savings, you anticipate a ROI of 11% yearly, 0.92% compounded monthly, that you believe is reasonable based on the mutual fund's past performance and long-term stock market returns. You then see that your monthly investment savings should be worth approximately $1,990.56 after one year. Stay with me, it gets better!

You are curious how this $1,990.56 breaks down month-by-month over the first full year. The next table is like a 1-year savings flow planner, showing each month's: starting balance, $156.25 added, interest or investment growth added, and month end balance. Your first year totals show $0 savings to start, plus $1,875 saved over the year, plus $115.56 investment growth, that all adds up to $1,990.56. If your income varies throughout the year, you can even adjust the green-cells to reflect monthly changes.

You also want to see the effects of saving small amounts monthly over your 30-years to retirement. The table to the right shows this for up to 50-years going forward. You realize that your net income and monthly savings should go up each year, but you are not sure by how much. So you assume they will go up by at least the 2.5% inflation rate set before.

Year-1 shows $156.25, year-2 is $160.16, all the way up to year-50 at $523.95 saved monthly. This all seems doable, right? It also shows year-1 future savings of $1,990.56, year-2 at $4,261.23, all the way up to year-50 at $5,160,783.87. No, that is not a typo, almost $5.2 million is correct. You started with $0 savings, saved $156.25 monthly, bumping this up by 2.5% every year, invested at an 11% return compounded monthly at 0.92%, in a tax-deferred retirement account for 50-years.

$5.2 million sounds great, but your goal was to retire much earlier than 50-years. You see the year-30 future value is $540,006.56, more than $63,000 over your target future savings of $476,719.90. You notice that you may even be able to retire a year earlier, as the year-29 future value is $480,347.78, a few thousand more than needed. You are wealthy… starting now, if this is you and you commit to this reasonable wealth plan. In 29-years you will also be independently wealthy and not dependent on a job anymore!

You then start to wonder what could happen if things change, as nobody has a perfect crystal ball. You would like to figure out high/low ranges and to build in a margin of safety. You can use these tables to factor-in all kinds of scenarios to help you stay on track. For example, what happens if inflation is higher than expected, or your tax rate, or if you want more at retirement than today's net income lifestyle? What happens if your return on investment is lower than expected, or you change your savings rate?

Inflation eats away at your savings value over time if your wealth plan doesn't keep pace! Your pay needs to grow by at least the inflation rate to maintain your current lifestyle and also to keep your savings on track. Pay increases tend to happen yearly, which is why the year-by-year net income and monthly savings increases every year at the inflation rate.

Inflation also affects the value of investments. If inflation is 3% and your return on investment is 11%, then your real return on investment is 8%. This is very good! However if your savings are growing at only 2%, your seemingly safe bank account is actually losing 1% in real value per year. Higher inflation means higher costs, from raw materials, to energy, to interest rates etc. Unexpected inflation rate changes can substantially affect the value of businesses, stocks and real estate in a hurry.

Every extra percentage point of investment return magnifies your overall results compounded over time. On the other hand going for higher returns is tempting but often means higher risk of losses, which can derail your wealth plan in a heartbeat. You need to find a comfort zone balance that meets your goals and is also predictably safe.

With all this in mind you want to see what can be done to increase your wealth to support double your current net income at retirement. You change the target net income blue-cell from $18,750 to $37,500. This increases target future savings to $953,439.81 and moves out your retirement to 35-years. This is no good; you want those 5-years back.

You are extra frugal with your money anyway, so you wonder if doubling your savings rate from 10% to 20% will do the trick. This puts your retirement plan back to 29-years, but you know that living off of $1,562.50 - $312.50 = $1,250 monthly is not easy. This doesn't leave any room for a better home, kids, or future extras you haven't even thought of yet. You don't want to lower your current lifestyle and need to find a middle ground.

You are young and feel confident that your career will advance quickly. Based on pay increases the last few years and how much others are making, you believe your pay will keep going up faster than 2.50% per year. You decide to change your year-by-year net income increases to 5%, which meets your target future savings in a little over 27-years.

Some of the amounts are so big that you see #### instead of numbers. Just stretch the columns wider, as described in the comment table to the left, to read these amounts.

To put your retirement back up to 30-years again, you start adjusting your savings rate down from 20%. After plugging in different amounts you find that 14.0614% works out to almost exactly the future savings needed to retire in 30-years. Round numbers are easier to work with so you decide to set your wealth savings rate at a more reasonable 15%. If you really can save 20%, just set aside 5% to allow for all those extras as needed.

Your ego believes you can do better than an 11% return on investment. Later you will read about legendary investors who regularly outperform the market, with my own methods to help you achieve this, but it is financially hazardous to assume upfront that you will beat long-term average investment returns. Instead you decide to round up your monthly save/invest blue-cell amount from $234.38 to an even $250.00 to start.

For simplicity and convenience, you also start rounding up all year-by-year monthly blue-cell amounts to the next $5. You then notice that these small extra amounts, pocket change really, start adding up to big money over time. The rounded-up year-1 to year-30 monthly savings amounts should have worked out to: $250, $265, $280, $295, $310, $330, $350, $370, $390, $410, $435, $460, $485, $510, $540, $570, $600, $630, $665, $700, $735, $775, $815, $860, $905, $955, $1,005, $1,060, $1,115, $1,175. After rounding-up year-30, you notice you can actually retire almost 2-years earlier. You now agree this is much safer and more reasonable than planning to beat an 11% return!

The year-30 future value is now $1,151,039.73, well above your $953,439.81 target. You then realize that you can start lowering your 11% return on investment, until your year-30 future savings is back down to your target future savings. You find that at 10.3287% your target future savings is $1,015,407.35 and your year-30 savings is $1,015,435.36, close enough to call them equal. In other words you have 11% - 10.3287% = 0.6713% as a return on investment margin of safety. This doesn't leave much room for error!

Investment returns have a huge impact on wealth results over time! You need to know how much lower your net income at retirement will be if returns are lower than expected, with everything else the same. At a 10% ROI your future net income needs to be adjusted down from $37,500 to $34,182 in today's dollars. At 9% it drops to $25,718, and at 8% this is down to $19,240, not even $500 more than today's net income in future dollars.

Change your target net income to $18,750, equal to today's net income, and then play around with the rate of return. You will find that you need 7.9122% returns for your year-30 future value to cover your target future savings. In other words you need 8% returns just to maintain current lifestyle at retirement, with everything else the same.

The point is to make reasonable predictions so that you can stay on track. An 11% long-term return is reasonable, as you will see later. However, if you ever thought there isn't much difference between 11% and 8%, you now realize it's the difference between retiring at today's net income lifestyle or double this amount, in future dollars.

In summary, starting with $0 savings and $25,000 yearly gross pay at a 25% tax rate, and saving 10% or $156.25 of your $1,562.50 monthly net income, increasing this yearly by 2.50%, invested at 11% yearly or 0.92% compounded monthly, the result is $540,006.56 in 30-years for retirement. This is $63,286.66 more than the $476,719.90 needed to retire independently wealthy on your investments alone. This wealth plan supports more than your current lifestyle, after factoring in taxes, expected yearly pay raises and inflation.

If you plan to retire independently wealthy at double your current net income lifestyle in 30-years, you need to save 15% of your monthly net income, instead of 10%, and round these amounts up to the next $5. You need investment returns of at least 10.33%, but you should have an additional 5% of net income saved to make up any shortfalls if needed. The bonus is that if you do achieve 11% returns, you will actually be able to retire early.

This simple wealth savings plan anticipates changes over time and builds in slack to get you back on track as needed. It helps you visualize and fully appreciate how one wealth factor affects several others over time.

Now it's time for you to play around with your numbers, to build your own target wealth savings plan. If the savings targets seem too aggressive, you may be able to find extra money in the next chapter, your Wealth Creation Budget.

Chapter 3
Wealth Creation Budget

Income	Guide	Per Year		Per Hour	
Income & Expense Planner (see **7 Easy Steps** below)					
Gross Income	<35k <75k $75k+	$ 25,000	$	12.50	gross wages
Tax Rate	25%, 30% or 40%	25%	$	3.13	tax deducted
Expenses					
Financial	20% of net income	$ 3,750	**Max.**		**Min.**
Paycheck Savings	10% of net income	$ 2,000	$ -	$	2,000
Personal Loans	10% of net, or pmt	$ 2,000	$ 6,000	$	2,000
School Loan	1.5x NI, or 15% net pmt	$ -	$ 9,000	$	3,000
Bank Charges	1% of net income	$ 200	$ 600	$	200
Professional Fees	2% of net income	$ 400	$ 1,200	$	400
Mini-Budget Target is over or under		-$850	$ 16,800	$	5,600
Health	5% of net income	$ 938	**Max.**		**Min.**
Insurance	3% of net income	$ 600	$ 1,800	$	600
Personal Care	1% of net income	$ 300	$ 1,200	$	300
Dental	1% of net income	$ 200	$ 600	$	200
Eye or Other	based on need	$ -	$ -	$	-
Other	1% of net income	$ 200	$ 600	$	200
Mini-Budget Target is over or under		-$363	$ 2,400	$	700
Home	25% of net income	$ 4,688	**Max.**		**Min.**
Mortgage or Rent	20% of net, or pmt	$ 6,000	$ 12,000	$	6,000
Property Tax & Water	1% of home value	$ -	$ 3,000	$	-
Insurance	.2% of home +$400	$ 200	$ 1,000	$	200
Maintenance	.3% of home value	$ 100	$ 900	$	100
Heat & Electric	.5% home + $1.5k	$ 600	$ 3,000	$	600
Phone, TV & Internet	1% net inc + $1.5k	$ 1,688	$ 2,100	$	1,500
Furniture & Appliances	.5% of home + $1k	$ 600	$ 3,500	$	600
Other	based on use	$ -	$ -	$	-
Mini-Budget Target is over or under		-$4,500	$ 25,500	$	9,000
Transportation	25% of net income	$ 4,688	**Max.**		**Min.**
Car Loan or Lease	15% of net income	$ 4,000	$ 9,000	$	4,000
License & Registration	$150 per vehicle	$ 150	$ 300	$	150
Insurance	2% of car + $800	$ 1,000	$ 2,000	$	1,000
Maintenance	1% of car + $400	$ 500	$ 1,000	$	500
Gas	2% of car + $800	$ 1,000	$ 2,000	$	1,000
Other	1% of car + $300	$ 400	$ 900	$	400
Mini-Budget Target is over or under		-$2,363	$ 15,200	$	7,050
Food, Clothing & Ent.	25% of net income	$ 4,688	**Max.**		**Min.**
Groceries	10% of net income	$ 2,000	$ 6,000	$	2,000
Restaurant & Snack	3% of net income	$ 600	$ 1,800	$	600
Clothing	3% of net income	$ 600	$ 1,800	$	600
Entertainment & Rec.	3% of net income	$ 600	$ 1,800	$	600
Vacation	4% of net income	$ 750	$ 2,400	$	750
Other	2% of net income	$ 400	$ 1,200	$	400
Mini-Budget Target is over or under		-$263	$ 15,000	$	4,950

Personal or Family Budget

per Work:	Day	Week	Month	Year
Gross Income	$98.04	$500.00	$2,083.33	$25,000.00
Less Taxes	$24.51	$125.00	$520.83	$6,250.00
Net Income	**$73.53**	**$375.00**	**$1,562.50**	**$18,750.00**
Expenses				
Paycheck Savings	$ 7.84	$ 40.00	$ 166.67	$ 2,000.00
Personal Loans	$ 7.84	$ 40.00	$ 166.67	$ 2,000.00
School Loan	$ -	$ -	$ -	$ -
Bank Charges	$ 0.78	$ 4.00	$ 16.67	$ 200.00
Professional Fees	$ 1.57	$ 8.00	$ 33.33	$ 400.00
Financial	**$ 18.04**	**$ 92.00**	**$ 383.33**	**$ 4,600.00**
Insurance	$ 2.35	$ 12.00	$ 50.00	$ 600.00
Personal Care	$ 1.18	$ 6.00	$ 25.00	$ 300.00
Dental	$ 0.78	$ 4.00	$ 16.67	$ 200.00
Eye Care	$ -	$ -	$ -	$ -
Other	$ 0.78	$ 4.00	$ 16.67	$ 200.00
Health	**$ 2.75**	**$ 14.00**	**$ 58.33**	**$ 1,300.00**
Mortgage or Rent	$ 23.53	$ 120.00	$ 500.00	$ 6,000.00
Property Tax & Water	$ -	$ -	$ -	$ -
Insurance	$ 0.78	$ 4.00	$ 16.67	$ 200.00
Maintenance	$ 0.39	$ 2.00	$ 8.33	$ 100.00
Heat & Electric	$ 2.35	$ 12.00	$ 50.00	$ 600.00
Phone, TV & Internet	$ 6.62	$ 33.75	$ 140.63	$ 1,687.50
Furniture & Appliances	$ 2.35	$ 12.00	$ 50.00	$ 600.00
Other	$ -	$ -	$ -	$ -
Home	**$ 36.03**	**$ 183.75**	**$ 765.63**	**$ 9,187.50**
Car Lease or Loan	$ 15.69	$ 80.00	$ 333.33	$ 4,000.00
License & Registration	$ 0.59	$ 3.00	$ 12.50	$ 150.00
Insurance	$ 3.92	$ 20.00	$ 83.33	$ 1,000.00
Maintenance	$ 1.96	$ 10.00	$ 41.67	$ 500.00
Gas	$ 3.92	$ 20.00	$ 83.33	$ 1,000.00
Other	$ 1.57	$ 8.00	$ 33.33	$ 400.00
Transportation	**$ 27.65**	**$ 141.00**	**$ 587.50**	**$ 7,050.00**
Groceries	$ 7.84	$ 40.00	$ 166.67	$ 2,000.00
Restaurant & Snack	$ 2.35	$ 12.00	$ 50.00	$ 600.00
Clothing	$ 2.35	$ 12.00	$ 50.00	$ 600.00
Entertainment	$ 2.35	$ 12.00	$ 50.00	$ 600.00
Vacation	$ 2.94	$ 15.00	$ 62.50	$ 750.00
Other	$ 1.57	$ 8.00	$ 33.33	$ 400.00
Food, Clothing & Ent.	**$ 19.41**	**$ 99.00**	**$ 412.50**	**$ 4,950.00**
Net Income or Loss	$73.53	$375.00	$1,562.50	18,750.00
- Total Expenses	$103.87	$529.75	$2,207.29	27,087.50
+ Paycheck Savings	$7.84	$40.00	$166.67	2,000.00
= Surplus or Deficit	-$22.50	-$114.75	-$478.13	-$6,337.50

Investment Planner $0.00

Next Home Affordability - Limits

Down Payment	% Down	Home Price	Mortgage	Monthly Pmt.
$ -	25.00%	$ -	$ -	$ 417

Children <18 Years	RRSP & RESP - Limits			
2	Year Max.	Unused Carry	Contr. Limit	Next Year
2006 RRSP	$ 4,500	$ -	$ 4,500	$ 4,500
2006 RESP	$ 8,000	$ 84,000	$ 8,000	$ 84,000

Investment Type	% Rate	Current Value	Contribution	Next Year
RRSP	8.00%	$ -	$0	$ -
RESP + CESG	6.50%	$ -	$0	$ -
Home	8.00%	$ -	$0	$ -
Other	0.00%	$ -	$0	$ -
Tax Sheltered	0.00%	$ -	$0	$ -
Personal Loans	15.00%	$ -	$0	$ -
Car Loan	8.50%	$ -	$0	$ -
School Loan	7.50%	$ -	$0	$ -
Business Loans	0.00%	$ -	$0	$ -
Mortgage	6.50%	$ -	$0	$ -
Other	0.00%	$ -	$0	$ -
Loans & Mortgage	0.00%	$ -	$0	$ -
Mutual Funds	8.00%	$ -	$0	$ -
Business	5.00%	$ -	$0	$ -
Other	0.00%	$ -	$0	$ -
Tax Deferred	0.00%	$ -	$0	$ -
Cashable GIC or CSB	3.00%	$ -	$0	$ -
Daily Interest Savings	2.50%	$ -	$0	$ -
Other	0.00%	$ -	$0	$ -
Taxable Cash	0.00%	$ -	$0	$ -
Personal Property	25.00%	$ -	$0	$ -
Car	20.00%	$ -	$0	$ -
Other	0.00%	$ -	$0	$ -
Depreciating Assets	0.00%	$ -	$0	$ -
Total Investments	0.00%	$ -	$0	$ -
- Loans & Mortgage	0.00%	$ -	$0	$ -
= Net Worth or Equity	0.00%	$0	$0	$0

Balance of Surplus or Deficit *to Contribute =* $0.00 *until = $0*

Simple Loan & Mortgage Calculator		Loan & Mortgage Payments Table		
		Loan Type	Monthly Pmt	# Payments
Loan or Mortgage	$ 100,000	Personal	$ -	0
Annual Interest Rate	6.50%	Personal	$ -	0
Amortization in Months	180	Car	$ -	0
Monthly Payment	**$871.11**	School	$ -	0
Yearly Payment	$ 10,453	Business	$ -	0
Total Interest	$ 56,799	Home	$ -	0
Total Principal & Interest	$ 156,799	Other	$ -	0
Interest is Compounded		12 times per yr., effective rate		6.697%

Your Financial Plan in 7 Easy Steps	Simple Math Calculator		
1. Enter all Investment & Loan details at	Add, Subtract, Multiply & Divide		
the Payments Table & Investment Planner	select a row by math function + - x /		
2. Modify blue cells at Income & Expense	1st $	2nd $	= Result
Planner. Aim for Mini-Budget Targets =>$0!	$4.00	$6.00	$10.00
3. Investment Planner. Modify Current Value	$4.00	$6.00	-$2.00
& Unused Carry blue cells = Next Year value	$4.00	$6.00	$24.00
4. Then make Contribution blue cells = $0	$4.00	$6.00	$0.67
5. Make Contributions until Balance = $0	wage per hr	hrs per week	wks per year
6. Reduce # of Payments by 12 (min. 0)	$ 12.50	40.00	50.00
7. To start a new year go back to step 2	Gross Income Per Year =		$ 25,000.00

A wealthy mindset must consider wealth in terms of reasonable expectations. For example, what happens to your wealth when you retire, and what are the chances of losing your employment suddenly? What about your family's wealth when you die?

The first goal of a wealth plan is being able to meet your needs for the foreseeable future. The second goal of a wealth plan is financial freedom and safety!

You may want to continue working your whole life. However, True Wealth is the ability to take care of all your needs from savings and other working capital that is fully under your control.

A wealthy mindset regularly evaluates these controls. How safe or at risk is your job, business, investments and property? What about your health, marriage and family needs? What about the economy and the effects of taxes and inflation?

You can prepare and have insurance, but there are always uncontrollable factors. However a wealthy mindset has a good understanding or feel of them all and considers everything discussed so far in terms of ones lifetime.

A business tracks results through yearly financial statements that include an income statement, balance sheet and net worth statement. The income statement shows all income less all expenses, and the net income or loss result. The balance sheet shows all assets owned versus all liabilities owed and shareholders equity, which must equal or balance. The net worth statement shows the value of all assets, less all liabilities.

Click on the second tab, 'Wealth Creation Budget', in your Wealth Plan excel workbook. Like any budget, it helps plan your reasonable income and expenses. The wealth creation budget is quick and simple to use, and focuses your cash flows with a goal of generating regular savings. It plans and tracks all investments and debt, and provides a net worth value. It is designed like a next year's combined income statement and balance sheet.

A year is a reasonable time frame to more precisely predict and plan income and expense value decisions. Loan interest, financial charges, rent or mortgage payments, property taxes and utility rates are usually set yearly. Medical and dental checkups, insurance premiums, licenses and memberships are usually renewed yearly. Planning for everything from your next vacation to filing income tax returns and contributing to a retirement saving plan is usually considered in yearly terms.

The goal of a wealth creation budget is to make the most out of the coming year by understanding where you are, and to appreciate what changes need to be made going forward, in order to build wealth. A wealth creation budget needs to balance; otherwise wealth is lost. It should plan for at least some yearly savings surplus as a wealth buffer just in case, or greater savings to support a higher lifestyle if desired.

The wealth creation budget provided is intuitive, as it has built in assumptions and minimum and maximum guidelines for when accurate amounts are not readily available. It can be used as a wealth snapshot to assess what happened last year, and to predict results for next year or future years.

It is a tool to predict financial results based on actual values, or can be used to show 'what if' scenarios. For example you might want to know how much income is needed to support buying your next house, a new car or more investments, within your current expenses. Or you may want to see where most of your income is going, in order to make value decisions to adjust certain expenses, reduce a loan, or pay off a mortgage faster.

Information is broken down in various ways, to help you view income and expenses from different value perspectives. By entering just your Gross Income, it calculates and auto fills your approximate hourly wage, tax rate, yearly taxes and after tax income.

If you are paid an hourly wage and don't know your yearly gross income, use the bottom section of the Simple Math Calculator provided and enter your wage per hour, hours per week and weeks per year. This will calculate and auto-fill your gross income above.

All income and expenses are preset based on $25,000 gross income and basic cost assumptions to start. Consumption tends to increase with higher incomes, but usually plateaus at some point. On the other hand consumption tends to decrease with lower incomes, limited by basic needs. This is why the expenses adjust automatically within minimum and maximum limits when your gross income is changed.

Everything is color coded for simplicity. The yellow and orange cells are simply labels that can be renamed as desired. Instead of a lengthy reference manual to explain the labels and what to do in more detail, comments are embedded that pop up by running your mouse-over the red flags in the corners of many of the cells.

For all the wealth plan excel spreadsheets, if any cell has a rounded number that you would like to see in more detail beyond the decimal point, simply right-click on the cell and then left-click: Format Cells, Number tab, and move up the Decimal places.

If a cell has several '#' in it, the value is too large to fit. Try changing the font size lower, or you can left-click on the right-edge of the cell's column-letter at the top and drag the edge wider. Cell height is adjusted the same way at the top-edge of cell's row-numbers.

You only need to change the blue-cells and the green cells will then auto-fill. You may of course change any cell, just know that the green-cells have formulas embedded, and if changed to a specific number they will not update again.

Hourly, daily, weekly and monthly green-cells are shown to the cent. However all yearly green-cells are formatted as more relevant dollar amounts, as they are more difficult to precisely predict. If you know the exact amount down to the penny enter it, which will be factored into calculations even though shown as rounded dollars. Accountants and even tax collection agencies expect reasonable yearly dollar rounding.

The dark-blue-cells tend to be longer term, larger loan amounts that will auto fill automatically based on Loan & Mortgage Payments Table values. Use the Simple Loan & Mortgage Calculator for your monthly payments and number of payments remaining. A Simple Math Calculator is also built in to use as needed!

The loan & mortgage calculator and payments table help you track and structure debt accurately and effectively. This calculator breaks down the 'Loan or Mortgage' amount, 'Annual Interest Rate', 'Amortization in Months' until the loan is paid off, 'Monthly Payment', 'Yearly Payment', 'Total Interest' and 'Total Principal & Interest' paid.

Annual interest rates may all seem the same, but they are very different depending on how interest is compounded. When we compare annual interest rates, it is the EIR Effective Interest Rate, APY Annual Percentage Yield or APR Annual Percentage Rate that we usually believe we are being quoted. This is usually false!

For example, U.S. mortgages and most loans compound monthly or twelve times per year, while Canadian mortgages compound semi-annually or twice per year. However credit cards compound daily, 365 or 360 times per year. A 10% annual interest rate converts to an EIR, APY or APR effective rate of 10.250% for a Canadian mortgage, 10.471% for a U.S. mortgage and 10.516% for most credit cards!

The bottom line blue-cell of the loan & mortgage calculator factors-in how many times interest is compounded per year. The green-cell to the right then updates to show you the effective rate you are really paying, based on the annual interest rate entered above.

A wealthy mindset compares apples to apples, and understands the effects of different compounding methods! The next chapter describes the detailed amortization table provided, to better plan long-term loans and mortgages. The effects of interest compounding are also discussed in more detail in chapter 5.4.

To better appreciate all loan costs versus just monthly payment affordability, play with the loan amortization in months and interest rate to see how they affect your monthly and yearly payments, and total interest paid. In other words slight changes in the monthly payment or interest rate can have a dramatic effect on the overall interest paid and number of years remaining to pay off a long term loan or mortgage.

To the immediate right of all income and expense planner blue-cells, you will see these values auto-fill into green cells, broken down as daily, weekly, monthly and yearly amounts. Instead of calculating them in simple calendar terms, 365 days or 52 weeks, it is more relevant to visualize them as income is earned throughout the year. In other words you should allow for any weekends, vacation time and holidays off work.

This is why the Personal or Family Budget displays income and expenses Days as averaged over an assumed 255 workdays per year, or Monday to Friday excluding holidays. Also Weeks are averaged over an assumed 50 workweeks, allowing for 2 weeks off for vacation and various holidays.

The effect is that average daily and weekly expenses are more accurate for planning purposes. Income and expenses are displayed per workday and per workweek, which is the only time income is earned to pay your expenses that occur all year. The purpose is to help you better visualize where all your money goes as it is earned!

The monthly income and expenses are simply the yearly amounts divided by 12. Expenses such as utilities, loans, rent, or mortgage payments are usually billed and paid by calendar months.

Yearly gross income is often based on a yearly salary. However if your income is a wage set hourly, weekly, bi-weekly, monthly or some other payment frequency you will have to calculate this over the year, to be entered as your gross income.

A wealthy mindset balances income and expenses over the entire year and understands why this is important. You need to allow for untimely expenses that tend to occur at different times than income is received. The opposite of this is living one day at a time, from paycheck to paycheck, without having any funds available for emergencies.

The payday loan business exists mainly because rent days are not usually the same as paydays. These types of high cost loans represent wealth destruction, which is usually avoidable with a little discipline and planning.

Not appreciating the importance of aligning income and expense timing is also why many find it extremely tight financially in February, after a vacation, after being ill, or after the Christmas holiday, that all have fewer workdays but the same or more monthly expenses.

To balance your wealth creation budget and generate savings, you only have 100% of after-tax income to work with. The Income and Expense Planner is arranged in sections called Mini-Budgets, which auto fill target expense amounts according to a set percentage of your net after-tax income.

Mini-budgets break down expenses by category to focus your spending in relation to other needs. If one mini-budget is over its target amount then other mini-budgets must be under budget, in order to balance out overall for the year.

The mini-budget target expenses of after tax income are based on published government statistics with some rounding for simplicity. You may change them as appropriate to your needs as long as the total equals 100%. For now they have been set as: Financial 20%, Health

5%, Home 25%, Transportation 25%, and Food, Clothing & Entertainment 25%.

Each mini-budget breaks down into various line expenses, to provide relevant detail while not being too complicated. The blue-cells will auto fill amounts as a guideline based on income and expense assumptions. More accurate actual amounts should always be used whenever possible.

A wealthy mindset is detailed, controls expenses, allocates resources purposefully, and estimates reasonably when actual amounts are not readily available!

A wealth plan and a wealth creation budget need to generate savings. Surplus savings should be viewed as a high priority wealth creation expense. In order to stay on track and not procrastinate, you need to set aside an amount from each paycheck for savings. In other words you need to pay yourself first!

As shown in the 'Your Wealth Now, in a Nutshell' spreadsheet, the amount of surplus savings needed is directly related to the level of eventual wealth or higher lifestyle desired. A reasonable savings surplus goal for most people, without affecting current lifestyle measurably, is to save 10% of your after tax income. You may of course decide more is reasonable, but to plan for less than 10% surplus savings usually prolongs your wealth goal and may not leave you enough of a wealth buffer.

This is why Paycheck Savings is built into your Financial expenses, calculated at 10% of after-tax Net Income. The result is that if your yearly budget balances at $0 and you are disciplined with your expenses, you will generate reasonable surplus savings to invest at the end of the year. Think of this as loan payments to you, or like a forced savings plan!

Your personal or family budget will either balance or show a Surplus or Deficit. By looking forward one year you will know this in advance, allowing you to decide what changes are needed now to meet 'Your Wealth Now, in a Nutshell' targets, instead of wondering why you are not any further ahead at the end of the year.

Once you have completed your income and expense planner, and made changes as best as reasonably possible, your Surplus or Deficit amount needs to be entered and allocated within the Investment Planner provided. Investment decisions such as contributions to a retirement or education savings plan, buying a new house or car, or to pay down a loan or mortgage, all tend to occur at the end of a year or early the next year around tax time.

The investment planner guides you by auto filling your retirement savings plan and education savings plan contribution limits, based on your gross income, number of children and previous contributions, within government guidelines. Any Unused Carry forward contribution amounts are tracked so they can be applied in future years.

The investment planner shows your Next Home Affordability Limits based on an adjustable percentage down and your down payment available from savings, factoring in assumed closing costs. It even calculates the monthly mortgage payment you may be able to afford, that meets most banks required minimum 32% GDSR Gross Debt Service Ratio and 40% TDSR Total Debt Service Ratio. These ratios are based on your income, and your income less all other loan payments and an assumed 1.5% of home value to cover heat, electric, insurance and property tax costs.

The investment planner helps you decide what to do with your surplus or deficit by making positive or negative contributions. Positive contributions increase wealth, adding value to an investment or lowering future costs by paying down a loan or mortgage.

Negative contributions decrease wealth because they reduce investment value or increase the future costs of a loan or mortgage. Continue making contributions until your surplus or deficit balance at the bottom equals zero.

The Investment Types are arranged in groups, listed according to common wealth creation priorities. At the top are Tax Sheltered investments like your home that allow tax-free growth, and RSP, RESP or in the U.S. 401k retirement plans, which create additional surpluses from tax deductions. The tax advantages plus safe wealth compounding of these investments should be the foundation for creating wealth.

If you enter a retirement savings contribution, you will see up top that your taxes, net income and year-end surplus or deficit change. They recalculate to factor in this RSP contribution, lowering your taxes. Your changed surplus or deficit amount should then be entered again at the top of the investment planner, so that these tax savings can also be invested.

Next are Loans & Mortgage, which have a cost to savings, therefore a good investment if paid off faster. Remember that it is the after-tax value of income that is important. Loans are paid with after tax dollars, whereas unsheltered investments are subject to tax.

Therefore if taxable investment returns are not substantially higher than loan rates, then paying off a loan is a better investment. Even if taxable investment returns are substantially higher than loan rates, you need to consider all costs and the level of risk involved. Paying off loans is a very good low risk way to add value and create wealth!

Next is Tax Deferred investments such as stocks, bonds and mutual funds, a business or collectibles that may have capital gains, usually taxed at a later date when sold. Next is Taxable Cash such as T-bills or other cash-like safe savings that can be turned into cash quickly, with yearly taxable interest and an overall low investment return.

Taxes owed for the interest received on taxable cash investments are calculated into income taxes up top. However capital gains taxes on taxable investments are not calculated, as they are assumed paid out of the gain when sold later. The goal is to create a meaningful and therefore simple to use and understand budget, not to overcomplicate or replace tax experts.

Last is Depreciating Assets that may have some cash value if sold, but lose value over a short period of time. They do not create wealth because they do not grow or even hold their value very well. Instead of a percentage rate of return, a depreciation rate is used to calculate next year's lower value. These assets should instead be seen as expenses as they need to be replaced often, but may have some resale value that is part of your net worth.

The investment planner also calculates your financial Net Worth or Equity, or the value left over if all investments were sold and all loans paid off. The net worth value is the most relevant measure of current financial wealth in basic dollar terms.

To start your wealth creation budget, follow the table called Your Financial Plan in 7 Easy Steps. The first tables to complete are the investment planner and the loan & mortgage payment tables, to set-up your current investments and loans.

Next make appropriate decisions and change the income and expense planner blue-cells as needed. Then return to the investment planner and make yearend adjustments and contributions. After the first year is set-up, it's really only two steps per year!

Once you are familiar using the wealth creation budget, you should find it quick and easy to set-up, and to track and plan yearly income and expenses, towards controlling and generating more wealth savings capital. You may of course change anything, however you should keep a clean copy unchanged as there are many formulas embedded that you may need later.

By anticipating and visualizing all of your income and expenses, and your investments and loans, you put yourself in position to take control of your wealth destiny. Your wealthy mindset should help provide the desire and discipline to make the right decisions.

The wealth creation budget is designed to be a powerful but simple to use planning tool. Great care was taken to detail as much as possible, to put you squarely in your financial drivers seat. It may even assist your accountant or banker, and will hopefully save you time or fees. However there are many other factors to consider that may limit its use.

For example, tax rates are approximate as they change regularly and also depend on where you live and other personal factors. Loan payments are anticipated as regular monthly payments, while there are many payment options. Similarly, loan interest and investment rates of return are based on annual percentage rates, which may be compounded differently.

It is too easy to just read a good wealth creation book, that may have excellent financial concepts, but to then not apply them. This wealth creation budget at the very least lays it all out for you, to know where you are. The goal is to put you in control financially by positioning your next year around a wealth plan.

In other words this wealth creation budget is an effective common sense tool that if used, forces you to put into action your wealthy mindset. Please use it, update it as needed and save dated copies to track each year's actual values or scenarios, as a reference later.

Chapter 3.1

Amortization Table

U.S. & Cdn. Mortage Amortization Table - 1 or 2 payments per month, any type of loan compounding

mortage amt.	interest rate	compound/yr.	effective rate	term in mths.	pays per mth.	# of payments	min. payment	add. payment	total payment	first & last pymt	dd/mm/yyyy	total interest
$100,000.00	6.500%	12	6.697%	180	2	360	$ 434.97	$ 15.03	$ 450.00	8-Jul-06	22-Jun-21	$ 53,090.59
payment date	8-Jul-06	22-Jul-06	8-Aug-06	22-Aug-06	8-Sep-06	22-Sep-06	8-Oct-06	22-Oct-06	8-Nov-06	22-Nov-06	8-Dec-06	22-Dec-06
payment	$ 450.00	$ 450.00	$ 450.00	$ 450.00	$ 450.00	$ 450.00	$ 450.00	$ 450.00	$ 450.00	$ 450.00	$ 450.00	$ 450.00
interest paid	$ 270.47	$ 269.98	$ 269.50	$ 269.01	$ 268.52	$ 268.03	$ 267.53	$ 267.04	$ 266.55	$ 266.05	$ 265.56	$ 265.05
principal paid	$ 179.53	$ 180.02	$ 180.50	$ 180.99	$ 181.48	$ 181.97	$ 182.47	$ 182.96	$ 183.45	$ 183.96	$ 184.45	$ 184.96
balance owing	$ 99,820.47	$ 99,640.45	$ 99,459.95	$ 99,278.96	$ 99,097.48	$ 98,915.51	$ 98,733.04	$ 98,550.08	$ 98,366.63	$ 98,182.68	$ 97,998.23	$ 97,813.28
payment date	8-Jan-07	22-Jan-07	8-Feb-07	22-Feb-07	8-Mar-07	22-Mar-07	8-Apr-07	22-Apr-07	8-May-07	22-May-07	8-Jun-07	22-Jun-07
payment	$ 450.00	$ 450.00	$ 450.00	$ 450.00	$ 450.00	$ 450.00	$ 450.00	$ 450.00	$ 450.00	$ 450.00	$ 450.00	$ 450.00
interest paid	$ 264.55	$ 264.06	$ 263.55	$ 263.04	$ 262.54	$ 262.03	$ 261.52	$ 261.01	$ 260.50	$ 259.99	$ 259.48	$ 258.96
principal paid	$ 185.45	$ 185.95	$ 186.45	$ 186.96	$ 187.46	$ 187.97	$ 188.48	$ 188.99	$ 189.50	$ 190.01	$ 190.52	$ 191.04
balance owing	$ 97,627.83	$ 97,441.88	$ 97,255.43	$ 97,068.47	$ 96,881.01	$ 96,693.04	$ 96,504.56	$ 96,315.57	$ 96,126.07	$ 95,936.06	$ 95,745.54	$ 95,554.50
payment date	8-Jul-07	22-Jul-07	8-Aug-07	22-Aug-07	8-Sep-07	22-Sep-07	8-Oct-07	22-Oct-07	8-Nov-07	22-Nov-07	8-Dec-07	22-Dec-07
payment	$ 450.00	$ 450.00	$ 450.00	$ 450.00	$ 450.00	$ 450.00	$ 450.00	$ 450.00	$ 450.00	$ 450.00	$ 450.00	$ 450.00
interest paid	$ 258.44	$ 257.93	$ 257.41	$ 256.89	$ 256.36	$ 255.84	$ 255.31	$ 254.79	$ 254.26	$ 253.73	$ 253.20	$ 252.67
principal paid	$ 191.56	$ 192.07	$ 192.59	$ 193.11	$ 193.64	$ 194.16	$ 194.69	$ 195.21	$ 195.74	$ 196.27	$ 196.80	$ 197.33
balance owing	$ 95,362.94	$ 95,170.87	$ 94,978.28	$ 94,785.17	$ 94,591.53	$ 94,397.37	$ 94,202.68	$ 94,007.47	$ 93,811.73	$ 93,615.46	$ 93,418.66	$ 93,221.33
payment date	8-Jan-08	22-Jan-08	8-Feb-08	22-Feb-08	8-Mar-08	22-Mar-08	8-Apr-08	22-Apr-08	8-May-08	22-May-08	8-Jun-08	22-Jun-08
payment	$ 450.00	$ 450.00	$ 450.00	$ 450.00	$ 450.00	$ 450.00	$ 450.00	$ 450.00	$ 450.00	$ 450.00	$ 450.00	$ 450.00
interest paid	$ 252.13	$ 251.60	$ 251.06	$ 250.52	$ 249.98	$ 249.44	$ 248.90	$ 248.36	$ 247.81	$ 247.26	$ 246.72	$ 246.17
principal paid	$ 197.87	$ 198.40	$ 198.94	$ 199.48	$ 200.02	$ 200.56	$ 201.10	$ 201.64	$ 202.19	$ 202.74	$ 203.28	$ 203.83
balance owing	$ 93,023.46	$ 92,825.06	$ 92,626.12	$ 92,426.64	$ 92,226.62	$ 92,026.06	$ 91,824.96	$ 91,623.32	$ 91,421.13	$ 91,218.39	$ 91,015.11	$ 90,811.28
payment date	8-Jul-08	22-Jul-08	8-Aug-08	22-Aug-08	8-Sep-08	22-Sep-08	8-Oct-08	22-Oct-08	8-Nov-08	22-Nov-08	8-Dec-08	22-Dec-08
payment	$ 450.00	$450.00	$450.00	$450.00	$450.00	$450.00	$450.00	$450.00	$450.00	$450.00	$450.00	$450.00
interest paid	$ 245.62	$ 245.06	$ 244.51	$ 243.95	$ 243.39	$ 242.84	$ 242.28	$ 241.71	$ 241.15	$ 240.59	$ 240.02	$ 239.45
principal paid	$ 204.38	$ 204.94	$ 205.49	$ 206.05	$ 206.61	$ 207.16	$ 207.72	$ 208.29	$ 208.85	$ 209.41	$ 209.98	$ 210.55
balance owing	$ 90,606.90	$ 90,401.96	$ 90,196.47	$ 89,990.42	$ 89,783.81	$ 89,576.65	$ 89,368.93	$ 89,160.64	$ 88,951.79	$ 88,742.38	$ 88,532.40	$ 88,321.85
payment date	8-Jan-09	22-Jan-09	8-Feb-09	22-Feb-09	8-Mar-09	22-Mar-09	8-Apr-09	22-Apr-09	8-May-09	22-May-09	8-Jun-09	22-Jun-09
payment	$ 450.00	$ 450.00	$ 450.00	$ 450.00	$ 450.00	$ 450.00	$ 450.00	$ 450.00	$ 450.00	$ 450.00	$ 450.00	$ 450.00
interest paid	$ 238.88	$ 238.31	$ 237.74	$ 237.16	$ 236.59	$ 236.01	$ 235.43	$ 234.85	$ 234.27	$ 233.69	$ 233.10	$ 232.52
principal paid	$ 211.12	$ 211.69	$ 212.26	$ 212.84	$ 213.41	$ 213.99	$ 214.57	$ 215.15	$ 215.73	$ 216.31	$ 216.90	$ 217.48
balance owing	$ 88,110.73	$ 87,899.04	$ 87,686.78	$ 87,473.94	$ 87,260.53	$ 87,046.54	$ 86,831.97	$ 86,616.82	$ 86,401.09	$ 86,184.78	$ 85,967.88	$ 85,750.40
payment date	8-Jul-09	22-Jul-09	8-Aug-09	22-Aug-09	8-Sep-09	22-Sep-09	8-Oct-09	22-Oct-09	8-Nov-09	22-Nov-09	8-Dec-09	22-Dec-09
payment	$ 450.00	$ 450.00	$ 450.00	$ 450.00	$ 450.00	$ 450.00	$ 450.00	$ 450.00	$ 450.00	$ 450.00	$ 450.00	$ 450.00
interest paid	$ 231.93	$ 231.34	$ 230.75	$ 230.15	$ 229.56	$ 228.96	$ 228.36	$ 227.76	$ 227.16	$ 226.56	$ 225.96	$ 225.35
principal paid	$ 218.07	$ 218.66	$ 219.25	$ 219.85	$ 220.44	$ 221.04	$ 221.64	$ 222.24	$ 222.84	$ 223.44	$ 224.04	$ 224.65
balance owing	$ 85,532.33	$ 85,313.67	$ 85,094.42	$ 84,874.57	$ 84,654.13	$ 84,433.09	$ 84,211.45	$ 83,989.21	$ 83,766.37	$ 83,542.93	$ 83,318.89	$ 83,094.24
payment date	8-Jan-10	22-Jan-10	8-Feb-10	22-Feb-10	8-Mar-10	22-Mar-10	8-Apr-10	22-Apr-10	8-May-10	22-May-10	8-Jun-10	22-Jun-10
payment	$ 450.00	$ 450.00	$ 450.00	$ 450.00	$ 450.00	$ 450.00	$ 450.00	$ 450.00	$ 450.00	$ 450.00	$ 450.00	$ 450.00
interest paid	$ 224.74	$ 224.13	$ 223.52	$ 222.91	$ 222.30	$ 221.68	$ 221.06	$ 220.44	$ 219.82	$ 219.20	$ 218.58	$ 217.95
principal paid	$ 225.26	$ 225.87	$ 226.48	$ 227.09	$ 227.70	$ 228.32	$ 228.94	$ 229.56	$ 230.18	$ 230.80	$ 231.42	$ 232.05
balance owing	$ 82,868.98	$ 82,643.11	$ 82,416.63	$ 82,189.54	$ 81,961.84	$ 81,733.52	$ 81,504.58	$ 81,275.02	$ 81,044.84	$ 80,814.04	$ 80,582.62	$ 80,350.57
payment date	8-Jul-10	22-Jul-10	8-Aug-10	22-Aug-10	8-Sep-10	22-Sep-10	8-Oct-10	22-Oct-10	8-Nov-10	22-Nov-10	8-Dec-10	22-Dec-10
payment	$ 450.00	$ 450.00	$ 450.00	$ 450.00	$ 450.00	$ 450.00	$ 450.00	$ 450.00	$ 450.00	$ 450.00	$ 450.00	$ 450.00
interest paid	$ 217.32	$ 216.69	$ 216.06	$ 215.43	$ 214.79	$ 214.16	$ 213.52	$ 212.88	$ 212.24	$ 211.60	$ 210.95	$ 210.31
principal paid	$ 232.68	$ 233.31	$ 233.94	$ 234.57	$ 235.21	$ 235.84	$ 236.48	$ 237.12	$ 237.76	$ 238.40	$ 239.05	$ 239.69
balance owing	$ 80,117.89	$ 79,884.58	$ 79,650.64	$ 79,416.07	$ 79,180.86	$ 78,945.02	$ 78,708.54	$ 78,471.42	$ 78,233.66	$ 77,995.26	$ 77,756.21	$ 77,516.52
payment date	8-Jan-11	22-Jan-11	8-Feb-11	22-Feb-11	8-Mar-11	22-Mar-11	8-Apr-11	22-Apr-11	8-May-11	22-May-11	8-Jun-11	22-Jun-11
payment	$ 450.00	$ 450.00	$ 450.00	$ 450.00	$ 450.00	$ 450.00	$ 450.00	$ 450.00	$ 450.00	$ 450.00	$ 450.00	$ 450.00
interest paid	$ 209.66	$ 209.01	$ 208.36	$ 207.70	$ 207.05	$ 206.39	$ 205.73	$ 205.07	$ 204.41	$ 203.74	$ 203.08	$ 202.41
principal paid	$ 240.34	$ 240.99	$ 241.64	$ 242.30	$ 242.95	$ 243.61	$ 244.27	$ 244.93	$ 245.59	$ 246.26	$ 246.92	$ 247.59
balance owing	$ 77,276.18	$ 77,035.19	$ 76,793.55	$ 76,551.25	$ 76,308.30	$ 76,064.69	$ 75,820.42	$ 75,575.49	$ 75,329.90	$ 75,083.64	$ 74,836.72	$ 74,589.13
payment date	8-Jul-11	22-Jul-11	8-Aug-11	22-Aug-11	8-Sep-11	22-Sep-11	8-Oct-11	22-Oct-11	8-Nov-11	22-Nov-11	8-Dec-11	22-Dec-11
payment	$ 450.00	$ 450.00	$ 450.00	$ 450.00	$ 450.00	$ 450.00	$ 450.00	$ 450.00	$ 450.00	$ 450.00	$ 450.00	$ 450.00
interest paid	$ 201.74	$ 201.07	$ 200.39	$ 199.72	$ 199.04	$ 198.36	$ 197.68	$ 197.00	$ 196.32	$ 195.63	$ 194.94	$ 194.25
principal paid	$ 248.26	$ 248.93	$ 249.61	$ 250.28	$ 250.96	$ 251.64	$ 252.32	$ 253.00	$ 253.68	$ 254.37	$ 255.06	$ 255.75
balance owing	$ 74,340.87	$ 74,091.94	$ 73,842.33	$ 73,592.05	$ 73,341.09	$ 73,089.45	$ 72,837.13	$ 72,584.13	$ 72,330.45	$ 72,076.08	$ 71,821.02	$ 71,565.27
payment date	8-Jan-12	22-Jan-12	8-Feb-12	22-Feb-12	8-Mar-12	22-Mar-12	8-Apr-12	22-Apr-12	8-May-12	22-May-12	8-Jun-12	22-Jun-12
payment	$ 450.00	$ 450.00	$ 450.00	$ 450.00	$ 450.00	$ 450.00	$ 450.00	$ 450.00	$ 450.00	$ 450.00	$ 450.00	$ 450.00
interest paid	$ 193.56	$ 192.87	$ 192.17	$ 191.47	$ 190.78	$ 190.07	$ 189.37	$ 188.67	$ 187.96	$ 187.25	$ 186.54	$ 185.83
principal paid	$ 256.44	$ 257.13	$ 257.83	$ 258.53	$ 259.22	$ 259.93	$ 260.63	$ 261.33	$ 262.04	$ 262.75	$ 263.46	$ 264.17
balance owing	$ 71,308.83	$ 71,051.70	$ 70,793.87	$ 70,535.34	$ 70,276.12	$ 70,016.19	$ 69,755.56	$ 69,494.23	$ 69,232.19	$ 68,969.44	$ 68,705.98	$ 68,441.81
payment date	8-Jul-12	22-Jul-12	8-Aug-12	22-Aug-12	8-Sep-12	22-Sep-12	8-Oct-12	22-Oct-12	8-Nov-12	22-Nov-12	8-Dec-12	22-Dec-12
payment	$ 450.00	$ 450.00	$ 450.00	$ 450.00	$ 450.00	$ 450.00	$ 450.00	$ 450.00	$ 450.00	$ 450.00	$ 450.00	$ 450.00
interest paid	$ 185.11	$ 184.40	$ 183.68	$ 182.96	$ 182.24	$ 181.51	$ 180.79	$ 180.06	$ 179.33	$ 178.59	$ 177.86	$ 177.12
principal paid	$ 264.89	$ 265.60	$ 266.32	$ 267.04	$ 267.76	$ 268.49	$ 269.21	$ 269.94	$ 270.67	$ 271.41	$ 272.14	$ 272.88
balance owing	$ 68,176.92	$ 67,911.32	$ 67,645.00	$ 67,377.96	$ 67,110.20	$ 66,841.71	$ 66,572.50	$ 66,302.56	$ 66,031.89	$ 65,760.48	$ 65,488.34	$ 65,215.46
payment date	8-Jan-13	22-Jan-13	8-Feb-13	22-Feb-13	8-Mar-13	22-Mar-13	8-Apr-13	22-Apr-13	8-May-13	22-May-13	8-Jun-13	22-Jun-13
payment	$ 450.00	$ 450.00	$ 450.00	$ 450.00	$ 450.00	$ 450.00	$ 450.00	$ 450.00	$ 450.00	$ 450.00	$ 450.00	$ 450.00
interest paid	$ 176.39	$ 175.65	$ 174.90	$ 174.16	$ 173.41	$ 172.67	$ 171.92	$ 171.16	$ 170.41	$ 169.65	$ 168.90	$ 168.14
principal paid	$ 273.61	$ 274.35	$ 275.10	$ 275.84	$ 276.59	$ 277.33	$ 278.08	$ 278.84	$ 279.59	$ 280.35	$ 281.10	$ 281.86
balance owing	$ 64,941.85	$ 64,667.50	$ 64,392.40	$ 64,116.56	$ 63,839.97	$ 63,562.64	$ 63,284.56	$ 63,005.72	$ 62,726.13	$ 62,445.78	$ 62,164.68	$ 61,882.82
payment date	8-Jul-13	22-Jul-13	8-Aug-13	22-Aug-13	8-Sep-13	22-Sep-13	8-Oct-13	22-Oct-13	8-Nov-13	22-Nov-13	8-Dec-13	22-Dec-13
payment	$ 450.00	$ 450.00	$ 450.00	$ 450.00	$ 450.00	$ 450.00	$ 450.00	$ 450.00	$ 450.00	$ 450.00	$ 450.00	$ 450.00
interest paid	$ 167.37	$ 166.61	$ 165.84	$ 165.07	$ 164.30	$ 163.53	$ 162.76	$ 161.98	$ 161.20	$ 160.42	$ 159.64	$ 158.85
principal paid	$ 282.63	$ 283.39	$ 284.16	$ 284.93	$ 285.70	$ 286.47	$ 287.24	$ 288.02	$ 288.80	$ 289.58	$ 290.36	$ 291.15
balance owing	$ 61,600.19	$ 61,316.80	$ 61,032.64	$ 60,747.71	$ 60,462.01	$ 60,175.54	$ 59,888.30	$ 59,600.28	$ 59,311.48	$ 59,021.90	$ 58,731.54	$ 58,440.39
payment date	8-Jan-14	22-Jan-14	8-Feb-14	22-Feb-14	8-Mar-14	22-Mar-14	8-Apr-14	22-Apr-14	8-May-14	22-May-14	8-Jun-14	22-Jun-14
payment	$ 450.00	$ 450.00	$ 450.00	$ 450.00	$ 450.00	$ 450.00	$ 450.00	$ 450.00	$ 450.00	$ 450.00	$ 450.00	$ 450.00
interest paid	$ 158.06	$ 157.27	$ 156.48	$ 155.69	$ 154.89	$ 154.09	$ 153.29	$ 152.49	$ 151.69	$ 150.88	$ 150.07	$ 149.26
principal paid	$ 291.94	$ 292.73	$ 293.52	$ 294.31	$ 295.11	$ 295.91	$ 296.71	$ 297.51	$ 298.31	$ 299.12	$ 299.93	$ 300.74
balance owing	$ 58,148.45	$ 57,855.72	$ 57,562.20	$ 57,267.89	$ 56,972.78	$ 56,676.87	$ 56,380.16	$ 56,082.65	$ 55,784.34	$ 55,485.22	$ 55,185.29	$ 54,884.55
payment date	8-Jul-14	22-Jul-14	8-Aug-14	22-Aug-14	8-Sep-14	22-Sep-14	8-Oct-14	22-Oct-14	8-Nov-14	22-Nov-14	8-Dec-14	22-Dec-14
payment	$ 450.00	$ 450.00	$ 450.00	$ 450.00	$ 450.00	$ 450.00	$ 450.00	$ 450.00	$ 450.00	$ 450.00	$ 450.00	$ 450.00
interest paid	$ 148.44	$ 147.63	$ 146.81	$ 145.99	$ 145.17	$ 144.34	$ 143.52	$ 142.69	$ 141.86	$ 141.02	$ 140.19	$ 139.35
principal paid	$ 301.56	$ 302.37	$ 303.19	$ 304.01	$ 304.83	$ 305.66	$ 306.48	$ 307.31	$ 308.14	$ 308.98	$ 309.81	$ 310.65
balance owing	$ 54,582.99	$ 54,280.62	$ 53,977.43	$ 53,673.42	$ 53,368.59	$ 53,062.93	$ 52,756.45	$ 52,449.14	$ 52,141.00	$ 51,832.02	$ 51,522.21	$ 51,211.56
payment date	8-Jan-15	22-Jan-15	8-Feb-15	22-Feb-15	8-Mar-15	22-Mar-15	8-Apr-15	22-Apr-15	8-May-15	22-May-15	8-Jun-15	22-Jun-15
payment	$ 450.00	$ 450.00	$ 450.00	$ 450.00	$ 450.00	$ 450.00	$ 450.00	$ 450.00	$ 450.00	$ 450.00	$ 450.00	$ 450.00
interest paid	$ 138.51	$ 137.67	$ 136.82	$ 135.98	$ 135.13	$ 134.28	$ 133.42	$ 132.57	$ 131.71	$ 130.85	$ 129.98	$ 129.12

U.S. & Cdn. Mortage Amortization Table - 1 or 2

mortage amt	interest rate	compound/yr	effective rate	term in mths	pays per mth	# of payments
$100,000.00	6.500%	12	6.697%	180	2	360

payment date	8-Jul-06	22-Jul-06	8-Aug-06	22-Aug-06	8-Sep-06	22-Sep-06
payment	$ 450.00	$ 450.00	$ 450.00	$ 450.00	$ 450.00	$ 450.00
interest paid	$ 270.47	$ 269.98	$ 269.50	$ 269.01	$ 268.52	$ 268.03
principal paid	$ 179.53	$ 180.02	$ 180.50	$ 180.99	$ 181.48	$ 181.97
balance owing	$ 99,820.47	$ 99,640.45	$ 99,459.95	$ 99,278.96	$ 99,097.48	$ 98,915.51

payment date	8-Jan-07	22-Jan-07	8-Feb-07	22-Feb-07	8-Mar-07	22-Mar-07
payment	$ 450.00	$ 450.00	$ 450.00	$ 450.00	$ 450.00	$ 450.00
interest paid	$ 264.55	$ 264.05	$ 263.55	$ 263.04	$ 262.54	$ 262.03
principal paid	$ 185.45	$ 185.95	$ 186.45	$ 186.96	$ 187.46	$ 187.97
balance owing	$ 97,627.83	$ 97,441.88	$ 97,255.43	$ 97,068.47	$ 96,881.01	$ 96,693.04

payment date	8-Jul-07	22-Jul-07	8-Aug-07	22-Aug-07	8-Sep-07	22-Sep-07
payment	$ 450.00	$ 450.00	$ 450.00	$ 450.00	$ 450.00	$ 450.00
interest paid	$ 258.44	$ 257.93	$ 257.41	$ 256.89	$ 256.36	$ 255.84
principal paid	$ 191.56	$ 192.07	$ 192.59	$ 193.11	$ 193.64	$ 194.16
balance owing	$ 95,362.94	$ 95,170.87	$ 94,978.28	$ 94,785.17	$ 94,591.53	$ 94,397.37

payment date	8-Jan-08	22-Jan-08	8-Feb-08	22-Feb-08	8-Mar-08	22-Mar-08
payment	$ 450.00	$ 450.00	$ 450.00	$ 450.00	$ 450.00	$ 450.00
interest paid	$ 252.13	$ 251.60	$ 251.06	$ 250.52	$ 249.98	$ 249.44
principal paid	$ 197.87	$ 198.40	$ 198.94	$ 199.48	$ 200.02	$ 200.56
balance owing	$ 93,023.46	$ 92,825.06	$ 92,626.12	$ 92,426.64	$ 92,226.62	$ 92,026.06

payments per month, any type of loan compounding

min. payment	add. payment	total payment	first & last pymt dd/mm/yyyy		total interest
$ 434.97	$ 15.03	$ 450.00	8-Jul-06	22-Jun-21	$ 53,090.59

8-Oct-06	22-Oct-06	8-Nov-06	22-Nov-06	8-Dec-06	22-Dec-06
$ 450.00	$ 450.00	$ 450.00	$ 450.00	$ 450.00	$ 450.00
$ 267.53	$ 267.04	$ 266.55	$ 266.05	$ 265.55	$ 265.05
$ 182.47	$ 182.96	$ 183.45	$ 183.95	$ 184.45	$ 184.95
$ 98,733.04	$ 98,550.08	$ 98,366.63	$ 98,182.68	$ 97,998.23	$ 97,813.28

8-Apr-07	22-Apr-07	8-May-07	22-May-07	8-Jun-07	22-Jun-07
$ 450.00	$ 450.00	$ 450.00	$ 450.00	$ 450.00	$ 450.00
$ 261.52	$ 261.01	$ 260.50	$ 259.99	$ 259.48	$ 258.96
$ 188.48	$ 188.99	$ 189.50	$ 190.01	$ 190.52	$ 191.04
$ 96,504.56	$ 96,315.57	$ 96,126.07	$ 95,936.06	$ 95,745.54	$ 95,554.50

8-Oct-07	22-Oct-07	8-Nov-07	22-Nov-07	8-Dec-07	22-Dec-07
$ 450.00	$ 450.00	$ 450.00	$ 450.00	$ 450.00	$ 450.00
$ 255.31	$ 254.79	$ 254.26	$ 253.73	$ 253.20	$ 252.67
$ 194.69	$ 195.21	$ 195.74	$ 196.27	$ 196.80	$ 197.33
$ 94,202.68	$ 94,007.47	$ 93,811.73	$ 93,615.46	$ 93,418.66	$ 93,221.33

8-Apr-08	22-Apr-08	8-May-08	22-May-08	8-Jun-08	22-Jun-08
$ 450.00	$ 450.00	$ 450.00	$ 450.00	$ 450.00	$ 450.00
$ 248.90	$ 248.36	$ 247.81	$ 247.26	$ 246.72	$ 246.17
$ 201.10	$ 201.64	$ 202.19	$ 202.74	$ 203.28	$ 203.83
$ 91,824.96	$ 91,623.32	$ 91,421.13	$ 91,218.39	$ 91,015.11	$ 90,811.28

This chapter is an extension of the wealth creation budget, as it provides the means to strategically plan long-term loans and mortgages. It is also a prelude to the next chapter, providing an effective tool to minimize how much compound interest you pay.

Bank, mortgage and financial websites often provide mortgage calculators and sometimes amortization tables. The information is presented in the most attractive way to market their services, and may not be enough for you to make fully informed loan decisions.

The following excel worksheet is a detailed amortization table to more effectively plan loans & mortgages. It provides the flexibility to change almost anything that effects how long-term loans are structured, showing how payments really breakdown over time.

On your wealth plan excel workbook, click the third tab at the bottom called 'Amortization Table'. This spreadsheet is another powerful wealth planning tool that is very easy to use. It is designed to better visualize all your payments over the entire term of your mortgage, with the full effects of compound interest factored in.

Using an automobile analogy, compound loan interest works like driving wealth with one foot always on the brake. If expenses and loan interest exceed net income and investment gains, this is like driving your wealth stuck in reverse, with both feet on the gas pedal!

Loans and mortgages also require collateral, meaning there are risks of your lender taking wealth away if you don't pay on time and in full! Compound loan interest needs to be managed well as your lender is driving the tractor-trailer riding your wealth rear bumper!

There are only seven blue-cells you need to consider, to accurately setup a long-term loan or mortgage amortization scenario. From this, every payment will show the 'payment date', 'payment', 'interest paid', 'principal paid' and 'balance owing' over the entire term of your mortgage or loan amortization, with the effects of compound interest factored in.

The first blue-cell is the 'mortgage amount', the total loan amount being borrowed, excluding your down payment. If your lender has added any fees or closing costs to your loan, these amounts should be included in the mortgage amount.

The second blue-cell is the quoted annual 'interest rate' percentage. The third blue-cell is how many times interest 'compounds per year'. This is how often your lender calculates interest on your loan – not to be confused with how many payments you make on your loan or mortgage per year. The last chapter explained the compounding effect and chapter 5.4 discusses this further.

Check with your lender to be sure, but U.S. mortgages and most loans compound 12 times per year, whereas Canadian mortgages compound 2 times per year. Credit cards usually compound daily, 365 or 360 times per year. In short, the more often interest compounds, the higher the effective rate or how much you are really paying!

Don't be surprised if your loan agent doesn't know or answers this incorrectly. Know that if your payment does not work out the same as this table indicates, then one of your blue-cells is incorrect, and it is usually the compounding factor!

The fourth blue-cell is the loan or mortgage amortization 'term in months'. A 15-year amortization is simply 15 x 12 = 180 months. To further clarify, this is the time in months to repay the entire loan, not the time until your mortgage is renewed again.

Canadian mortgages are usually required to be renewed more often than U.S. mortgages. For example, a typical U.S. 15-year amortization might have a 15-year mortgage term, whereas a Canadian 15-year amortization may have a shorter mortgage term. For both examples the term in months is 180, not to be confused with a shorter renewal term.

The fifth blue-cell indicates 1 monthly or 2 semi-monthly 'payments per month'. Your bank can setup your mortgage to automatically take payments twice per month, instead of once per month, which is very practical if your income is paid twice per month.

This small change in loan payment frequency lowers your monthly and total mortgage interest costs. Using convenient bank automated deposits and withdrawals this should be seen as free money! Alternatively you can shorten your loan term, by paying the same amount as the monthly payment but instead cutting in half into two semi-monthly payments.

For simplification, the amortization table accurately shows up to 360 payments for a 30-year 1-payment per month mortgage, or 15-year 2-payments per month mortgage. You can imagine how large this table would have to be for a 30-year weekly payment mortgage, requiring the breakdown of 1560 payments.

If you are paid weekly, bi-weekly or some other pay frequency, your bank may be able to further align your loan payments with your income as received, to more efficiently pay down your loan even faster. There may be timing issues and potential service charges to consider, but the point is to have your money working for you, instead of sitting there and working for your bank!

The sixth blue-cell is 'additional payment', a voluntary amount to top-up all your minimum payments. Your lender will not require more than the minimum payment, which is mostly spent on interest at the beginning of your mortgage. Most people budget for the minimum payment but can usually afford to pay a little more.

Additional payments are investments, with 100% used to pay-down your principal loan balance faster. This also reduces your interest costs substantially over time. If you don't want to be locked into more than the minimum payment, a little discipline to top-up each payment by a small amount can shorten your loan by years!

The seventh blue-cell is your 'first payment date'. This is almost always one month after your loan or mortgage starts. The format to enter this date is dd/mm/yyyy where dd is a day between 1 and 31, mm is a month between 1 and 12 and yyyy is the year. For example, 08/07/2006 will display as 8-Jul-2006.

From these seven blue-cells, the green-cells up top will auto-update the: 'effective rate', 'number of payments', 'minimum payment', 'total payment, 'last payment' date and 'total interest'. Each loan payment also auto-fills, broken down to the last payment date.

Most banks tell you the interest rate, monthly payment and the last payment date, and that's about it. If your loan agent is helpful, or you read all the small print, you might discover the APY, APR or EIR effective interest rate. If you ask nicely, they might even provide a loan or mortgage amortization schedule that should show almost as much loan detail as this table.

However, this table allows you to see all the effects when changing the various blue-cell amounts to structure your loan or mortgage to best meet your needs, within your budget. You can even plan occasional payment changes, like adding an extra $50 or $500 or whatever amount to any number of the blue-cell payments at any time.

For example, the wealth creation budget shows a $100,000 mortgage, 6.50% annual interest that is compounded monthly, 180-month 15-year loan term, which equals $871.11 in monthly payments. The amortization table uses this same mortgage scenario, but instead calculates two semi-monthly minimum payments of $434.97.

If you multiply $434.97 by 2, this equals $869.94 per month, $1.17 less than one monthly payment. On the other hand, if you divide $871.11 by 2 and increase your semi-monthly payments by $0.59 to $435.56, this shows that your mortgage is paid off 2-weeks earlier.

The difference amounts may seem small, but remember this is free money if you are paid twice a month anyway. This free money changes proportionally to the size of the loan, and substantially more if interest rates are higher or loan amortization terms are longer.

Look at the cost and time saving effect of rounding-up your $434.97 semi-monthly payments to $450.00. The additional payment blue-cell is $15.03, which results in all but $90.35 of your mortgage being paid off on August 22, 2020, instead of June 22, 2021.

Budgeting for an extra $15.03 per payment pays your mortgage off 20-payments earlier. At the minimum payment you would have been paying $434.97 x 20 = $8,699.40 over those 20-payments. Paying an extra $15 per payment now, saves you $8,700 later!

Rounded-up to $500 per payment and all but $123.57 is paid off on June 22, 2018. An extra $65.03 per payment now will save you paying $434.97 x 72 = $31,317.84 later. This also reduces your mortgage or loan amortization from 15 to 12-years!

A hidden bonus is that three years of mortgage insurance payments will totally disappear!

Simple rounding up of payments is easier to remember, convenient and lowers loan terms and interest costs significantly. You don't want to stretch yourself too thin with payments higher than you can reasonably afford, but you also don't want to set payments too low as most of us tend to procrastinate on well intentioned but soon forgotten extra payments.

Some borrowers, such as commission sales people, may not have steady income and can only commit to the minimum monthly payment. When there is expected extra cash flow, you can use the amortization table to factor-in extra lump sum payments by changing the payments blue-cells at any desired payment date.

The amortization table is very accurate but there are a few points to keep in mind. Each calculated interest paid has to be rounded somehow, to account for fractions of a cent. The most common way, and how this table works, is to round one-digit after the cent, rounding up if $0.005 or more, otherwise rounding down to the nearest cent.

Lenders may round fractions of a cent off, up or down, to different number of digits after the decimal point. Don't worry about this; we are talking pennies over long-term loans. However, if each payment is significantly different than your bank indicates, it is usually because your bank is adding home and life insurance, property taxes or other amounts to each loan payment.

Budgeting is simpler, and it may save time or be more convenient to allow your lender to collect and pay these amounts for you. They are more than happy to do this, and often require it! This is not a goodwill service, your bank is simply protecting their loan collateral by making sure your home insurance, mortgage life insurance and property taxes are paid!

Find out exactly what these extra amounts are per payment, and subtract them from the loan payment indicated by your bank. The result should then equal the amortization table minimum payment amount, if their loan terms are the same as all your blue-cell amounts.

Use this table to more effectively plan long-term loans. Play with different scenarios in the privacy of your home, considering every angle without being rushed, until you decide on the loan structure that works best for you!

You now fully appreciate how compound loan interest is a drag on wealth, with the tool to manage this properly. The next chapter explains how compound investment returns build savings and enhance wealth, with different ways to plan your lifetime wealth goals.

Chapter 4

Second Key to Wealth: Time & Compounding

You already know that a wealthy mindset has a wealth plan with reasonable expectations.

The 'Your Wealth Now, in a Nutshell' worksheet helped determine your monthly savings rate and target future wealth needs. Your 'Wealth Creation Budget' has helped determine your immediate level of surplus savings to expect over the next year, and where adjustments are needed to stay on track. Your 'Amortization Table' has helped you strategically plan mortgages and long-term loans, to lower interest costs and reduce the time it takes to payoff your debt.

In order to fully achieve your lifetime wealth goals, you need to further define, reinforce and look for other ways to enhance your wealth plan. You should reference your list of things of value again, and consider how this list will change over time.

The current lifetime expectancy in the United States and Canada is around 80 years, with women still expected to outlive men by a few years on average. Obviously nobody has a perfect crystal ball, but this can be useful for wealth planning purposes to visualize snapshots of your lifetime in twenty-year quarters.

Twenty-Year Lifetime Quarters are a practical timeframe as we usually take around 20 years from birth to gain an education, grow into an adult and start earning an income. The second twenty-year quarter from age 20 to 40 is when most people get married, buy a home and raise a family, and set career and lifestyle decisions.

The third quarter from age 40 to 60 is usually when career, income and living standards are established, and debt repayment and retirement savings need to be accelerated. The fourth quarter from 60 to 80+ is usually when income and lifestyle may again change considerably, as retirement costs and health concerns become your main focus.

It is reasonable to expect needs to change over time, and as surplus savings build to reward yourself by acquiring some of your wants. It can be useful to develop separate lists of things of value for each of the lifetime quarters you are looking forward to.

Similarly it may be very useful to mock up future wealth creation budgets with reasonable assumed gross income, expenses, loans, mortgages and investments. In other words you should have a good idea how you want your income and expense planner, yearly savings, investment planner and net worth to look like at ages 20, 40, 60 and 80.

Breaking down your wealth goals into lifetime quarters helps you focus on the next 20 years. This is practical because even though you expect to retire some day, if you are 20 or 30 years old, retirement seems too long away to be thinking about and planning now.

However for the next 20 years, you may see your life as not that different than today, with the same health, house, marriage and profession. Otherwise you may need a 10-year plan, for example. At the end of 20 years, or when major lifestyle changes occur, you need to review your quarterly lifetime goals!

Time and compounding is a key to wealth because it shows you how you need investment savings to perform each year, in order to meet your lifetime wealth goals. The important point is to move ahead financially each year, and not let time slip away!

Most people want to retire as early as possible! You need to first set a reasonable target retirement age, which is the easy part. Then you need to produce a wealth creation budget that supports your retirement expense needs and any remaining debt costs at that time.

The tricky part is that during retirement your gross income is your pension income, which is considerably less. Lower retirement income is even more pronounced for those who do not have a pension to look forward to, other than very low social security payments!

The future tangibility of a government pension, Medicare, and even many corporate pension plans are very much in question these days. In any event government social security and even corporate pension plans are not in your control and may be at risk.

If a pension is not available or is uncertain, this leaves only retirement savings and the income produced from all investments to rely on for your needs. If after tax income from all savings is not enough to support your retirement needs, then the principal value of savings is consumed just to pay the bills. This can result in even lower investment income that can accelerate wealth destruction and negatively affect lifestyle in a short time.

For example, it is a fact that most people consume 80% of their total lifetime medical needs in the last two years alive. A wealthy mindset is careful and plans for savings to outlive him or her, and not the other way around!

Your wealth plan goal should have adequate savings and investment income goals that support all your retirement needs. You are not in control of your eventual lifestyle and Wealth Destiny if you plan for anything less!

Alternatively you could set a wealth plan goal based on a net worth value, instead of savings and investment returns. However this assumes that you have sold all assets and repaid all loans at retirement, in order for the remaining net worth cash to be available to support your needs.

Either wealth plan goal is appropriate, as long as you consider all debt and the lifestyle adjustments implied! The important point is to set a retirement age wealth plan goal that is reasonable! Use 'Your Wealth Now, in a Nutshell' targets if you are not sure.

You should also notice that the wealth creation budget has cells called Total Investments and Net Worth or Equity, in the investment planner. Under % Rate, this shows the approximate rate of return for all your investments and a net worth value for that year. While the future always brings change, these amounts and % rates should be seen as a reality check on how your investments are performing now.

Quarterly lifetime wealth creation budgets help you determine 20-year wealth plan savings goals. You then need to take your current and expected savings, yearly surplus savings, investment return and tax rate, and project these forward. Only then will you know if your goals are reasonable, or if adjustments are needed to get back on track!

Depending on your financial situation and the lifetime quarter you are in, you may have determined from your quarterly snapshots that one million dollars may not be enough. A million dollars today and especially in the future is not the status symbol it used to be. This is discussed in more detail in chapter 4.5 on the cost of inflation.

However, if you have just started to save, or your age is in the first or second lifetime quarters, a million dollars is still a substantial amount. It is also a common round number that many people still shoot for as their first reasonable wealth goal.

On your wealth plan excel workbook, click the fourth tab at the bottom called 'Time & Compounding'. This spreadsheet is another powerful wealth planning tool that is very easy to use. It was designed to better visualize your yearly savings over your entire lifetime, with various compounding effects factored in.

Using another automobile analogy, the Compounding Effect is like the gas pedal and odometer of your investment savings. It is the speed at which your investments grow in value, and over time is extremely important in determining how far your savings will go.

You also need a reasonable level of Wealth Acceleration, investment compounding, to get you to the retirement finish line on time. There are also unreasonable speed limits; inappropriately high or low risk investment returns, both dangerous to wealth results.

The time and compounding tools go beyond 'Your Wealth Now, in a Nutshell'. They help you better visualize various compounding effects by structuring savings plans in different ways. They can also be used to determine needed yearly surplus savings and investment rates of return so that you don't fall behind on your wealth goals.

Like the other worksheets, the time and compounding tools are intuitive. They factor in the negative effects of taxes against taxable savings returns, and the positive effects of tax savings on tax sheltered retirement savings and education savings plans. They even factor in Canadian Education Savings Grants added to RESP contributions.

The time and compounding tools are long-term savings plans with four easy ways to build wealth. They are called: The Wealth Fountain of Youth, The Simple & Steady Savings Plan, Tax Sheltered RSP Wealth on Steroids, and The Education No Brainer.

There is even a table called The Cost of Inflation, used to compare future dollars to today dollars, to better visualize results in a relevant time value perspective.

It's quick, easy and even fun playing around with the following time and compounding savings tables. You will notice subtle differences between them that change results over time in a big way. The point is to recognize and understand these differences and how they might relate to your own personal financial situation, and to then choose the best fit to meet your own personal wealth plan goals.

Chapter 4.1
Wealth Fountain of Youth

enter your age	invest your birthday times	start of year investment funds	end of year investment at return rate of 10.00%	end of year investment after taxes at 25.00%
1	$ 150	$ -	10.00%	25.00%
1	$ 150	$ 150	$ 165	$ 161
2	$ 300	$ 461	$ 507	$ 496
3	$ 450	$ 946	$ 1,040	$ 1,017
4	$ 600	$ 1,617	$ 1,778	$ 1,738
5	$ 750	$ 2,488	$ 2,737	$ 2,675
6	$ 900	$ 3,575	$ 3,932	$ 3,843
7	$ 1,050	$ 4,893	$ 5,382	$ 5,260
8	$ 1,200	$ 6,460	$ 7,106	$ 6,944
9	$ 1,350	$ 8,294	$ 9,124	$ 8,916
10	$ 1,500	$ 10,416	$ 11,458	$ 11,197
11	$ 1,650	$ 12,847	$ 14,132	$ 13,811
12	$ 1,800	$ 15,611	$ 17,172	$ 16,782
13	$ 1,950	$ 18,732	$ 20,605	$ 20,137
14	$ 2,100	$ 22,237	$ 24,460	$ 23,904
15	$ 2,250	$ 26,154	$ 28,770	$ 28,116
16	$ 2,400	$ 30,516	$ 33,568	$ 32,805
17	$ 2,550	$ 35,355	$ 38,890	$ 38,006
18	$ 2,700	$ 40,706	$ 44,777	$ 43,759
19	$ 2,850	$ 46,609	$ 51,270	$ 50,105
20	$ 3,000	$ 53,105	$ 58,416	$ 57,088
21	$ 3,150	$ 60,238	$ 66,262	$ 64,756
22	$ 3,300	$ 68,056	$ 74,861	$ 73,160
23	$ 3,450	$ 76,610	$ 84,271	$ 82,356
24	$ 3,600	$ 85,956	$ 94,551	$ 92,402
25	$ 3,750	$ 96,152	$ 105,768	$ 103,364
26	$ 3,900	$ 107,264	$ 117,990	$ 115,309
27	$ 4,050	$ 119,359	$ 131,294	$ 128,311
28	$ 4,200	$ 132,511	$ 145,762	$ 142,449
29	$ 4,350	$ 146,799	$ 161,479	$ 157,809
30	$ 4,500	$ 162,309	$ 178,540	$ 174,482
31	$ 4,650	$ 179,132	$ 197,045	$ 192,567
32	$ 4,800	$ 197,367	$ 217,103	$ 212,169
33	$ 4,950	$ 217,119	$ 238,831	$ 233,403
34	$ 5,100	$ 238,503	$ 262,354	$ 256,391
35	$ 5,250	$ 261,641	$ 287,805	$ 281,264
36	$ 5,400	$ 286,664	$ 315,330	$ 308,164
37	$ 5,550	$ 313,714	$ 345,085	$ 337,242
38	$ 5,700	$ 342,942	$ 377,237	$ 368,663
39	$ 5,850	$ 374,513	$ 411,964	$ 402,602
40	$ 6,000	$ 408,602	$ 449,462	$ 439,247
41	$ 6,150	$ 445,397	$ 489,936	$ 478,801
42	$ 6,300	$ 485,101	$ 533,612	$ 521,484
43	$ 6,450	$ 527,934	$ 580,727	$ 567,529
44	$ 6,600	$ 574,129	$ 631,542	$ 617,189
45	$ 6,750	$ 623,939	$ 686,333	$ 670,734
46	$ 6,900	$ 677,634	$ 745,398	$ 728,457
47	$ 7,050	$ 735,507	$ 809,057	$ 790,670
48	$ 7,200	$ 797,870	$ 877,657	$ 857,710
49	$ 7,350	$ 865,060	$ 951,566	$ 929,939
50	$ 7,500	$ 937,439	$ 1,031,183	$ 1,007,747
total contrib's				total tax paid
$ 191,250				$ 272,166

Wealth Fountain of Youth shows how even very small amounts of savings started early in life, with gradual increases over time, can produce real wealth. It is an ideal way to demonstrate to even a young child, the importance and power of savings invested as early as possible. Newborn gifts are soon forgotten, but this is the plan that really keeps giving!

Let's assume a wealth fountain of youth 50-year goal of one million dollars. You start the plan off with $150 on the baby's first birthday. Each birthday you add $150 multiplied by the child's age. Parents and grandparents may wish to chip in together each year, as the contributions are $1,050 by year 7.

However the yearly savings become very reasonable when you look out 20 or 25 years, when the young adult should be working and making their own contributions. Even at age 50, the last year's contribution is only $7,500.

Like the other worksheets, the wealth fountain of youth and all four savings plans are flexible and color-coded for simplicity. The blue-cells up top should be changed as needed and the green cells throughout will then auto-fill, but can also be changed.

$150 is multiplied by age because this is how much it worked out to, in order to reach our 50-year million-dollar goal. Actually to be precise the amount is $148.85 times your age. Scroll down and you will see that the total contributions over 50 years are only $191,250, with a $1,007,747 wealth result, assuming a 10% investment return and 25% tax rate.

Any of the blue-cell assumptions can be changed to show any number of scenarios desired. For example, if the child is older, you can change the 'enter your age' blue-cell and the light-green age cells will automatically update.

If you have some savings already, you can enter this amount into the 'start of year investment funds' blue-cell, and this will be factored into all results. Change the 'end of year investment return rate' blue-cell, if a 10% rate of return doesn't seem appropriate.

The 'end of year investment after taxes at' 25% blue-cell should be updated. The tax rate will depend on actual earned and investment income, which may change over time. In Canada your child or anyone doesn't pay tax until earned income exceeds approximately $8,500 per year. However this may affect your taxes if you gift the contributions.

Therefore you may wish to set the tax rate at 0% to start, for a child. Let's then assume by age 25, for example, this person will be paying taxes at a 25% tax rate. All you need to do is find the age-24 line, and re-enter the 'end of year investment after taxes' amount. This is the last green cell, and these amounts should be re-entered for all the same cells back to year one.

The numbers don't change, but by re-entering them, the formulas in these cells are changed to set amounts. If we didn't do this, these cells would update automatically when you then adjust the tax rate from 0% back to 25%, which you may only want to apply to years going forward from age 25.

This same process of changing certain green cells with formulas embedded to set amounts, and then changing that column's blue-cell amounts, to update the other green cells, can be used to vary the yearly contribution amount, the investment return rate, or to adjust any projected amount to an actual result as received over time.

When you update the tax rate to 25%, you will notice the year 50 results are now $1,195,376. They were $1,007,747 with the tax rate at 25% for all years. This small change of reducing taxes to 0% until age 25, improves total age 50 results by $187,629.

Remember that these tax savings applied to only the first 24 years, and we started with just $150. At age 24 the total results are $121,023, however the compounded tax savings for the first 24 years produced an additional $187,629 at age 50.

One of the inherent values of the Wealth Fountain of Youth is that as children grow up, they may not earn much, but they can earn up to approximately $8,500 per year tax-free!

The wealth fountain of youth savings plan is most effective if you are starting to save in the first or second lifetime quarter, with at least

20 years until retirement. However it is still useful for wealth-planning purposes at any age, especially if you can only save and invest a small amount at first, but plan to accelerate savings every year.

The purpose of all four plans is to motivate you to start and commit to save and invest regularly! The wealth fountain of youth helps demonstrate the value of saving, even small amounts of money, versus just spending. This is especially important to learn at the same time a young person discovers money!

Chapter 4.2
Simple & Steady Savings Plan

The Simple & Steady Savings Plan!

invest equal amount each year of	start of year investment funds	end of year investment at return rate of 10.00%	end of year investment after taxes at 25.00%
$ 1,928	$ -	10.00%	25.00%
$ 1,928	$ 1,928	$ 2,121	$ 2,073
$ 1,928	$ 4,001	$ 4,401	$ 4,301
$ 1,928	$ 6,229	$ 6,852	$ 6,696
$ 1,928	$ 8,624	$ 9,486	$ 9,271
$ 1,928	$ 11,199	$ 12,318	$ 12,038
$ 1,928	$ 13,966	$ 15,363	$ 15,014
$ 1,928	$ 16,942	$ 18,636	$ 18,213
$ 1,928	$ 20,141	$ 22,155	$ 21,651
$ 1,928	$ 23,579	$ 25,937	$ 25,348
$ 1,928	$ 27,276	$ 30,003	$ 29,321
$ 1,928	$ 31,249	$ 34,374	$ 33,593
$ 1,928	$ 35,521	$ 39,073	$ 38,185
$ 1,928	$ 40,113	$ 44,124	$ 43,121
$ 1,928	$ 45,049	$ 49,554	$ 48,428
$ 1,928	$ 50,356	$ 55,392	$ 54,133
$ 1,928	$ 56,061	$ 61,667	$ 60,265
$ 1,928	$ 62,193	$ 68,413	$ 66,858
$ 1,928	$ 68,786	$ 75,665	$ 73,945
$ 1,928	$ 75,873	$ 83,460	$ 81,563
$ 1,928	$ 83,491	$ 91,841	$ 89,753
$ 1,928	$ 91,681	$ 100,849	$ 98,557
$ 1,928	$ 100,485	$ 110,534	$ 108,022
$ 1,928	$ 109,950	$ 120,945	$ 118,196
$ 1,928	$ 120,124	$ 132,136	$ 129,133
$ 1,928	$ 131,061	$ 144,167	$ 140,891
$ 1,928	$ 142,819	$ 157,101	$ 153,530
$ 1,928	$ 155,458	$ 171,004	$ 167,118
$ 1,928	$ 169,046	$ 185,950	$ 181,724
$ 1,928	$ 183,652	$ 202,017	$ 197,426
$ 1,928	$ 199,354	$ 219,289	$ 214,306
$ 1,928	$ 216,234	$ 237,857	$ 232,451
$ 1,928	$ 234,379	$ 257,817	$ 251,958
$ 1,928	$ 253,886	$ 279,274	$ 272,927
$ 1,928	$ 274,855	$ 302,340	$ 295,469
$ 1,928	$ 297,397	$ 327,137	$ 319,702
$ 1,928	$ 321,630	$ 353,793	$ 345,752
$ 1,928	$ 347,680	$ 382,448	$ 373,756
$ 1,928	$ 375,684	$ 413,253	$ 403,860
$ 1,928	$ 405,788	$ 446,367	$ 436,223
$ 1,928	$ 438,151	$ 481,966	$ 471,012
$ 1,928	$ 472,940	$ 520,234	$ 508,410
$ 1,928	$ 510,338	$ 561,372	$ 548,614
$ 1,928	$ 550,542	$ 605,596	$ 591,832
$ 1,928	$ 593,760	$ 653,136	$ 638,292
$ 1,928	$ 640,220	$ 704,242	$ 688,237
$ 1,928	$ 690,165	$ 759,181	$ 741,927
$ 1,928	$ 743,855	$ 818,241	$ 799,644
$ 1,928	$ 801,572	$ 881,730	$ 861,690
$ 1,928	$ 863,618	$ 949,980	$ 928,390
$ 1,928	$ 930,318	$ 1,023,350	$ 1,000,092

total contrib's			total tax paid
$ 96,400			$ 301,231

The second plan, called 'Simple & Steady Savings Plan', demonstrates another perspective on the power of time and compounding in meeting reasonable wealth goals! This plan is like 'Your Wealth Now, in a Nutshell' except that savings are assumed invested and compounded yearly, instead of monthly, for simplicity and visual affect.

Like the wealth fountain of youth, this savings plan factors in yearly savings, starting funds, and rates of investment return and taxes. The main difference is that instead of using a dollar multiplier times your birthday, it assumes a fixed savings amount invested every year. Like the name suggests, it is simple to use and the easiest plan to follow!

The simple and steady savings plan is perfect to use at any age, especially when yearly savings are not expected to change much for the foreseeable future! Use this plan to set a yearly savings amount, to see the results over time, or to determine how much you need to save each year in order to reach your wealth goal by a certain age.

$1,928 per year is how much it worked out to, in order to reach our 50-year million-dollar goal. Actually to be precise the amount is $1,927.83 per year. The total contributions over 50 years are only $96,400, with a $1,000,092 wealth result.

The first three savings plans all assume a 10% investment return and 25% tax rate for easy comparison. Saving and investing $1,928 every year, instead of $150 the first year and more each year going forward, results in you contributing $94,850 less overall than for the wealth fountain of youth savings plan. Also the 50th year contribution is up to $7,500 in the first plan, but it is still only $1,928 in the last year of this plan.

This is an excellent way to visualize how more invested upfront, will save you a bundle of money later, in more than one way. Also $1,928, or $161 per month, is usually a reasonable amount to plan to save, even within tight budgets.

You may remember that the wealth creation budget suggests a minimum $2,000 yearly savings goal. The point is to plan for tomorrow today, as yearly savings will have to be substantially more if started later, investment returns are lower, or if tax rates are higher.

To further this point let's assume you don't start saving until age 25. Change the 'enter your age' blue-cell to 25. In order to accomplish your million-dollar age 50 goal, you will have to change the 'invest equal amount each year of' blue-cell to $12,557.78.

In other words, putting off saving until age 25 means that you will have to contribute over 6.50 times as much each year, in order to catch up and meet your wealth goal. Starting 5-years earlier at age 20 lowers the yearly savings amount to $8,294.22. This is down to $5,576.25 per year if you start saving at age 15. The earlier the better, as time and compounding determines everything!

Realistically it may not be possible for a young person to save these amounts at this time, or you may be reading this at a much later age, or your wealth goals may be higher or lower, or the investment return or tax rate may not be appropriate etc. This plan is a reality check, to help you know what you should expect and changes that are needed, in order to set-up and catch-up your wealth savings plan.

Over time you may find that your yearly savings are not exactly as planned. You can easily reflect this by changing green cell results to actual amounts. You would then review how this affects all your results and make adjustments as needed to stay on track.

For example, let's say you want to start a million dollar wealth savings plan at age 30. You have already saved $25,000, invested in unsheltered taxable stock and bond mutual funds. They have been yielding 11.25% overall and are expected to continue at this rate.

Your tax rate is 30%. Your net income is $35,000 and you expect to be able to contribute 10% of this amount each year. You will also be able to increase your savings gradually by $500 per year with annual pay raises expected. Your other goal is to retire by age 60.

First update the blue-cells. Change 'enter your age' from 1 to 30. Enter $25,000 at 'start of year investment funds'. Change the 'end of year investment after taxes at' 25% to 30%. Change the 'end of year investment at return rate of' 10% to 11.25%. Then Change 'invest equal amount each year of' $1,928 to $3,500.

Your savings contributions change each year, therefore you will need to update the 'invest equal amount each year of' green cells as well. Change them for all years from age 31 to age 60, increasing the amount by $500 each year.

You will notice that when you change the age-31 first green cell to $4,000, the later years green cells change to this amount as well. This makes it easier to calculate yearly savings contributions, as you only need to add $500 to the previous year amount.

The last yearly contribution at age 60 should work out to be $18,500. The total wealth savings result should be $1,329,411. You should also see that under this plan, you could achieve your million-dollar retirement goal as early as age-57!

These tools are meant to be quick and simple to use, based on reasonable long-term expectations. However with a little practice and simple tweaking, your plan can be very accurate and reflect a variety of year-to-year changes.

To do this, simply re-enter all the green cells for the year before future changes occur, and for all prior years going back in time. Then change the blue-cells up top as needed, to project future results from that year forward. Do this as often as you wish going forward in time and your plan will accurately reflect all year-to-year changes desired.

Chapter 4.3
Tax Sheltered RSP, Wealth on Steroids

Tax Sheltered RSP, Wealth on Steroids!						
your tax rate:		25.00%	start of year		end of year	
your current		tax savings	retirement		investment at	
RSP contrib.		reinvested	savings plan		return rate of	
$	625	$	156	$	-	10.00%
$	625	$	156	$	781	$ 859
$	625	$	156	$	1,641	$ 1,805
$	625	$	156	$	2,586	$ 2,845
$	625	$	156	$	3,626	$ 3,988
$	625	$	156	$	4,770	$ 5,247
$	625	$	156	$	6,028	$ 6,631
$	625	$	156	$	7,412	$ 8,153
$	625	$	156	$	8,934	$ 9,828
$	625	$	156	$	10,609	$ 11,670
$	625	$	156	$	12,451	$ 13,696
$	625	$	156	$	14,477	$ 15,925
$	625	$	156	$	16,706	$ 18,377
$	625	$	156	$	19,158	$ 21,074
$	625	$	156	$	21,855	$ 24,041
$	625	$	156	$	24,822	$ 27,304
$	625	$	156	$	28,086	$ 30,894
$	625	$	156	$	31,676	$ 34,843
$	625	$	156	$	35,624	$ 39,187
$	625	$	156	$	39,968	$ 43,965
$	625	$	156	$	44,746	$ 49,221
$	625	$	156	$	50,002	$ 55,002
$	625	$	156	$	55,783	$ 61,362
$	625	$	156	$	62,143	$ 68,357
$	625	$	156	$	69,139	$ 76,052
$	625	$	156	$	76,834	$ 84,517
$	625	$	156	$	85,298	$ 93,828
$	625	$	156	$	94,609	$ 104,070
$	625	$	156	$	104,852	$ 115,337
$	625	$	156	$	116,118	$ 127,730
$	625	$	156	$	128,511	$ 141,362
$	625	$	156	$	142,143	$ 156,358
$	625	$	156	$	157,139	$ 172,853
$	625	$	156	$	173,634	$ 190,997
$	625	$	156	$	191,779	$ 210,957
$	625	$	156	$	211,738	$ 232,912
$	625	$	156	$	233,693	$ 257,062
$	625	$	156	$	257,843	$ 283,628
$	625	$	156	$	284,409	$ 312,850
$	625	$	156	$	313,631	$ 344,994
$	625	$	156	$	345,775	$ 380,353
$	625	$	156	$	381,134	$ 419,248
$	625	$	156	$	420,029	$ 462,032
$	625	$	156	$	462,813	$ 509,094
$	625	$	156	$	509,876	$ 560,863
$	625	$	156	$	561,644	$ 617,809
$	625	$	156	$	618,590	$ 680,449
$	625	$	156	$	681,230	$ 749,353
$	625	$	156	$	750,135	$ 825,148
$	625	$	156	$	825,929	$ 908,522
$	625	$	156	$	909,304	$ 1,000,234
total contrib's		tax contrib's			total tax paid	
$	31,250	$	7,813		$	-

The third time and compounding tool is your most powerful wealth creation savings plan! It is called Tax Sheltered RSP, Wealth on Steroids. This plan has two key advantages, it removes the drag on investment performance of taxes, plus tax refunds are re-invested to turbo charge results.

Many countries such as Canada and the United States provide Retirement Savings Plan tax incentives to save for your own retirement. This is not government tax charity; they know there is a real need, as millions of baby boomers will be retiring soon. There simply is not be enough medical, pension or social assistance money to go around for everyone.

Savings invested within a Retirement Savings Plan are tax sheltered until withdrawn, plus your current taxes are reduced. When withdrawing funds from an RSP, presumably for retirement needs, you are taxed at your tax rate at that time, which is usually lower than your current tax rate.

In other words an RSP offers a triple wealth bonus; your savings grow tax-free for now, plus you pay taxes later at a lower rate, plus you pay less tax now or receive a tax refund. Sometimes this can even result in lowering your tax bracket, your percentage tax rate, which may further reduce your current taxes.

To better visualize the impact of taxes, go back to the first two savings plans and change just the blue-cell 'end of year investment after taxes at' 25% to 30%. You will see that even a small tax rate change has a dramatic effect on results over time.

The third savings plan reveals the powerful wealth effect of contributing to a tax sheltered plan, compared to unsheltered plans. In addition your tax rate determines a yearly tax savings bonus, instead of a yearly tax drag cost, on investment returns!

The government sets Registered RSP's and 401k plans contribution limits. For example in Canada, the 2006 contribution limit is 18% of earned income, up to a maximum of $18,000. Contributing to an RSP reduces your taxable income by this amount. This lowers your tax obligation, or results in a tax refund on your tax return.

There are options if you cannot afford to contribute the maximum each year to your RSP or 401k. Unused contribution room is not lost, as it is carried forward for future years use when more affordable. This also provides some flexibility for tax planning purposes. For example it might be more beneficial to hold off or apply a contribution next year, if your income and tax rate is then expected to be substantially higher.

However a wealthy mindset knows the value of time and compounding, which also needs to be factored into these decisions. Unless your income from year to year is very erratic, it is usually best not to procrastinate.

Therefore, even if you cannot fully afford to maximize your RSP or 401k contributions, the tax benefits plus time and compounding investment returns, often warrant borrowing to top-up your contribution. This is usually true even if the loan rate is somewhat higher than your RSP investment return rate, if the loan is paid off quickly within a year.

If you do borrow to top-up RSP or 401k contributions, your tax savings or refund should be used to pay down the loan faster. This type of loan should be worked into your wealth creation budget investment planner and income and expense planner for the next year.

The tax sheltered RSP wealth on steroids savings plan, encourages you to also contribute your yearly tax saving. This will dramatically accelerate your savings wealth, assuming you don't need to use these tax savings to pay off a contribution top-up loan. In other words put these tax refunds or tax reductions to work, to build wealth faster!

$625 per year is how much it worked out to, to reach our 50-year million-dollar goal. The precise amount is $624.86 per year. The total contributions over 50 years are only $31,250, plus $7,813 in re-invested tax savings or refunds, with a $1,000,234 wealth result. This savings plan also assumes a 10% investment return and 25% tax rate.

Now change 'your current RSP contribution' blue-cell to the same $1,928 amount used in the simple and steady savings plan. This produces a 50-year result of $3,085,522! The effect of tax-sheltered investment growth, plus adding yearly tax savings or refunds to your RSP contribution, is an additional $2,085,430!

Out of pocket contributions are the same, but the wealth opportunity of this tax sheltered investment savings plan is over triple the result! Now you understand why "steroids" was added to this plans name!

This is an exciting way to demonstrate the importance of effectively managing taxes. To be practical, you still need to factor in the taxes that are paid as you make withdrawals. However, with an extra $2 million this shouldn't be a problem!

This is a substantial amount of money and you should be using a qualified tax advisor by then, to minimize tax withdrawal costs. However, even if your tax rate is much higher, you will still be way ahead, plus your remaining RSP continues growing tax deferred.

This can also be used to demonstrate why it is far more important to position your investments tax effectively, rather than only focusing on higher returns. High investment returns are always desirable, but they also imply more risk of capital loss, or wealth destruction. In other words tax sheltered RSP's provide a very safe way to ramp up or leverage time and compounding results!

For example let's revisit our million-dollar wealth savings plan at age 30. This time your starting $25,000 is already in a tax-sheltered self-directed RSP, invested in the same stock and bond mutual funds yielding 11.25%. Your tax rate is still 30%, net income is $35,000, and yearly contributions are the same $3,500 that increases yearly by $500.

First change the 'enter your age' blue-cell to 30. Then change the tax sheltered RSP wealth on steroids blue-cells; 'your current RSP contribution' is $3,500, 'start of year retirement savings plan' is $25,000, 'end of year investment at return rate of' is 11.25% and 'your tax rate:' is 30%.

You will see this auto-fills $1,050 per year in all 'tax savings reinvested' blue and green cells. If your tax rate is 30%, a $3,500 RSP contribution will reduce taxes or provide a tax refund of $1,050, which should also be contributed to your RSP. $3,500 x 0.30 = $1,050.

This extra $1,050 contribution actually produces a further $315 tax refund that we didn't factor in to keep things simple. For the same reason, we didn't factor in the approximate $7,500 in tax refunds received over prior years while building up your $25,000 RSP. If you do have $25,000 in unused RSP contribution room, you can add this to the age-30 contribution green cell, and then change the age-31 contribution back to $3,500.

However, large lump sum RSP contributions like this may warrant additional tax planning to maximize value. Income and timing questions such as whether to claim this as a current year or future years contribution, and whether to contribute this to your RSP or a spousal RSP may need further consideration.

For our million-dollar RSP wealth savings plan at age 30, we are keeping things simple by assuming the $25,000 in previous savings was already contributed to an RSP, entered into the 'start of year retirement savings plan' blue-cell. You still need to increase all 'your current RSP contribution' green cells by $500 for each year from ages 31 to 60.

Your objective is to find out if this tax sheltered plan allows you to retire even earlier than age 57, as under the simple and steady savings plan. You also want to know how much of a retirement wealth buffer you have, if investments don't perform as expected.

Your age 60 results are now $3,162,382. Your million-dollar retirement goal is achieved after only 22 years at age 51. You can retire six years earlier, but to be safe you plan to actually retire at age 52, to have a buffer available to pay taxes on future withdrawals.

Your age-60 retirement wealth buffer is also determined by changing the 'end of year investment at return rate of' blue-cell. If your compound annual returns are only 5.035%, your one million dollar by age-60 goal is still achievable. This implies that you have 11.25% minus 5.035% as an investment return buffer, or a 6.215% margin of safety. To again allow for taxes, and for yearly investment return fluctuations, you should roundup your reasonable yearly minimum investment return goal to at least 7%.

If for some reason you don't want to re-invest your tax refunds, simply change the 'tax savings reinvested' green cells to $0. This will reduce your results, meaning you will have to increase your contributions in order to meet your wealth goals. An easier way to calculate yearly RSP contributions without re-investing tax savings, is to use the simple and steady savings plan and set the tax rate to 0%.

For example, let's say you started your first real job at age 20, your tax rate is 25% and you plan to contribute $2,000 per year to an RSP. You want to keep things simple and will spend any tax refunds received, but you want to know if this is still enough to produce any real wealth by age 60, assuming a 10% investment return.

Use the simple and steady savings plan like a tax sheltered plan by changing the tax rate to 0%. Change the age to 20 and yearly contribution to $2,000. The age 60 results work out to $1,073,274. This should be enough to inspire you to get going with an RSP, and to explore various other wealth planning scenarios.

Now go back to the tax sheltered RSP wealth on steroids plan and look at how much you could have, if you instead put those $500 tax refunds to work as well. The age 60 results are now $1,341,592. Surely whatever you bought with that $500 tax refund each year didn't add up to the extra $268,318 you would have if your refunds were reinvested?

The downside of RSP tax savings is that many forget that tax is paid on the full amount of RSP withdrawals, and not just on the interest earned or capital gains. Tax refunds should be seen as a future tax loan, and not as extra current consumption. Otherwise wealth is reduced if you spend tax savings, and you should think of them this way!

You could even view tax savings and tax refunds as an RSP mortgage. You need to save and invest tax savings today, because at least some of this will be clawed back later when tax is deducted on RSP withdrawals. In other words, if you spend the RSP mortgage money instead of investing it, the remaining value of your RSP house will have to pay off this mortgage some day.

RSP's are really just tax deferred savings plans, which work to your advantage if there is enough time and compounding left, or your retirement tax rate will be lower than your current tax rate. To avoid paying more tax than you receive in current tax savings, you may need to consider the timing of your last few yearly contributions before withdrawals are needed.

Unless you are self-employed, your employer usually takes taxes off each paycheck. In a way your employer, or really the government, makes you budget for taxes by collecting them upfront. This forces you to budget for all your other bills with the remainder.

Since you are already meeting your needs with after tax income, this is why the wealth creation budget adds RSP contribution tax savings to your surplus savings for investment. Similarly the tax sheltered RSP wealth on steroids plan treats tax savings or tax refunds as a savings bonus, or extra wealth value to be re-invested.

RSP's have other perks as well. You are allowed to borrow up to $20,000 from your RSP to buy your first home. You can even borrow from your RSP to buy or start a private business, or as a short-term loan if needed under certain conditions.

In these situations you would repay your RSP loan over a set timeline. You can even pay interest to your RSP within guidelines. Borrowing from your RSP is not subject to early withdrawal taxes and is a great way to fund a first home down payment or a prudent business loan, while keeping your tax-sheltered retirement plan on track.

For all these reasons you can see why a RSP should be the foundation of your wealth plan!

Chapter 4.4
Education No Brainer

The Education No Brainer!

invest equal amount each year to RESP	CESG Grant is added, * calculated at	end of year investment at R.O.R. of
$ 2,000	20.00%	6.00%
$ 2,000	$ 400	$ 2,544
$ 2,000	$ 400	$ 5,241
$ 2,000	$ 400	$ 8,099
$ 2,000	$ 400	$ 11,129
$ 2,000	$ 400	$ 14,341
$ 2,000	$ 400	$ 17,745
$ 2,000	$ 400	$ 21,354
$ 2,000	$ 400	$ 25,179
$ 2,000	$ 400	$ 29,234
$ 2,000	$ 400	$ 33,532
$ 2,000	$ 400	$ 38,088
$ 2,000	$ 400	$ 42,917
$ 2,000	$ 400	$ 48,036
$ 2,000	$ 400	$ 53,462
$ 2,000	$ 400	$ 59,214
$ 2,000	$ 400	$ 65,311
$ 2,000	$ 400	$ 71,774
$ 2,000	$ 400	$ 78,624

total contrib's	* total CESG	
$ 36,000	$ 7,200	

balance	school year	allocation
$ 78,624	$ for year 1 =	$ 19,656
$ 62,506	$ for year 2 =	$ 20,835
$ 44,171	$ for year 3 =	$ 22,085
$ 23,411	$ for year 4 =	$ 23,411

total contrib's	+ all gains =	edu. funds
$ 36,000	$ 49,987	$ 85,987
contributions overall return =		138.85%

RESP / CESG Limits

* RESP maximum contribution per child:
$4,000 per year
$42,000 lifetime total

* CESG maximum grant per child:
$400 per year
$800 per year if carried forward
$7,200 lifetime total

* if net family income is less than $35,595
CESG is 40% of first $500 contributed

* if net family income is less than $71,190
CESG is 30% of first $500 contributed

* otherwise the minimum CESG is 20%

total contrib's	tax contrib's	total tax paid
$ 36,000	$ 7,200	$ -

The fourth time and compounding tool is called 'Education No Brainer'. The main purpose of this savings plan is to fund family education needs.

This type of plan usually does not create wealth for you, but should for your children. However, if you believe you are responsible for helping your children with their education costs, this really is a wealth plan for you as well.

Strategically planning a tax-sheltered RESP Registered Education Savings Plan early minimizes your costs later in a big way. This provides wealth value for you because it reduces your future expenses. Like they say a penny saved is a penny earned!

Education costs in Canada over the past ten years have been going up 7.6% per year on average, and are expected to maintain this pace going forward for the foreseeable future. Students at most post-secondary schools today pay around $15,000 to $20,000 or more per year, depending on the school's tuition, residence, materials and other costs. Ivy League and specialty schools usually cost considerably more.

Looking forward 18 years, a child born in 2006 may be paying at least $125,000 over four years. This does not include residence, which might add another $30,000. If you don't plan for this expense now, it could send your wealth plan off track in a hurry later.

An RESP is an education no-brainer because it offers many advantages that allow you to leverage results safely. Like an RSP, an RESP is tax-sheltered and provides tax-free returns until withdrawn. The taxes owed may actually be very low, if any, as RESP funds are taken out to pay your child's education and related costs.

In other words RESP funds are deemed a taxable benefit to the person in school. Any tax owed is based on your child's income and not yours. Presumably your child's income is low or $0, and their tax rate will be lower than yours.

Also, unlike an RSP, you do not receive RESP tax refunds. Therefore the only amount subject to tax is on the investment growth or interest earned, and not on the principal amount contributed over the life of the plan.

The contributors, usually parents or grandparents, may withdraw the balance of their principal tax-free at any time. However, the usual intent is to apply these funds to the child's first year education costs.

The tax advantages alone are enough reason to build an RESP into a family wealth plan, but there is more! In 1998 the Canadian government started the CESG Canadian Education Savings Grant, to further encourage parents to save for education costs.

Again this is not just tax philanthropy, they are aware post-secondary education costs have skyrocketed, expected to continue at 7.6% per year. Federal and provincial governments spending on education is one of their largest expenses. Just like government pensions and social security, there may not be enough money to go around some day.

Governments need to lower this education burden; otherwise they will have no choice but to raise taxes. Higher taxes are unpopular and bad for the economy, and usually not a wise move for any politician hoping to be re-elected.

The smart alternative is to leave these funds in taxpayers' hands and provide more incentives to save for their child's education. The CESG is the government's way of topping up your RESP. This significantly boosts RESP value and your return on investment. The CESG is effectively a guaranteed 20% education savings bonus?

As of 2006, the RESP contribution limit per child each year is $4,000. The overall RESP limit is $42,000 per child. CESG limits are up to $7,200 in government grants added per child, determined by your yearly RESP contributions and net family income.

If your net family income is less than $35,595, the CESG on your first $500 contributed per child yearly is 40% up to $200. If net family income is higher, but less than $71,190, the CESG on your first $500 contributed per child yearly is 30% up to $150. For higher family incomes and the balance of contributions over $500, the CESG is 20%.

The CESG limit per child for each year is $400. You will notice the education no-brainer suggest a yearly contribution of $2,000 per child, if this fits into your budget. This is how much it worked out to, in order to get the full $400 added, assuming only a 20% CESG.

There are a variety of convenient ways to schedule and make RESP payments. Most people contribute yearly or monthly, by check or automatic bank debit. A yearly contribution of $2,000 works out to $166.66 monthly.

For higher income families this is a reasonable amount to set aside. For lower income families this could be a very wise investment for part of the monthly child tax benefit check. You can buy RESP units for as low as $9.50 per month in some plans. Even a small RESP goes a long way, plus you can catch-up and buy additional units later!

For wealth planning purposes, you get the biggest bang for your time and compounding buck if you can maximize all CESG payments as early as possible. As the CESG limit per child is $400 yearly, you should apply for a SIN Social Insurance Number and start soon after the child is born.

Any unused portion of the CESG can be carried forward to future years, however the maximum CESG that can be received yearly per child is $800. In other words you can usually catch up, but if you wait too long you won't receive the full $7,200 CESG. It is best to plan for 18 years of contributions, or at least 9 years, to receive the full grant.

For decades only a few companies offered an RESP, managed like a bond mutual fund. They were originally designed to offer safe interest returns, tied to prevailing near and long-term government bonds and mortgage-backed securities. They filled a need and performed reasonably well then, and still do today even with lower interest rates.

Since the CESG came into effect in 1998, greater demand has resulted in more RESP options. Today most banks and other financial institutions now offer RESP products. You may even be able to set-up a self-directed RESP through a financial planner.

However, don't forget this is needed education money, and you only have a limited time to make it work. You need a plan that offers predictable returns in order to meet 18-year education goals. With all the grants and tax savings available to safely enhance returns, risk should be minimized. In other words, you can't afford to ride-out a bad investment.

You need to review your options and the various advantages and disadvantages, to decide which plan best fits your needs. Does your RESP have a history of safe and predictable returns, and regular reporting? Do they offer convenient contribution payment options and helpful customer support? Is all the CESG paperwork automatically done for you? How knowledgeable and dedicated is the firm and its representatives, or is an RESP just a way to get you in the door to transfer other higher paying business? Do some homework!

An RESP has various value options that may differ by company or by plan. Flexible new bells and whistles are being added often. They all do basically the same thing and must keep within government regulations. However there are some important differences!

To get the most RESP value, generally you need to make all withdrawals for education before age 26. If your child doesn't pursue post-secondary education, most plans can be transferred between siblings or to other beneficiaries if needed.

Some plans allow you to transfer RESP interest to an RSP tax-free, or to withdraw it as income and pay tax at your marginal rate, plus an additional tax of 20%. Some plans use unclaimed interest to top-up other plans, or offer scholarships from any surplus revenue.

You can even set-up a plan for yourself to return to school. The student must be enrolled a minimum 13 weeks to qualify to receive interest and CESG payments. The school can be anywhere in the world as long as it qualifies under the income tax act. This includes most colleges, universities, trade and correspondence schools.

Your wealth creation budget and the investment planner will help you determine an affordable amount to save for education expenses. The education no-brainer will help you determine if this is a reasonable amount, after all RESP contributions plus added CESG funds, plus tax-sheltered time and compounding growth are factored in.

The education no-brainer 'invest equal amount each year to RESP' blue-cell should be changed based on your yearly education savings budget per child. Spread out over 18 years, $2,000 is the maximum yearly amount in order to receive the full $7,200 CESG.

This assumes that you only qualify for a 20% CESG, based on family net income. If you qualify for a higher percentage CESG, you may need to contribute less to get the maximum $400 CESG per year. Just be aware that even $2,000 per year will probably not be enough to fully cover all education costs.

Every budget has limits, but something is always better than nothing! Use the 'RESP / CESG Limits' table at the bottom of the plan, to make sure you are getting the most value and that any adjustments are within CESG and RESP yearly and lifetime limits.

You will notice that yearly RESP contributions of $2,000, plus a $400 CESG, results in approximately $78,624. This continues to grow tax-sheltered until fully withdrawn. In other words $36,000 contributed evenly over 18-years, plus 20% CESG's added, invested at only 6% will return 138.85% or $85,987 over a typical four-year education program.

There is an allocation table built in to the education no-brainer to calculate this for you. Basically the $78,624 is divided by four, equalling $19,656 withdrawn over the first year that is added to the student's yearly taxable income. The $58,968 balance remains tax-sheltered in the RESP and by the second year should be back up to $62,506. This amount is then divided by the remaining years and so on until all funds are fully withdrawn.

For the four school years this should work out to $19,656 for year 1, $20,835 for year 2, $22,085 for year 3 and $23,411 for year 4. This will not fully cover all education costs, but will at least help your child keep school loans down to a reasonable level.

It is common knowledge that higher education tends to lead to higher incomes. However the high costs of education can seriously jeopardize the standard of living that it was supposed to provide. Far too many young families are not prepared for this and are dealing with the reality of being the educated poor!

Servicing high education debt levels can be a real threat to lifestyle standards, and may derail wealth plans for many years. If you have children or plan to, future education costs need to be factored into your wealth plan. As you can see, a RESP is the best way to reasonably achieve this goal, especially with free CESG money and tax-sheltered growth available!

A wealthy mindset knows the first two keys to wealth are saving, and time and compounding. The wealth creation budget puts you in control of your next year. Now the time and compounding saving tools puts you in position to control your wealth lifetime!

The time and compounding tools are another effective common sense way to further put into action your wealthy mindset. All you then need to do is review at least yearly, reasonably update the details, save and print time dated copies for your wealth plan file, and most importantly stay committed!

Achieving your actual wealth goals will then simply be a matter of time, or rather time and compounding!

Chapter 4.5
Cost of Inflation

The Cost of Inflation

start of year current value or dollar cost	end of year dollar cost of inflation at
$ 36,000	7.60%
$ 36,000	$ 38,736
$ 38,736	$ 41,680
$ 41,680	$ 44,848
$ 44,848	$ 48,256
$ 48,256	$ 51,923
$ 51,923	$ 55,870
$ 55,870	$ 60,116
$ 60,116	$ 64,685
$ 64,685	$ 69,601
$ 69,601	$ 74,890
$ 74,890	$ 80,582
$ 80,582	$ 86,706
$ 86,706	$ 93,296
$ 93,296	$ 100,386
$ 100,386	$ 108,016
$ 108,016	$ 116,225
$ 116,225	$ 125,058
$ 125,058	$ 134,562
$ 134,562	$ 144,789
$ 144,789	$ 155,793
$ 155,793	$ 167,633
$ 167,633	$ 180,373
$ 180,373	$ 194,082
$ 194,082	$ 208,832
$ 208,832	$ 224,703
$ 224,703	$ 241,781
$ 241,781	$ 260,156
$ 260,156	$ 279,928
$ 279,928	$ 301,202
$ 301,202	$ 324,094
$ 324,094	$ 348,725
$ 348,725	$ 375,228
$ 375,228	$ 403,745
$ 403,745	$ 434,430
$ 434,430	$ 467,447
$ 467,447	$ 502,973
$ 502,973	$ 541,198
$ 541,198	$ 582,330
$ 582,330	$ 626,587
$ 626,587	$ 674,207
$ 674,207	$ 725,447
$ 725,447	$ 780,581
$ 780,581	$ 839,905
$ 839,905	$ 903,738
$ 903,738	$ 972,422
$ 972,422	$ 1,046,326
$ 1,046,326	$ 1,125,847
$ 1,125,847	$ 1,211,411
$ 1,211,411	$ 1,303,478
$ 1,303,478	$ 1,402,543

$1 at 7.6% inflation will cost
$38.96 in 50 years!

Inflation is defined as a persistent increase in the level of consumer prices. Subsequently this results in a persistent decline in the purchasing power of money. Inflation is caused by an increase in available currency and credit, beyond the proportion of available goods and services.

The Inflation Rate is the rate at which the general level of prices for goods and services is rising. Similarly it is also the rate at which purchasing power is falling. As inflation rises, every dollar will buy a smaller percentage of a good or service.

For example, if the inflation rate is 2%, then a $1 pack of gum will probably cost $1.02 in a year. While this may not seem that important, inflation affects the value of everything and is one of the biggest threats or challenges to achieving lifetime wealth goals.

Even a small change in the inflation rate has a dramatic effect on the value of money and cost of goods and services over time. Inflation affects everything from trade and employment to interest rates and investment returns.

Back to our driving analogies, inflation is like climbing an unavoidable and never ending wealth hill. Inflation needs to be factored into wealth goals, to keep your wealth plan from stalling or rolling backwards in value. The inflation rate is like the angle or slope of the hills on your wealth highway!

A wealthy mindset factors in all costs, including inflation; otherwise your wealth plan is driving at night without headlights, to see what hidden dangers lie ahead. A wealth plan that reasonably anticipates inflation is equipped with wealth safety high beams!

In other words, adequate investment returns are needed just to maintain the future buying power of today's savings. You need enough growth to offset the effects of inflation, with not too much exposure to risk of capital loss. An investment that provides high safety but inadequate returns, at less than the inflation rate, actually reduces future buying power and overall wealth!

Understanding the real value of investment returns is important to your wealth plan. Returns should be seen not only in after-tax and after all costs terms, but even after inflation. For example, if your investment return is 5%, but only 3% after deducting all taxes and fees, you need to know you really are no further ahead at a 3% inflation rate.

This is also extremely important to the health of the overall economy. Controlling inflation through interest rate adjustments and how much currency is issued, in a Goldilocks not too hot and not too cold way, is one of the government's top priorities in order to maintain consistent long-term growth and employment.

Statistics Canada, the Bank of Canada and similar government agencies in the United States track prices over time. The CPI or Consumer Price Index is a broad measure of the cost of living, used widely to compare current prices to a base year index of $100.

For example the CPI in the year 2000 had reached $113.50 compared to a 1992 base of $100. The CPI tracks an average basket of about 600 goods and services such as housing, transportation, food, clothing, recreation and consumer staples etc.

To better put this into perspective, a basket that cost $1,000,000 in 1966 would cost approximately $3,747,573 in 1986 and $6,276,699 in 2006. Another way of looking at this is a basket that costs $1,000,000 today; projected forward at the government's average 2% inflation rate target will cost $1,485,947 in 2026.

In other words, if your 20-year savings goal is to achieve the equivalent of a million dollars today, you need to plan for a future value of almost $1.5 million. Similarly, if you have a million dollars today, you need to invest and grow it by almost 50% over the next 20 years, just to maintain its present value.

At the current 3% inflation rate, just 1% above the average inflation target, today's million would cost an extra $320,164, or $1,806,111 in 2026. Time and compounding of investment returns builds wealth, but inflation in the same way works against wealth. Let's hope that 1980 inflation rates of over 14% were just an anomaly that doesn't repeat!

You now have tools to effectively budget for savings, and to reasonably predict future results based on investment returns and tax rate assumptions. Just keep in mind that these are absolute dollar results. You now need to also value savings results in relative or inflation adjusted dollars, in order to fine-tune your wealth plan.

The Cost of Inflation tool helps you figure out how much your future savings are really worth in today's dollars, after factoring in the negative time and compounding effects of inflation. Or use this tool to more realistically determine your wealth plan savings and investment return goals, adjusted for future inflation.

For example, let's look at the importance of factoring inflation into future education costs. You will notice the 'end of year dollar cost of inflation at' blue-cell is 7.60%. As discussed in the last chapter, this is the ten-year average inflation rate for education costs, which are expected to continue at this rate for the foreseeable future.

The 'start of year current value or dollar cost' blue-cell is $36,000. One year of university today costs approximately $9,000 for tuition, books, fees etc. This does not include living costs such as residence, food and long-distance transportation. Therefore a four-year university degree is approximately $36,000, plus living costs.

Most young adults commence a post-secondary education at around age 18. You will see that a present value of $36,000 results in an 18-year future value of $125,058. If the student doesn't go to school until they turn 19-years old, you would instead use the $134,562 future value at the end of 18-years.

To allow for residence and other living costs, you would estimate the present value of these costs and project them forward 18-years as well. For example, let's assume an apartment is shared, plus food, utilities, sundries etc. total an average of $700 a month. Over an 8-month school term you estimate $5,600 per year.

To be conservative you round this up to $6,000 and assume the higher end of the government's 1% to 3% inflation rate target. If you change the blue-cells to $6,000 and 3%, the 18-year result is $9,917. Therefore, under this scenario looking out 18 to 22-years, living costs over 4-years will be approximately $40,000.

You would then add $40,000 to $125,058, which results in total 4-year education plus related inflation-adjusted reasonable living costs totalling approximately $165,000. This is the result to plan for with RESP savings, if you want or need to cover all of your child's education costs under these assumptions.

Like 'Your Wealth Now, in a Nutshell', the cost of inflation tool can be used to more accurately plan your retirement savings goals. For example, you are happy with your lifestyle and just want to maintain your current standard of living. Your wealth creation budget indicates you will be debt-free after 20-years, when you plan to retire.

Your current yearly expenses, excluding all debt and savings costs, are approximately $26,500. You determine that even if you were debt-free today, you need to allow for some retirement extras to pay future life insurance premiums and medical costs, and for more travel and some perks. Therefore you estimate that you will need $30,000 per year in today's dollars to comfortably meet your 20-year future retirement needs.

You then need to factor-in taxes on RSP withdrawals. You estimate that at $30,000 yearly, or $2,500 monthly; your tax rate will be 30%. To calculate how much you need to withdraw from your RSP before taxes, convert 30% to a decimal or 30 / 100 = 0.30. Then subtract this from 1, equalling 0.70. Then divide $30,000 by 0.70, which equals $42,857.14. This is the pre-tax withdrawal present value that you will need each year.

You then need to factor-in inflation. Let's use an inflation rate of 2.5%, the average of the current 3% and the government's target of 2%. Enter $42,857.14 and 2.5% in the cost of inflation blue-cells. The 20-year result is $70,226 in yearly RSP withdrawals needed in order to maintain your current standard of living under these reasonable assumptions.

Let's also assume that at retirement your RSP is re-structured to provide lower but safer annual investment income returns of 7%. Use the following formula to calculate how much your RSP needs to be worth in 20-years, in order to maintain its value while providing yearly pre-tax withdrawals of $70,226. Convert 7% to a decimal, 7 / 100 =

.07. Then divide this into your yearly pre-tax amount needed, $70,226 / .07 = $1,003,229.

In other words a 20-year RSP future value of $1,003,229, returning 7% yearly pre-tax income of $70,226, provides the after-tax equivalent of $30,000 present value today, with the effects of 2.5% inflation factored in. This may also result in an estate value of one million dollars, which perhaps wasn't such an arbitrary RSP goal after all!

However, unless you plan to live forever, you may decide to plan for a lower RSP result that uses the principal over your expected retirement lifetime. You can also purchase financial products that provide predictable lifetime income streams at a fixed cost.

For example, life annuities do this while factoring in actuarial life data, based on a group of investors. Products like this may offer advantages that allow you to lock in a fixed or increasing income over time, and may provide a death benefit to your spouse or estate.

Chapter 5.4 describes a simple value calculator provided to help you plan a life annuity. It extends your time and compounding RSP wealth on steroids results, to plan out pre-retirement savings, plus in-retirement annuity payments and estate plan values.

You need to factor in as much detail as possible, while not over complicating things, to determine realistic results. The time and compounding tools offer a reasonable way to build taxes and inflation into various savings results and your wealth plan.

You may then determine if your current actual savings plans are adequate, under-funded or over-funded. The important point is to know, either way. Then you can make informed decisions how you need to change things going forward. Only then are you in control of your wealth destiny!

Having adequate or over-funded savings plans is a great feeling! However, even if you are under-funded, you are still in control, as long as you know this! As long as you have enough time, you may still be able to get your wealth plan back on track.

Your wealth creation budget shows where you are this year. Your wealth now, in a nutshell, and the time and compounding tools, shows where you need to go over your wealth lifetime. If your income, expenses, taxes and savings have been optimized, and you still can't get to where you need to be, this only leaves higher investment returns to reach your wealth goals. Value Investing is the third key to wealth and the focus of the next chapter.

Chapter 5
Third Key to Wealth: Value Investing

We started by defining wealth as a store of value, that meets all your current and future needs. The most common store of value today is money.

If your wealth creation budget balances, then you should have enough money coming in over the next year. If you have enough money safely stored and under your control to predictably meet your needs for the foreseeable future then you are wealthy.

This is why the first key to wealth is savings and the second key to wealth is time and compounding. The wealth creation budget and time and compounding tools help measure your tangible working capital and savings, used to predict future wealth in money terms.

We also discussed personal needs and intangible working capital, valued usually in spiritual, mental, and physical health terms. These personal features are beyond the scope of this book, except to say that you need reasonable health to carry out a wealth plan.

Money buys most common needs such as food, clothing, housing, transportation and entertainment etc. We usually think of and value money in terms of currency, or the dollar, yen, euro, peso or pound etc., depending on where you live and spend money. In chapter 6 we will get into this further, when we explore the value of money itself.

Accepting money for now as our common measure of value, how do you save more money than your current wealth plan supports? The safe way is to earn more income or reduce expenses, thereby increasing savings that are invested at reasonably predictable rates of return.

The other way is to achieve a higher investment rate of return. However, you need to fully appreciate that higher rates of return usually imply more risk. At best, higher risk investments result in less predictable returns; at worst you can lose some or all value.

A fair assumption is that even if your wealth plan needs were fully funded, you would still want to enhance investment returns, within reasonable safety limits. In other words you want more value from your investments, without incurring more risk.

The third key to wealth is Value Investing, which focuses on identifying Undervalued Investments. To be undervalued, the cost must be less than its Intrinsic Value, which is simply its Present Value. The overall gain or loss when the investment is sold, determines your Return On Investment. The concept is simple, but only if fully appreciated!

The Perception of Value may differ by a large degree from person to person. This is only reasonable as information is valued and weighed differently. Even if everyone has the same information, with no unknowns, people will still negotiate varying perceptions of value as a natural result of human behaviour and attitude.

If the perception of value is not the same when everything is known, then predicting future investment values is extremely tricky. Future values must be assessed in terms of all risks, balancing the odds of success under all reasonable scenarios. Risk must factor-in many assumptions good and bad, including uncertain future conditions that may change!

This is Investment Speculation, and even if you are eventually right, you still have to ask yourself if many other people are making the same guess. If so, how much of your perceived future value is already built into the current price. Even then if your investment speculation guess or bet does come true, there must still be willing buyers that recognize its perceived value and are willing to buy it from you at that price.

A value investor defines an investment as that which offers favourable odds of reasonably predictable returns. If the odds of success are too high or unpredictable, a value investor considers this a speculation. A value investor carefully and conservatively measures the odds of success, and then weighs this against other opportunities.

In a casino you have specific outcomes that determine your result. Whether your card, dice roll, or slot combination hits or not, at least you know for certain if and how much you won or lost. However, casino odds are always stacked against you winning and in the long-term end, gamblers lose! Speculation is like gambling, with many uncertain results!

Investment speculation is not only high risk in absolute terms, but also in relative or risk-adjusted terms. In other words a reasonable person knows that all investment bets will not work out. Your winners and losers must both be reflected in overall returns, and then compared to more certain lower-risk rates of return.

For example, let's assume over time you believe that higher-risk investment speculations may actually result in an overall gain of 15%. You then realize that lower-risk rates of return, including dividends, are available that will produce a more predictable 10% rate of return. If investment speculations work out, you will pick-up an extra 5% return.

However, you need to weigh this result against the probabilities of your higher-risk return actually being realized. You believe you have a 50% chance of a 15% or better overall rate of return, and a 50% chance of a 10% or less return. You must then decide if this extra 5% uncertain gain is worth betting on a coin toss, plus the long-term implications to your wealth plan if you are wrong.

You need to also factor-in all costs associated with taking on more risk, including extra time and worry that may drain various tangible and intangible working capitals. A wealthy mindset balances all risks, and stays focused on long-term wealth plan results.

Future value is even more difficult to predict if current and past information is not accurate or reliable. Look at the investment value lost by once considered safe growth stocks, like Enron, Worldcom and Nortel as past results were revised lower and lower.

Relevant value information is not readily available to all people at the same time. If the present value is perceived to be so much higher or lower than the current price, you need to ask why? Before a major announcement, is your stock price running up or down on speculation, or because some investors know the value outcome before others?

Are you buying or selling based on outdated, incomplete or outside information, that is materially different than insiders are aware of when making their own buy or sell decisions? In other words, are you aware of all the risks?

One of the main reasons value is not perceived the same way is simply because people are different. They have different wealth and lifestyle goals based on their own needs, wants, and risk tolerance. In any event there are always two sides to any trade, a buyer and seller who both perceive an opportunity based on any number of reasons.

Value investing reasonably identifies tangible intrinsic value! I'm sure you will agree that the future is less certain than the past. Similarly future investment results are usually more reliable if past results were reliable. In other words a value investor projects present values into the future, based on a history of consistently reliable results.

If the current price of the investment is lower than its present value, then it is undervalued if your information and reasonable assumptions are correct. However, this does not necessarily mean the price has bottomed in the short-term, for a variety of reasons.

Emotions such as fear and greed can influence trading decisions, sometimes resulting in irrational stock prices. This has nothing to do with the intrinsic or present value of the company or its stock. Instead buy and sell decisions are affected by personal events or other less relevant conditions. Therefore value and price are often not the same!

A value investor perceives an investment as undervalued only after all conditions or events that may affect value are carefully considered and weighed. These risks are many and may include the condition of the economy, currency or stock market crisis, political events such as war, legal liabilities such as lawsuits and patent protection, labour disputes, insolvency debt risks etc. The list is endless!

Some of these risks are complex, unknown or not controllable, that can only be weighed in the context of a value investor deciding whether to invest now or later. Timing investments must be considered, however this also involves speculation.

Investment stock prices tend to climb a so-called wall of worry. There is always something going on somewhere, which may impact short-term stock market prices. However, substantial companies with sustainable long-term earnings usually have the flexibility to manage or mitigate uncontrollable risks, which tend to work out over time.

Skilled management is key to growing long-term earnings, value and investment returns. A company with effective management anticipates and is positioned to efficiently deal with controllable risks and to take advantage of opportunities. Consistency of past results is often the most reliable indicator of skilled management and predictable future performance.

How does a value investor manage controllable and uncontrollable risks that affect investment values? The answer is simply by narrowing stock selection to only substantial companies with sustainable earnings and skilled management at fair prices!

Value investing focuses on long-term intrinsic value, which is an investment's price compared to the present value of reasonable future earnings, with skilled management. If both conditions are true, and investment prices are depressed as a result of exaggerated short-term risk perception by the stock market, then this may represent an undervalued investing opportunity.

All buying and selling, rational or irrational, affects stock prices. Even when value is perceived, some timing consideration should be given to other conditions affecting price. In other words, if the stock is undervalued but still selling off, or overvalued but going higher, a little patience until trading momentum ends may present even better prices.

Value investing focuses on fundamental values, and not on stock popularity or lack of it. Value investors often trade against the current trend, especially when stock prices become irrationally extended to extreme highs or lows as compared to actual value. This is why value investors are often considered Contrarian Investors.

A value investors reasonable bet is that at some time in the future, an undervalued investment is likely to be priced closer to its then present value. Historically this has worked well to provide reasonably predictable results.

Value investing offers far superior odds of success compared to investment speculation. Speculators accept high-odds, betting on uncertain future results. Value investors only bet that reasonably certain results eventually will be fairly reflected in the price.

Again nobody has a perfect crystal ball to predict the future. The best we can do is to learn from past experiences, and use all reliable current information available to make reasonable assumptions going forward. A value investor makes investment decisions based mostly on calculated intrinsic values, with as little guesswork as possible.

Value investing is the most consistent way to invest and build wealth. This holds true for both publicly traded and privately owned companies. Your personal needs and various wealth capital assets are also important investment factors, especially relating to private businesses that involve a great deal of your time, effort and emotions.

Therefore it would be more useful if we focus on value investing as it relates to more common investments, such as the stock market. The principles are really the same, as a value investor only sees the stock market as another way to buy or sell businesses.

The following is a 70-year summary of historical rates of return from 1926 to 1996, breaking out the average rate of return and the real rate of return after taxes and inflation.

Investment Type	Rate of Return,	Less 31% Tax,	Less 3.1% Inflation
Small Company Stocks	12.6%	8.7%	5.6%
S&P 500 Common Stocks	11.3%	7.8%	4.7%
Real Estate	11.1%	7.7%	4.6%
Long-Term Government Bonds	5.1%	3.5%	0.4%
United States Treasury Bills	3.8%	2.6%	- 0.5%

If you perceive Bonds or even T-Bills as an acceptable low-risk return, you must remember to factor-in taxes and inflation. The long-term real rate of return for bonds is barely a breakeven proposition. T-bills actually produce a negative real rate of return as they lose buying power or relative value over time, unless they are tax-sheltered.

You can see that stocks and real estate offer the best chance of any real return growth after the effects of taxes and inflation. However the stock market may have a broader tangibility advantage, with more buyers and sellers readily available to trade its shares.

This is not to knock real estate as an investment, but only to point out that real estate is often specialized and may involve more time than you have available. However some real estate offers tax advantages, such as your home, plus it is a good idea to spread out your bets or diversify risk by owing different investment types.

Diversification hedges bets against significant short-term losses in any single type of investment. If the real estate or stock market has a few bad years, owning various types of investments may help offset short-term losses. Pay attention to how your wealth is concentrated and be careful to not put all your investment eggs in one basket.

In any event you need some real estate, if for no other reason you need a home to live in. Just be aware that real estate liquidity and tangibility related to a specific property's investment features must also be considered, such as zoning, maintenance and location.

Stocks and real estate have historically created more wealth than other investment types. This book focuses on the stock market because we assume that your wealth plan involves you earning an income, with only limited time to spend investing surplus savings. One major advantage of the stock market is that shareholders don't have to run the companies they own.

However, a value investor believes the stock market does not always represent the real value of a business. Instead stock prices are just what you may buy or sell the business for today, which may be different than your perceived present value of the business.

Some people argue that value investing is not reliable. They believe the stock market price reasonably reflects all information available to buyers and sellers, and therefore represents the company's real value. If this were true, a value investor's return on investment would not reasonably be able to outperform the stock market over time.

In fact the vast majority of stock mutual funds under-perform the market over time. Even most value investing mutual funds tend to under-perform. However, most of this probably has more to do with sales, management and transaction fees than actual returns.

The best-known value investors in the world consistently outperform the stock market. Warren Buffett has made a name as the most successful investor of the twentieth century. A student and friend of Benjamin Graham, the father of value investing, Buffett has built one of the largest fortunes in history, estimated at over $40 billion.

Warren Buffett is now and has been for over a decade, the second richest man in the world. The first is Microsoft chairman Bill Gates, estimated to be worth over $50 billion. The holding company Mr. Buffett founded and still manages is called Berkshire Hathaway, which trades on the New York Stock Exchange under the symbol BRKA.

Berkshire is the highest priced stock on the NYSE, currently trading at around $90,000 per share. To make the stock lower priced for investors, $1/30^{th}$ of a Berkshire share trades under the symbol BRKB, currently just under $3,000 per share.

Berkshire is a substantial company with a market capitalization over USD $110 billion. This is the overall stock market value of the company, calculated by multiplying the stock market price of one share, times the total number of shares issued and outstanding.

Berkshire owns some or all of many companies, both private and publicly traded. The media and the investment community in general, closely follow Mr. Buffett's comments and actions as a result of Berkshire's famously successful investments.

Most of Berkshire's stock market investments would be considered old school or boring, blue-chip companies like Coca Cola, American Express, Wells Fargo, General Dynamics, The Washington Post and Geico Insurance. Mr. Buffett doesn't invest in high-tech companies because they don't have easy to understand transparent earnings.

This investment philosophy tends to protect value investors from having to time boom and bust stock market cycles. Value investors like Mr. Buffett totally avoided trendy dot-com concept companies that traded at astronomically high prices in the 1990's.

These dot-com companies offered no real value other than the promise of very high-risk future potential. By 2001 many of these companies had gone broke and disappeared. The few surviving dot-coms still trade at a fraction of their previous highs.

On the other hand, Berkshire's investors enjoyed enviable returns for decades, beating the S&P 500 in 20 out of 24 years. If you had invested $10,000 in Berkshire Hathaway when Mr. Buffett took control in 1965, your holdings would be worth more than $50 million today!

This has resulted in loyal investors who regularly participate in Berkshire Hathaway's Omaha Nebraska annual shareholders meetings. You can see why Mr. Buffett is often referred to endearingly as the Oracle of Omaha!

Mr. Buffett prefers to buy into well-run companies with consistent results, rather than trying to turn around poorly managed companies. Books about Mr. Buffett are widely read best sellers, about his time-tested value investing principles anyone can apply easily.

Back to our driving analogies, value investing is your wealth creation plan tune-up. This is needed to make your wealth journey more consistent, efficient, safe and reliable to travel long distances. A finely tuned wealth plan also tends to perform better overall!

History has shown that a company's primary investment value is a function of its current earnings and its ability to produce future earnings. If earnings are realized and used to create shareholder equity and value, this tends to be reflected in stock prices over time.

To use a baseball analogy, value investing focuses on identifying earnings base hits that may lead to future home run investment values. Base hits are easier and more predictable than home runs, and therefore offer a much higher percentage to score.

Value investors simply try to reasonably identify companies with consistent yearly earnings that have been overly discounted by the stock market. If your perceived present value of a future series of earnings is significantly greater than the current market price, this unrecognized or discounted earnings growth may represent a value investing opportunity.

If you are right, as the market eventually realizes the company's earnings and growth rate is actually higher, this reasonably should translate into higher prices. Earnings are not the only consideration, but have been the most predictable way to determine value.

This is why value investing primarily focuses on identifying undervalued earnings. A value investor also wants earnings growth, but again this involves predicting an uncertain future. A value investor believes that a well-managed company that produces consistent earnings is more likely to do so again. This is usually safer than betting on a new company with unproven management, with only inconsistent or hopeful future earnings.

Value investing is no different than how personal wealth is valued. This involves your income, savings and investment growth, and your expenses and debt service. The yearly result is your net savings surplus or deficit.

Your yearly net savings represents how much extra you can buy each year. In other words net savings determine additional consumption ability or extra wealth, just like a company's yearly earnings. If your earnings are saved and invested instead of spent, this increases your wealth just like retained earnings increase shareholders equity value.

Earnings can be used to create shareholder value in several ways. The company may pay a cash dividend, to return some of the earnings to its shareholders. They may invest in productive assets such as plant and equipment, or pay down debt to reduce future costs, or grow the business by acquiring another company for cash or stock.

If well managed, this leads to even more earnings and shareholder value. The company may even decide the best use of earnings is to buy its own shares, to reduce the number outstanding and thereby increase the earnings value per remaining share.

Debt may be used to do some of these things, but shareholder value is then offset by all debt costs. If the company is under duress or can't readily access credit, they will usually have to pay an interest premium, sell valuable assets or issue more shares in order to secure debt.

If expected future earnings do not materialize, shareholder value is further eroded while paying set debt costs. As debt costs become unmanageable, the viability of the company is at risk. You can see why debt represents higher risk of capital loss if not well managed.

The important point to remember is that earnings represent tangible value. Reinvested earnings are a safe and flexible way to grow future earnings and shareholder equity value.

A value investor practices the saying "Buy Low, Sell High". Value investing is simply buying or selling stock in valuable companies, when you perceive they are accordingly undervalued or overvalued. This is determined by comparing the current price to its intrinsic value.

A company's intrinsic value factors in all reasonable current and future cash flows, discounted to allow for the time value of money at a comparable investment rate of return. The present values of all future cash flows or earnings, added together determine a company's reasonable intrinsic value. Tools to do this are provided in chapter 5.4.

Management skills and consistency of past earnings growth should guide a value investor as to how accurate and reliable future earnings growth may be.

The next chapter discusses value investing in mutual funds versus individual stock and bond holdings and the many advantages and disadvantages you need to consider.

Chapter 5.1
Mutual Funds vs. Trading Stocks & Bonds

With thousands of publicly traded companies, how can the average person find enough time to reasonably sift through mountains of information in order to make reasonable value investing decisions?

One answer is to invest in a mutual fund, or a few different funds, that are simply pools of professionally managed money. To quickly narrow your choices, focus on fund companies and money managers with a solid long-term track record.

Past performance does not guarantee future performance, but is a reasonable indicator. Compare both the 1 to 3 year short-term returns and the 5 to 10 year or longer term returns to similar fund types. You are looking for consistent above average performance.

Mutual funds allocate return distributions in cash or more commonly extra fund units, based on your proportionate ownership of the entire pool. Investment returns are based on fund distributions, plus unit value capital gains or losses on your original investment.

You don't need to figure all this out as the mutual fund industry is regulated, with returns easily comparable to other funds, presented in similar formats on regular statements. Just make sure you are comparing returns after all costs have been factored in!

Mutual funds charge around 1% to 2% of the funds NAV net asset value in management fees per year. This lowers your yearly investment return significantly, and is calculated after all expenses such as transaction costs have been deducted.

For example, let's say you invest $10,000 and over the next year the funds investments increase by a 10% net return after all expenses. Your $10,000 should be worth $11,000, but if the fund charges 2%, or $220 in management fees, your result is $10,780. Your 10% net return is now only 7.8%, or 2.2% lower. Management fees alone may lower your net return on investment by 10% to 20%, or as in this example 2.2 / 10 x 100 = 22%!

However if you traded your own investments, most stockbrokers usually charge 1% to 3% in commissions for every buy and sell transaction. Again this is based on the value of the investment being bought or sold, whether you make or lose money.

Let's say you buy $10,000 in stocks and then decide to sell them at the same price. You will pay commissions on both the buy and sell of usually $100 to $300 each way, totalling $200 to $600. Your net result, assuming no change in price and no dividends have been paid to you, is a loss of 2% to 6% just to buy and sell once.

Results are significantly at risk if you trade often! Let's again invest $10,000 and assume $200 or approximately 2% for all buy and sell commissions. Let's assume the same $1,000 yearly investment gain, and every time your stocks go up $500 you decide to sell.

You invest $10,000 including a $200 commission on your first buy of $9,800 worth of stock. You then sell for $10,300 that nets you $10,100. You invest all of this again and buy $9,900 in stock after paying a third $200 commission. Lastly you sell it all again for $10,400, netting you $10,200 after your fourth $200 stock trading commission.

All of your money was invested each time and your stocks went up $1,000 over the year. Your stocks actually performed better than 10%, but only two in-and-out, also called round trip, trades chewed up 80% of your $1,000 stock gains.

In other words the four 2% commissions total $800, while your $10,000 investment nets you only $10,200. Your broker made 8% on your investment capital with no risk! Your money was at risk, your investments performed well, but you only netted $200 or 2%!

Most brokers also have flat minimum transaction fees that can drive commission percentages even higher. This is especially true for small dollar value investments, low priced stocks, or odd-lot trades of less than a standard 100-share board-lot.

Remember that a wealthy mindset factors-in all costs, so for stock market day-traders, who really makes 2% commissions.... if they are lucky? For a lot of practical cost reasons, it makes sense to invest in mutual funds until you have accumulated at least $25,000 in investment savings!

Mutual funds also provide an effective way to diversify risk, especially when small amounts of money are invested. Most financial experts agree that you need to own at least 5, or preferably 10 or more different company stocks to reasonably diversify risk.

Diversification spreads-out or limits the negative impact of a few bad investments on overall returns. However you don't want to diversify too much, called diworsification, as this dilutes the positive impact of successful investments on overall returns. In other words choosing the best stocks help you outperform the market, but if you choose too few stocks then your overall returns are at risk if one of your investments performs badly.

Mutual funds are also a convenient way to invest as you can start with $500 or less, and buy additional units in increments of around $50 or more. For example, periodic bank withdrawals can be set-up to automatically invest your monthly surplus savings.

Dollar Cost Averaging through regular mutual fund purchases means you don't need to worry about timing the stock market in general, or when to buy or sell specific stocks managed by the fund. Dollar cost averaging helps to smooth out short-term stock market price spikes and is an effective way to plan for long-term expected average returns.

Mutual funds are professionally managed according to each fund's stated investment objectives. The fund manager makes all investment decisions, saving you time and effort. Mutual funds also have economies of scale advantages.

Mutual funds are considered Institutional Investors as they invest large amounts of money on behalf of unit holders, and therefore usually pay lower percentage transaction fees. Institutional investors often have better or timelier access to financial information and are in a preferred position to receive high demand IPO's, Initial Public Offerings.

Mutual funds are a simple and effective way to start investing in stocks, bonds and other investment securities. They are also a great way to participate in investment opportunity themes that involve specialized knowledge or might not otherwise be accessible.

For example there are mutual funds that invest only in specific countries, industries or technologies. There are mutual funds that invest in any combination of financial assets from different classes of common, preferred or convertible company shares, to debt instruments such as various bonds, treasury bills or mortgage-backed securities.

Mutual fund holdings may even include speculative derivatives such as futures or options on various currencies, indexes, precious metals, grains, or other farming or resource based commodities. There are mutual funds that leverage market performance or hedge against a downturn by shorting or selling securities not owned in the hopes of buying them back cheaper. These are very risky but show how fund combinations are endless!

There are thousands of mutual funds that trade any number of financial assets, managed according to varying degrees of risk tolerance and investment return objectives. As retirement savings have grown, so has the size of the mutual fund industry. Today there are as many mutual funds as there are publicly traded securities to invest in!

Therefore, back to our original question, how can the average person find enough time to reasonably sift through mountains of information in order to make reasonable value investing decisions?

If you are starting to invest savings of less than $25,000, mutual funds may be the most practical way to achieve reasonable cost returns with diversification safety. However $25,000 is not a magical number as your minimum amount to consider investing in individual stocks may be higher depending on your objectives and risk tolerance.

This amount is just a guideline, and assumes yearly net income is around $25,000. In other words, if you have investment savings equal or more than one year's net income, this may suggest that you can afford the extra risk that may be associated with concentrating investments into 5 or 10 individual stocks, in the pursuit of higher long-term returns.

$25,000 is also a practical amount if you assume 5 different stocks are purchased, worth around $5,000 each. For example, if your stockbroker charges a 2% commission with a minimum transaction fee of $100, then a $5,000 trade would result in a $100 charge. The point is to keep the percentage paid for each trade down, as commissions significantly eat into returns.

However if you were trading smaller amounts of $2,500, the commission may still be $100, doubling your trading commission to 4%. Remember this is 4% to buy, plus 4% to sell, based not on your potential profits but on the entire value of the stock you trade.

Another option is to use a Discount Broker that offers internet trading. Online Trading has empowered individual investors with opportunities to save on commissions, execute trades effectively and access financial information faster. You may want to explore this and decide if you are comfortable with how all this works and how it fits your personality.

There are pros and cons to online trading that relate mainly to how computer and market savvy you are, and how much customer service you require. You should compare these options to local full-service broker commissions as many have lowered their rates due to competitive pressures. In any event it is a good idea to be informed about all costs versus service value, and how the differences may affect your investment returns.

A reasonable guideline for people with lower risk tolerances, is to stay in mutual funds and not invest in individual stocks until you have investment savings equal or more than $50,000 or two year's net income, whichever is greater. This assumes half of savings will be invested in 5 or more quality stocks and the other half placed in government bonds, T-bills or similar safe, near cash investments to balance out your risk and reward profile.

For example, let's assume you have $50,000 to invest, excluding real estate, and you have a 7% return goal. You also want to keep your risk down as much as possible. However cash savings and T-Bill rates are too low and don't keep up with inflation.

Instead you choose government bonds that offer some growth potential with a higher 5% expected safe net return that you are comfortable with, for 50% of your investments. You diversify the good or bad effects of sudden interest rate changes by spreading the duration of the bonds over time, with each $5,000 bond set to mature in 2, 4, 6, 8 and 10 years.

Bond prices change to reflect prevailing interest rates. When interest rates go up, bond prices go down and the opposite is also true. This may create a short-term capital gain or loss if you sell the bonds. If you hold the bonds until maturity when the face value is due, the yield, interest plus capital gain or loss, is exactly the same as when you purchased it.

Bonds offer safe and predictable investment returns if held to maturity. Bonds can also be traded as an investment speculation based on expected interest rate swings. By spreading out the duration of bond maturities you can safely have the best of both worlds.

If interest rates go up, maturing bonds may be reinvested at lower bond prices and higher yields. If interest rates go down, long-term bonds may go up in value allowing you to sell and lock in capital gains, or switch short-term bonds at maturity to other investments.

Bonds have four value features. First, long-term nominal rates of return at maturity are safely locked in. Second, interest rates affect short-term prices. Third, relative real rates of return may change due to inflation. Fourth, every investment needs to be compared to others available and the potential opportunity costs of missing out on better investment returns.

Bond investors should see the last three value features as crystal ball speculations. You should consider them all so that you don't commit too much of your savings to long-term bonds, bank certificates etc. just because rates are somewhat better at this moment.

If a reasonable portion of savings is allocated to various bond durations, the only real risk for bond investors is the safety of the bond itself. A bond is a debt obligation, and is only as safe as the quality of the issuer. In other words corporate bonds usually offer higher yields than government bonds because they are more likely to fail to pay back the bond.

Government bonds can fail as well, however governments have one key advantage as they can increase revenues by raising taxes. If government bonds fail to pay, this usually means dire consequences for the whole economy, currency values and most investment values in general. This is discussed further in chapter 6 on global value perspectives.

The other 50% of your $50,000 you decide to invest in 5 different quality company stocks that pay dividends. Your goal is for reasonable growth and safety, targeting the historic 11% growth rate, 10% net rate of return after all eventual commissions.

Let's assume you are bang on and your $25,000 in bonds returns 5% net or $1,250 the first year in higher bond prices and coupon interest payments. Your $25,000 in stocks returns 10% net or $2,500 the first year in dividends and higher priced share appreciation.

You reinvest all interest, plus principal payments as bonds mature, into more bonds. Dividends received on stocks are also reinvested over time as reasonable funds become available. Perhaps the companies' chosen offer a DRIP or dividend reinvestment plan that automatically buys more shares commission free to minimize your trading costs.

Your overall $50,000 investment return would be calculated as $1,250 + $2,500 = $3,750 / $50,000 x 100 = 7.50%. This meets your 7% return goal, with a small margin of safety. If this was higher or lower than your return goal, you may change the Asset Allocation percentage of stocks versus bonds within your reasonable safety limits and re-calculate.

These safety limits depend on your risk tolerance or acceptable loss of capital under reasonable worst-case scenarios. You can calculate this by estimating high and low returns expected by each investment class.

You then determine an approximate high, low and overall expected rate of return range and compare this to your objectives.

Asset allocation aims to structure and balance your investment plan to consistently meet objectives. This simply means that certain percentages of your savings are put into various investment classes of stocks, bonds, real estate etc. This diversifies your risk further as investment classes do not tend to perform the same at all times.

When one investment class under performs, another investment class may over perform. Results tend to work out in the long-term, and short-term price extremes in one asset class may be offset by opposite extremes in other asset classes. In other words real estate, bonds and the stock market all have good and bad years that often don't align.

Asset Allocation is half the battle in determining your expected overall investment returns. It is just as important to get the asset class ingredient mixture or percentage of real estate, stocks, bonds and cash right, as is it is to pick the best stocks.

Financial analysts regularly update their recommended asset allocation based on their view of the financial markets and how certain assets are expected to perform versus other asset classes. Professional brokers and financial planners are expected to further refine this asset allocation in the context of your personal goals and risk tolerance profile and recommend that you invest accordingly.

Asset allocation seems complicated but really isn't! When predicting market performance for any asset class, history show that a simple and steady long-term asset allocation plan tends to perform as well or better than trying to time short-term investment changes.

However, shifting assets around often does help generate commissions for your broker. If you instead target a simple asset allocation between stocks, bonds and real estate, you have done 99% of what most people need in order to reach long-term objectives.

For example, a reasonable long-term asset allocation is 25% real estate, 25% stocks, 25% bonds, and 25% in cash and personal assets. Just remember this is based on resale prices less debt, or how much equity you have in your home, stocks, bonds and personal assets.

Over time you may become more or less comfortable with certain asset classes. The most cost effective way to adjust your asset allocation is to shift cash flows such as interest, dividends or rent into other assets, or into cash or T-Bills as a temporary parking place.

Most people start out saving for a needed home with real estate as your largest asset. At the same time retirement savings are usually invested in stock mutual funds while you are young. Individual stocks and bonds may be a good idea as wealth and financial savvy grows over time. In essence your lifestyle needs end up determining your asset allocation to a large extent. Asset allocation is very important, look at it as your wealth investment recipe!

Mutual funds have several advantages and are a reasonable way to grow long-term savings. This is especially true when investing small amounts of money, if you are not interested in trading stocks or time is limited. You need to ask yourself if a mutual fund can add more investment value than you can on your own, versus time spent earning money elsewhere.

Just keep in mind that mutual funds also have disadvantages. You need to minimize costs and remain in control of your own wealth destiny. Mutual funds essentially trust your investment savings to someone who doesn't know you, your goals or risk tolerance.

Mutual fund managers' compensation is usually based on a combination of salary, fund performance and assets under administration. Their interests are aligned with yours, long-term investment growth, but are also motivated by popular perception. Mutual fund trading decisions may be influenced by short-term events, rather than long-term value.

Quarterly or year-end holdings are often bought or sold to pretty up the fund portfolio, also called window dressing. Losers that might come back are sold, while hot-stocks that have already made their price run are purchased, sometimes just for appearances.

Popular mutual fund holdings may present a better marketing opportunity to existing and new fund purchasers. However today's popular stocks are often tomorrow's dogs, with the opposite also true.

I'm not suggesting deception, just that mutual funds are focused on maintaining assets and management fees, which is sensitive to popular value perception.

Let's face the fact that when it's time for your fund manager's job review, it's easier for him or her to explain stock picking mistakes that a herd of other investment professionals have made as well. This is often preferred instead of putting one's neck on the line by sticking with an unpopular short-term stock price loser that may still represent great long-term value.

Mutual fund performance also often becomes a victim of its own success. As the fund performs well, more investors want to buy-in. The fund manager may then not be able to find enough stock opportunities within his style of investing to keep up results. This is especially true if the fund manger's returns were based on small-cap, low-priced or thinly traded stocks.

In the long-term, mutual funds usually under-perform the Standard & Poors and Dow Jones stock indexes, which are standard mutual fund performance benchmarks. This is often a result of fees, fund size, diworsification and consensus-herd stock picking.

Mutual funds also may find it difficult to efficiently trade holdings worth millions or even billions of dollars, without negatively affecting stock market prices. On the other hand individual investors have a significant mobility advantage as they can buy or sell small amounts of shares in an instant.

Value stock investing is all about picking undervalued stocks. This implies that you perceive value that others do not yet recognize. General market perception does not agree with you at this point. Your investment decision is contrary to the consensus herd.

When the consensus-herd accepts this value, the price appreciates as individual and institutional investors bid-up the stock. At some point the stock may become overvalued which is when a value investor sells, again trading contrary to popular perception.

If you have over $25,000 in savings for stock investments, instead of spending all your time capital researching which mutual funds are best, maybe it makes sense to learn more about value investing in quality companies on your own?

This can be as simple or as complex as you want to make it! The next chapter discusses a value-investing tool that I developed to help me quickly identify relatively undervalued quality stocks.

Chapter 5.2

Value Stock Selector

Value Stock Selector - Using 30 Stocks, from the Dow Jones Industrial Average (DJIA 27-Jun-08							
company name	rank	symbol	share price	52-wk high	52-wk low	earn/sh	dividend
Dow Jones Inds. Avg.	N/A	DJIA	11,346.51	14,279.96	11,248.48	$123.99	$ 311.00
Exxon Mobil	25	XOM	$ 86.55	$ 96.12	$ 77.55	$7.69	$ 1.60
Boeing	16	BA	$ 66.92	$ 107.83	$ 66.38	$5.75	$ 1.60
Caterpillar	24	CAT	$ 73.75	$ 87.00	$ 59.60	$5.59	$ 1.68
Johnson & Johnson	23	JNJ	$ 63.57	$ 68.85	$ 59.72	$4.01	$ 1.84
Du Pont	7	DD	$ 42.69	$ 53.90	$ 41.26	$3.52	$ 1.64
Chevron	29	CVX	$ 97.80	$ 104.63	$ 76.40	$9.07	$ 2.60
McDonalds	26	MCD	$ 56.50	$ 63.69	$ 46.64	$2.11	$ 1.50
Walt Disney	14	DIS	$ 31.57	$ 35.69	$ 26.30	$2.23	$ 0.35
United Technologies	18	UTX	$ 61.15	$ 82.50	$ 61.05	$4.48	$ 1.28
Bank of America	3	BAC	$ 24.59	$ 52.96	$ 24.25	$2.37	$ 2.56
General Electric	1	GE	$ 26.26	$ 42.15	$ 26.15	$2.16	$ 1.24
3M Company	15	MMM	$ 69.51	$ 97.00	$ 68.89	$5.13	$ 2.00
Home Depot	2	HD	$ 24.02	$ 41.01	$ 23.77	$2.00	$ 0.90
American Express	13	AXP	$ 38.04	$ 65.89	$ 37.94	$3.33	$ 0.72
Proctor & Gamble	17	PG	$ 60.49	$ 75.18	$ 60.49	$3.39	$ 1.60
Citigroup	20	C	$ 17.25	$ 52.97	$ 16.91	-$1.31	$ 1.28
IBM	30	IBM	$ 120.05	$ 129.99	$ 97.04	$7.62	$ 2.00
Hewlett Packard	20	HPQ	$ 44.58	$ 53.48	$ 39.99	$3.09	$ 0.32
AT&T	6	T	$ 32.76	$ 42.97	$ 32.76	$2.06	$ 1.60
Microsoft	10	MSFT	$ 27.63	$ 37.50	$ 26.87	$1.72	$ 0.44
Verizon Comm.	8	VZ	$ 34.28	$ 46.24	$ 33.15	$1.96	$ 1.72
Intel	12	INTC	$ 21.49	$ 27.99	$ 18.05	$1.15	$ 0.56
Wal-Mart	27	WMT	$ 56.30	$ 59.95	$ 42.09	$3.24	$ 0.95
Coca Cola	11	KO	$ 51.84	$ 65.59	$ 51.79	$2.67	$ 1.52
JP Morgan Chase	5	JPM	$ 35.05	$ 50.48	$ 34.20	$3.72	$ 1.52
Amer Intl Group	27	AIG	$ 27.75	$ 70.97	$ 27.41	-$0.70	$ 0.88
Alcoa	18	AA	$ 35.38	$ 48.77	$ 26.69	$2.55	$ 0.68
Pfizer	4	PFE	$ 17.28	$ 26.15	$ 17.12	$1.12	$ 1.28
General Motors	20	GM	$ 11.55	$ 43.20	$ 11.21	-$82.19	$ 1.00
Merck	9	MRK	$ 36.98	$ 61.62	$ 34.49	$2.23	$ 1.52
blue cells - user set	averages-->		$ 46.45	$ 63.08	$ 42.21	$0.39	$ 1.35
green cells - auto fill	Buy equal $ amounts of the top ranked 5 or 10 stocks. Only 1 stock p						
yellow cells - pre set	Balance every year. Sell stocks that are no longer a top 10 ranked sto						

Note: Updated 2008 illustrations do not reflect the same 2006 stock values mentioned herein. Stock values change constantly!

30 Stock Index) p/e ratio	div yield	income div yield vs DJIA	rel value div vs earnings	rel value p/e vs DJIA	contrarian momentum 52-wk hi/lo	low price lever	score
91.51	2.74%	N/A	0.40	N/A	3	N/A	3.40
11.25	1.85%	-2	3.00	3	0	-3	1.00
11.64	2.39%	-1	3.00	3	3	-3	5.00
13.19	2.28%	-1	3.00	3	0	-3	2.00
15.85	2.89%	0	2.18	3	0	-3	2.18
12.13	3.84%	2	2.15	3	3	0	10.15
10.78	2.66%	-1	3.00	3	-3	-3	-1.00
26.78	2.65%	-1	1.41	3	0	-3	0.41
14.16	1.11%	-3	3.00	3	0	3	6.00
13.65	2.09%	-2	3.00	3	3	-3	4.00
10.38	10.41%	3	0.93	3	3	3	12.93
12.16	4.72%	3	1.74	3	3	3	13.74
13.55	2.88%	0	2.57	3	3	-3	5.57
12.01	3.75%	2	2.22	3	3	3	13.22
11.42	1.89%	-2	3.00	3	3	0	7.00
17.84	2.65%	-1	2.12	3	3	-3	4.12
999.99	7.42%	3	-3.00	-3	3	3	3.00
15.75	1.67%	-3	3.00	3	-3	-3	-3.00
14.43	0.72%	-3	3.00	3	0	0	3.00
15.90	4.88%	3	1.29	3	3	0	10.29
16.06	1.59%	-3	3.00	3	3	3	9.00
17.49	5.02%	3	1.14	3	3	0	10.14
18.69	2.61%	-1	2.05	3	0	3	7.05
17.38	1.69%	-3	3.00	3	-3	0	0.00
19.42	2.93%	0	1.76	3	3	0	7.76
9.42	4.34%	3	2.45	3	3	0	11.45
999.99	3.17%	0	-3.00	-3	3	3	0.00
13.87	1.92%	-2	3.00	3	0	0	4.00
15.43	7.41%	3	0.88	3	3	3	12.88
999.99	8.66%	3	-3.00	-3	3	3	3.00
16.58	4.11%	2	1.47	3	3	0	9.47
91.51	3.54%	0.03	1.78	2.40	1.60	0.00	5.81
er industry sector		max 3	max 3	max 3	3,0 or -3	3,0,-3	value if
ck		min -3	min -3	min -3	low,0,high,	lo,0,hi	5+

First image above shows where you input current share price, 52-week high & low, and earnings & dividend per share. Second image shows how these input values get broken down & scored.

The following value investing technique is not for everyone! I don't know your needs or wants, or greed and fear risk profile. In any event you may learn from it, and it may help stimulate ideas to better develop and adapt your own reasonable stock trading style.

On your wealth plan excel workbook, click the fifth tab at the bottom called 'Value Stock Selector'. This spreadsheet is another powerful wealth planning tool that is easy to use, designed to identify quality stocks that may be undervalued or overvalued.

This value-investing tool may work well for any number of quality companies that have earnings and pay dividends. For simplicity and practical reasons it focuses on just 100 stocks that makeup the Standard & Poors S&P 100 index, which includes the 30 stocks that comprise the Dow Jones Industrial Average or DJIA.

The S&P 100 is a subset of the S&P 500. Both stock indexes are standard mutual fund performance benchmarks. The S&P 100 ticker symbol is OEX; the most heavily traded index option worldwide. In short the S&P 100 measures the largest blue-chip stocks.

When referring to stock market performance in general, most people quote the DJIA, also simply called The Dow. The DJIA is comprised of 30 of the largest industrial companies that are also within the S&P 100. Think of the Dow as the bluest of blue-chip stocks.

Economists regularly review how the stock market, the economy or Corporate America is performing. It's usually these stock indexes and the 30, 100 or 500 companies involved that matter most and is really being referred to.

There are many advantages in narrowing your value investing focus to only blue-chip stocks. These are my Top-10 Reasons:

First, you only have to identify undervalued or overvalued stocks within a total universe of 100 quality companies. This makes stock investing focused, easier and saves time.

Second, these 100 stocks represent diverse industry groups, representing almost all major businesses. This provides adequate selection to properly diversify opportunities and risk.

Third, these companies are the largest publicly traded U.S. companies, with established businesses that may represent future safety value. If you worry about investments, you should sleep better owning these stocks. Call it the peace of mind factor!

Fourth, these stocks are the most widely held and most liquid stocks and options to trade. Unlike thinly traded stocks, these stocks trade millions of shares per day, allowing an individual investor to trade large long and short positions without affecting prices.

Fifth, these companies and their products have been around, allowing a value investor to better understand and appreciate what they do. Call it a common sense feel-appeal.

Sixth, these companies provide guidance and a history of producing positive earnings, dividends and growth rates. This makes predicting future values easier and more reliable.

Seventh, these companies have cost and opportunity economies of scale. They buy in large quantities and can demand the best price from suppliers. Their large capital base, brand prestige and human resources may provide efficiencies, when adjusting operating costs, or to attract, fund and market new products or technologies. They have flexibility and strengths to adjust to business threats or to buyout competitors with cash or stock.

Eighth, these companies diversify their business risks and opportunities. Many of them are geographically diversified, selling worldwide. You may need to consider the effects of currency fluctuations and economic conditions, both at home and abroad. These companies are also sales diversified, with several established revenue streams. In other words they have the means to sell their many products wherever they are needed.

Ninth, these companies usually have skilled management. It's how they became so big in the first place. If new management is needed, large salaries and the ego value of running these big companies, with stock options, usually attract the best management talent.

Tenth, these companies are usually big enough to deal with short-term negative events or management mistakes. Similarly, when you make an investment mistake, lower short-term stock prices usually recover over time. Any investment can fail but these stocks offer reasonable odds of surviving mishaps.

In summary, value stock investors should start by narrowing focus to only the S&P 100 and DJIA 30 stocks because they represent:

1.   30 to 100 stocks, focused, easier and save time.
2.   Adequate selection to properly diversify.
3.   The largest companies, peace of mind factor.
4.   The most widely held liquid stocks.
5.   Understandable common-sense feel-appeal.
6.   Guidance, earnings, dividends and growth history.
7.   Cost and opportunity economies of scale.
8.   Business diversification, geographically, many products.
9.   Skilled management.
10.   Reasonable odds of surviving mishaps.

You are probably wondering about the disadvantages from restricting stock selection to only the 30 or 100 largest companies? Surely a broader selection of big, medium and small cap stocks, from the thousands available, provides even more opportunities to outperform these stock market averages?

I don't believe this is true, especially if returns are risk adjusted with the extra costs, time and effort factored in. Investing in companies would then turn into stock trading speculation, or playing the market with unpredictable and often undesirable results.

The consensus herd cycles in and out of the stock market at the wrong time during both boom and bust years, reacting mainly to stock market hype and trading momentum. They repeatedly buy when they should be selling, and sell when they should be buying, often giving up on the stock market eventually, seeing it as gambling.

This is what you are up against when trying to outperform the market in this way. Remember that the 70-year average return on small company stocks is 12.6% versus 11.3% for the S&P 500, a difference of 1.3%. After tax it is 8.7% versus 7.8%, and after taxes and inflation the real return is down to 5.6% versus 4.7%, or 0.9%.

This suggests that if you accept significant added risk, there may be an extra 1% long-term average return by broadening your stock selection. This also suggests that you may need to spend considerably more time getting to know about many companies, distracting you from earning your regular income and balancing your expenses.

It takes time to really get to know the Dow 30 companies, with lots of tangible information available. Imagine how much time it will take to get to know 300 or 3000 companies, some with sketchy information at best to base investment decisions on.

You simply can't reasonably do it; nobody can! Tangible financial information readily available on the Dow 30 stocks is then substituted with technical analysis or trading patterns on risky stocks. In other words value investing business fundamentals are diluted or ignored.

Instead you trade stocks based mainly on what other people are buying, selling or recommending. This is like surfing stocks blindly, one stock wave to the next, hoping to be lucky enough to get off a stock wave before it crashes.

You don't know or care if you overpay, your bet is simply that others will join the bandwagon and pay even more. This is how stock prices get overvalued and undervalued.

Buying and selling in this way is based mainly on greed and fear emotions, in a greater fools momentum trading fashion. This is what created the dot-com boom, bubble and bust. It can happen for any investment that seems to have unlimited potential!

A similar real-estate bubble may be occurring for two simple reasons. Homeowners are encouraged to take advantage of low interest rates, borrow and leverage home equity to own multiple homes to flip or rent out, driving up real-estate demand and prices. At the same time renters realize they can afford to own a home as well. No down payment or documents supporting your mortgage payments... no problem, everyone was upsizing!

Interest rate costs are now going up and this trend is starting to cool down. There will be a crunch time when a lot of equity will be wiped out, like in past real-estate cycles. The past 5-years speculative high-priced sellers-market has finally evened out. The cycle usually ends in depressed prices and a buyers-market.

Homeowners are starting to realize they can no longer afford more than one home and for renters the no-money-down mortgages are drying up. Homes do have tangible long-term value and prices will recover eventually. In the meantime much of this capital will look for higher returns elsewhere, such as the stock market and other investments.

The point is that if more stocks, real-estate etc., are followed than needed, there is a natural tendency to ignore risks and get caught up in the excitement of boom cycles, chasing prices higher. Stock speculations especially tend to have volatile price swings; resulting in more trading to quickly lock-in profits or to minimize losses.

This means paying higher commissions and unpredictable returns while trying to outsmart the market's long-term average return. Short-term capital gains are also taxed at a higher rate than if capital gains are realized after one year.

Instead, why not rationalize it this way. The majority of mutual funds and other institutional money managers, and financial analysts cannot meet, let alone beat, the long-term market averages. They are fully trained, experienced, have better access to information and other resources, and follow many stocks. This is all they do!

How can you beat them at their game, when they can't even win? Instead, why not stay within the biggest and safest companies, get to know them well, and try and find the best out of these 30 to 100 quality stocks? The best of the best if you will!

This only makes sense as some quality stocks outperform others. If we can identify the undervalued and overvalued stocks within the index, and eventually our value perspective is proven right, we will reasonably outperform the market without extra cost, time or risk.

The value stock selector was designed to help value investors compare all stocks within the Dow 30, and then the S&P 100 with these Dow 30 stocks removed. All you need to do is enter amounts into the blue-cells and the green-cell values will auto-fill.

The value stock selector compares stocks within the Dow 30 separately because they are the bluest of the blue-chip stocks. Any of these 30 stocks may be worth owning, if the price is right. I look at the remaining 70 S&P 100 stocks simply as quality alternatives.

Most financial websites and newspapers provide stock quote information, referenced by ticker symbols. You will see the value stock selector lists all of the Dow 30 and S&P 70 company names, followed by their ticker symbol under the column called 'symbol'.

Use these symbols to get current stock and index quotes. You are looking for the current price, the 52-week high and 52-week low, and the annual earnings and dividend per share. Enter these amounts into all value stock selector blue-cells.

Be careful entering dividend values, which should always be yearly amounts. Most companies pay dividends every 3-months, while some pay only once or twice a year. Multiply quarterly dividends by four, or multiply semi-annual dividends by two, and enter this as the yearly dividend. Annual per share dividends should be entered as-is.

If you are not sure how often dividends are paid, compare the value stock selector 'div yield', or divide the dividend by the current price, and then multiply this by 100. Check if the result is the same as the percentage dividend yield indicated by your stock quote.

For example GE General Electric's stock quote currently shows a dividend of .25 per share, and a dividend yield of 2.89% at $34.61 per share. I know GE pays a quarterly dividend because .25 x 4 = $1.00 / $34.61 x 100 = 2.889%.

You would enter $1.00 as the 'dividend' and $34.61 as the 'share price'. You will then see that the 'div yield' green-cell auto-fills as 2.89%, the same as the dividend quote.

Some financial websites or newspapers provide more detailed stock quotes than others! You may have to look around or click a detailed quote link to get everything needed. GE's current '52-week high' is $37.13 and '52-week low' is $32.21.

Current earnings per share are $1.78, which you would enter in the 'earn/sh' blue-cell. You will then see that the 'p/e ratio' green-cell auto-fills as 19.44. The p/e ratio is a common quick value measure of earnings related to price. The p/e ratio is also called the p/e multiple, as the earnings multiplied by the p/e ratio equals the current price.

In other words the p/e ratio shows how many years it may take current earnings, added together over time, to equal the current share price. The p/e ratio is a value measure because the smaller the p/e ratio is, the fewer years this may take.

The p/e ratio is also considered a quick indicator of expected earnings growth. In other words a stock with a higher p/e ratio may imply that a stock's price factors in earnings that are expected to grow faster than a comparable stock with a lower p/e ratio.

Growth stock investors reason that a stock with a p/e ratio of 10 is expected to grow earnings at a significantly lower rate than a stock with a p/e ratio of 40. They argue that a higher p/e ratio stock may be better value than a comparable lower p/e ratio stock.

They may be right, but only if their earnings growth assumptions are eventually proven correct. Growth companies and analysts who forecast stock earnings estimates are often way off. Short-term earnings are uncertain; long-term earnings are unpredictable at best.

Value investors are concerned with relative value, with a margin of safety. A stock with a 10 p/e may not be good value if the company is expected to lose money. Similarly, a stock with a 40 p/e may be undervalued if earnings end up growing faster than expected.

The problem is that you pay-up for high growth expectations on a 40 p/e stock. This in itself may limit your upside. Also, if earnings miss for any quarter, your stock price may go down substantially as earnings estimates and growth rates are revised lower.

This is why value investors tend to favour low p/e stocks, of companies with a proven earnings track record, with less that can go wrong. Also, better than expected earnings are usually good for stock prices of both low and high p/e ratio stocks, with an added leverage affect for low p/e stocks when they start to be perceived and recommended as growth stocks again.

When valuing dividends, it is important to compare a stock's dividend yield to similar types of stocks, the market index in general and to alternative investments such as bonds. It is also important not to over or under weigh the importance of just one value indicator.

The value stock selector uses your current stock quote information to score stocks in different ways. The 'income div yield vs DJIA' column scores a stock between –3 and +3, after comparing its dividend yield to the dividend yield of the DJIA index.

If a stock's dividend yield is more than 1.5% higher than the DJIA dividend yield, the stock score is +3. If a stock's dividend yield is less than 1.0% lower than the DJIA dividend yield, the stock score is –3. Otherwise the score is somewhere in between.

Dividend yields represent tangible safety value because they are paid in cash. They may also represent additional investment growth and dollar cost averaging value if the company offers a DRIP or dividend reinvestment program, where dividends can be used to automatically purchase more shares commission free.

Dividends are important but their value must be kept in context with other investment value measures. For example, if the stock price goes down at a higher rate than the dividend yield, then your overall investment return is negative if you sell the stock.

If the company's dividend yield is unusually high, or dividends are higher than earnings, you need to question the reliability of future dividend payments. Also low dividend yields don't necessarily mean less value, as a company may be able to create higher yielding shareholder value using earnings to grow the business, future earnings and share prices.

The 'income div yield vs DJIA' assigns a maximum score of +3 and minimum of –3 so that overall value scores are not unreasonably skewed by dividend yields alone. Actually all of the value stock selector scores are kept within +3 to –3 ranges for this reason.

The 'income div yield vs DJIA' scores dividend yields in absolute terms, or the size of one dividend yield compared to others. The 'rel value div vs earnings' column scores a stock's dividend compared to its earnings. This is important to value for several reasons!

Dividends are usually paid out of earnings; therefore a company should earn at least as much as they are paying out. Otherwise dividends may create a drag on the company's other working capital, growth prospects and overall shareholder value.

This is called Dividend Coverage, or how many times current earnings cover dividends. If someone promises to pay you a high return, what value is this if they can't afford to pay? The 'rel value div vs earnings' scores this easily, dividing earnings by dividends.

If the dividend coverage is more than 0 but less than 1, the company is paying out more in dividends than they are currently earning. You need to question if this is a temporary event, or are future earnings and dividends at risk.

If the company doesn't pay a dividend, has no earnings, or is in the red with negative earnings, the 'rel value div vs earnings' penalizes these stocks with a minimum –3 score. Negative earnings mean the company is losing money, which implies higher risk. Similarly, a bird in the hand cash dividend is safer than two in the bush future growth.

The opposite is also true. A company that produces significantly more than adequate earnings to cover its dividend payments may indicate additional opportunity value. These surplus earnings add to working capital, growth prospects and overall shareholder value.

The bigger the dividend coverage, the more cash the company may have available to increase future dividends, buyback shares and other ways of adding shareholder value.

Dividend coverage is a relative value measure of the quality and safety of dividends!

You can see that all DJIA stocks except GM currently have adequate dividend coverage! GM gets top marks for its high dividend yield, but this is fully offset by the 'rel value div vs earnings' for safety reasons, because they are currently losing money.

In this way, companies that have and return to shareholders a reasonable amount of earnings through dividends are favoured over stocks that do not. We then need to measure the relative value of a stock's earnings as compared to other stocks.

The 'rel value p/e vs DJIA' scores stocks based on how much higher or lower a stock's p/e ratio is compared to the DJIA index p/e. Value investors are mainly concerned with company values, however general stock market conditions may also be important.

Comparative values of alternatives affect all investments. A stock's value is affected by competing returns on other stocks, bonds, real estate and other investment opportunities. This is one of the reasons why interest rates affect stock prices so much.

When the risk-free interest rate return of savings accounts, T-bills, bonds etc. goes up, the stock and real estate markets may look less attractive, especially on a risk adjusted basis. The reverse is usually also true when interest rates are low.

In other words the supply and demand of an investment class in general tends to affect prices. A stock's p/e and the stock market's p/e in general tends to go higher when stocks are in high demand during Bull Markets. The reverse is also true during Bear Markets.

The DJIA p/e is currently around 20. Some would argue this is good value as it implies a 5% return, $1 / 20 \times 100 = 5\%$, plus over 2% in dividends, which may be reasonably higher than competing bond interest rates. One could argue that a p/e of 20 is reasonable as earnings have been positive, growing and are expected to keep growing.

Others may argue interest and inflation rates are going higher, and earnings growth is now questionable due to higher operating and capital costs. The point is that a stock's p/e is affected by the stock market's p/e and some reasonable value comparison is needed.

Other investment values such as real estate prices fluctuate in the same way. As demand exceeds supply during hot real estate markets, it is not uncommon for competing bids to push prices higher, even beyond asking prices. The reverse is also true when sellers lower sale prices to stay competitive with similar properties for sale.

As prices go higher, more properties are built or listed for sale. As prices go lower, fewer properties are built and listings are cancelled. Real estate markets, like stock markets, eventually stabilize, finding value and price equilibrium, when supply meets demand.

It may be difficult to reasonably achieve long-term goals when fundamental values indicate prices are too high. On the other hand if fundamental values indicate prices are low, it still is not easy to invest against the trend, if it seems that prices may go even lower. How long can you wait to start investing when the risk-free return is not enough?

Late in the 1990's bull market, the stock market p/e was around 40. On the other hand, during past bear markets it was not unusual for p/e's to be lower than 10 for several years. The best way to even out irregular markets is to invest gradually and regularly!

If you had decided to stay out of the stock market in the mid 1990's only because the DJIA p/e of 25 seemed too high, you would have missed out on some great growth years. Similarly, if you had invested during past bear markets only because the DJIA p/e of 13 seemed low, you may have seen negative returns and even lower p/e's for years.

This demonstrates why waiting, in an attempt to better time the stock market in the short-term, is usually not reasonable. However it is reasonable to assume stock market prices will eventually stabilize to normal p/e's, as they return to a value and price equilibrium.

In the meantime you need to invest regularly to receive long-term investment returns. This is why the 'rel value p/e vs DJIA' scores a stock's relative p/e value compared to the current DJIA p/e. Assuming long-term returns eventually work out to historic averages, there may be added margin of safety value in owing stocks that have a relatively low p/e!

If a stock's p/e is equal to or less than 75% of the DJIA p/e, the score is +3. For example, if the DJIA p/e is 20, a stock's p/e of 15 or less would score +3. If a stock's p/e is more than 125% of the DJIA p/e, the score is –3, in this case if a stock's p/e is more than 25. The other scores are simply 10% intervals up from 76% to 125% of the DJIA p/e.

I just explained how timing the stock market is usually not reasonable. My next value measure may seem to contradict this point. The 'contrarian momentum 52-week hi/lo' scores a stock's price relative to its high and low price range over the last year.

In this way a stock's near-term price volatility is factored into value. This score favours stock prices that are closer to the low end of its 52-week trading range, over stock prices that are closer to the high end of its 52-week trading range.

Value stock investors tend to find more value in beaten-up quality stocks currently out of favour. When everything else is equal, the lower a stock's price, the more value it may offer. This assumes the company's value is the same as when stock prices were higher.

Value investors prefer to buy low and sell high and the 'contrarian momentum 52-week hi/lo' recognizes that stock prices often fluctuate considerably in any given year. If we can buy quality stocks near the low end, instead of the high end, of its yearly trading range, this may enhance overall returns and provide an added margin of safety.

This value indicator is called contrarian because it values quality stocks opposite to the current trading momentum or price trend. It favours quality stocks when the market sells them down, and penalizes quality stocks when the market bids prices higher.

Notice the word 'quality' has been used repeatedly! This is because the stock must have tangible value with established earnings and dividends to reasonably expect prices to recover. This is not the same as so-called bottom-fishing speculative stocks after their prices implode; simply hoping prices will recover with no established value to rely on.

As quality stock prices become extended, too high or too low, eventually they may correct to a more normal value and price equilibrium. The 'contrarian momentum 52-week hi/lo' values a stock in the context of its near-term stock price ebb and flow.

Volatile stock prices attract short-term momentum traders who push prices even higher, but will instantly bail out on a whim. They also try and push stocks even lower by shorting them when prices have fallen off. Eventually momentum changes, with their buys reversing into sell orders, and their short sales reversing into closing-out buy orders.

This value indicator favours quality stocks that are currently out of favour, and the opposite is also true. It reasonably assumes that some stocks perform better than others during any given year, as some industries perform better than others at different times.

This year's darlings are often next year's dogs. Assuming this evens out over time, if you wanted to own 5 or 10 quality stocks on the DJIA in any given year, it may be reasonable to prefer those stocks that have not performed that well lately and avoid the stocks that have already gone up in price substantially.

There are several Dogs of the Dow formulas that apply a simple approach to investing in the DJIA stocks. Most of them factor-in dividend yields, or p/e multiples as their only value indicator. Even for quality DJIA stocks, this may reasonably not be enough!

The value stock selector tries to keep things simple as well, while factoring in several value indicators and weighing them against each other. Fundamental values are of most importance to a value investor, but price momentum may offer some value as well.

Momentum can change quickly for any number of reasons. Management gets pressured by shareholders to boost stock prices when they are low. These are big companies and while turning them around may take considerable time, resources exist to do it.

To use a train analogy, this value indicator tries to identify stocks before they leave the station. It seems reasonable that within long-term investment return averages, this may provide a longer and safer journey than trying to jump on a stock train that is already moving ahead at full steam. In other words, stock prices tend to run in spits and starts.

Your stock may go down further in the short-term and you may have to wait a while longer than expected. However if the value is there, this is usually worth the wait for when momentum turns back in your favour.

The 'contrarian momentum 52-week hi/lo' value indicator simply scores a stock as –3, +3 or 0. If the current stock price is at the higher end of its 52-week trading range, more than 2/3^{rds} of the way between its 52-week low and 52-week high, the score is –3.

If the current stock price is at the lower end of its 52-week trading range, less than 1/3rd of the way between its 52-week low and 52-week high, the score is +3. Otherwise the stock price is somewhere in the middle, receiving a neutral score of 0.

The last value indicator is somewhat controversial as well. Between similar types of stocks, I wanted some way to favour lower priced stocks over higher priced stocks. With all other values comparable, the lower priced stock may provide added leverage value.

The lower a stock's price is, the more shares you can buy for the same dollars invested. Also, to keep commissions down and for convenience, we tend to buy in even board lots of 100 shares. This may favour lower priced stocks, especially for retail investors.

A good example of how the affordability factor of lower priced stocks may positively affect returns is when stocks split. This is when shareholders receive additional shares and the stock price is then adjusted lower to reflect this change in per share value.

For example when a stock splits 2 for 1, the price is cut in half and you end up with twice as many shares. In a 3 for 2 stock split, you get 3 new shares for every 2 old shares held, and the price is reduced to 2 / 3^{rds} of its old price.

The old and new investment value should total the same when you multiply the price by the number of shares. However, forward stock splits like these tend to result in prices shooting up, when company value has not changed. Only the stock price has changed!

Some argue this phenomenon is coincidence, and is irrelevant to value in the context of long-term returns. Perhaps, however you should ask why then do companies bother with the costs associated with stock splits, if this has no real impact on value.

This has nothing to do with actual fundamental values, but does affect the perception of value. Buying half of something may seem less valuable than splitting it into two halves that are each perceived as a new whole. They are really the same overall value.

Perception of value affects demand, especially for retail investors when one stock is significantly higher or lower in price as compared to a similar stock. There are practical costs and simplification reasons why investors want to buy in even 100 share board lots.

Many retail investors can't afford even one share of BRKA Berkshire Hathaway, which trades at around $90,000 a share. Retail investor demand is the main reason why Berkshire started offering its BRKB share, which is 1/30th of a BRKA share.

The value stock selector shows that the average share price of the DJIA is currently around $45. This is a convenient share price for a retail investor to invest $5,000 and buy 100 shares. If the stock price is $25, you can then buy 200 shares. However if it is $100 you can only buy 50 shares, which psychologically may seem like less value.

If share price affordability affects the demand for shares, then perhaps this added demand can drive-up prices faster. If so, lower priced stocks may have a leveraged return advantage. Some may argue this is nonsense, in any event I prefer lower priced stocks!

The 'low price lever' value indicator simply scores a stock as –3, +3 or 0. If the current stock price is one of the 10 highest DJIA stock prices, the score is –3. If the current stock price is one of the 10 lowest DJIA stock prices, the score is +3. Otherwise the stock price is somewhere in the middle, receiving a neutral score of 0.

I have played around with the weightings of these various value indicators, but have found that a simple +3 to –3 score value works best. This is not and end all by any means to identify overall stock value. It is simply a snapshot or guide to focus your research.

Green-cell value indicator scores are then added together to produce an overall DJIA or S&P 70 comparative stock value 'score'. This overall score can range from +15 to –15. 3/5[ths] of this score is based on dividend yield, dividends versus earnings and earnings versus price. 2/5[ths] of this score is based on the stock's relative price, and its 52-week trading range.

The current DJIA average score is under 3, and for the S&P 70 it is slightly negative. This does not seem too attractive overall, as the value stock selector does not perceive value until the score is +5 or higher. A score of +10 really gets my attention!

Only 8 stocks out of 30 in the DJIA currently have a score of +5 or more, and only 11 out of 70 in the S&P 70. Remember that value is a matter of perception, eventually proven right or wrong, that can change often for a variety of reasons.

You need to update and track prices regularly, research as best as possible for a gut feel, and do some value calculations like in chapter 5.4 and only pull the investment trigger when your instinctive common sense says to, within your goals and risk tolerance!

You may even want to project scenarios and change values such as the stock price or earnings per share to see how this will affect the overall score. The value stock selector was designed to use actual reported values instead of projected values, but even I like to play with the price and earnings occasionally to see how a stock could score a 10.

This value investing method needs time to work. Value stock investors usually do not trade a stock more than once a year, for various reasons already explained. A guideline is to gradually buy equal dollar amounts of the 5 or 10 stocks that 'rank' best overall.

Gradually refers to spreading out your buys over weeks or even months until your full stock position is acquired. This is simply to average into falling prices, instead of trying to pick one moment in time when you feel the stock has bottomed. This requires some judgement and may not be practical if it unreasonably drives-up your stock commissions.

Then wait! If after a year a stock's 'rank' falls out of the top 10, you may wish to sell this stock to buy another stock ranked in the top 5 or 10. Your goal is to own the top 5 to 10 quality stocks to try and regularly beat the DJIA or S&P 100 3-to-5-year average return.

These quality stocks should make-up only part of your diversified portfolio of stocks, bonds, real estate and other investments. Since you are concentrated into only 5 or 10 stocks at one time, it is important that you only buy one stock within any industry!

It is not reasonable to try and time investing in the stock market. However you should regularly invest and find the best quality stock values within the stock market at any given time!

Now that you have reasonably identified the top 5 or top 10 value stocks, you then need to confirm or reject them as an investment. You need to dig deeper into each company's story and consider all other risk and reward conditions that may reasonably affect a company's value, and how this fits within your objectives and comfort level.

Chapter 5.3
Company Value Perspectives

Y ou need to get to know companies beyond their stock quote! You need to fill in the value picture details by researching a company's history, what they do, their financial situation, management skills and how to estimate their future growth prospects.

In short you need to understand and have a feel for the various conditions that may affect a company's value, beyond the value stock selector score. The following is examples of things to watch out for or to keep in mind. They are opinions, which may be right or wrong, and not meant to substitute for other opinions or more exhaustive research.

In 2005 General Motors, symbol GM, started to look attractive as it continued to sink in price below $25. This was the lowest price GM traded in over 10-years. They also paid an extremely attractive $2 dividend, yielding 8% at the time.

However GM was losing market share and billions of dollars per year. The magic question is, can they turn it all around and is GM worth the risk?

My rough math indicated GM held around $15 billion in cash, almost the same as its stock market capitalization value or company worth. I figured they could tap their bank lines, pension plan credits, sell GMAC and cut their dividend to bring this cash up to around $40-$45 billion if needed, or around three times as much cash as the stock market was valuing all of GM's common shares.

This may mean some flexibility, but it is highly unlikely there would be any value left over if GM decided or was forced to sell everything off. I've read that GM's debt is around $300 billion, most owed by GMAC, but in any event debt far exceeds assets.

Cash to a bondholder may mean there are liquid assets to pay back debt. To a common shareholder this only means there may be time to turn around the business. GM traded even lower to around $18 in early 2006, when the value stock selector ranked it Top 5.

GM's business was not a pretty picture then, with many risks and uncertainties. It could be a great value investing stock as it turns around. For now GM is out of market favour and I needed to decide if it is an appropriate value investing stock for my risk profile.

I feel GM's stock is down mainly because their credit rating was downgraded several times as they were quickly losing money and market share. The big question is can GM restructure their operating and legacy costs lower, and at the same time revamp their product line quickly to less gas guzzling hybrid vehicles, to make the company profitable again.

I believe there may be value in GM, but I also realize things could get much worse. Layoffs are expected, as some plants need to close. Union contracts, pension plans and parts supplier costs all need to be renegotiated. Gas prices and interest rates could go higher, and GM's credit rating, market share, sales and margins could go even lower.

You could argue the risks are too many, too high, and therefore unreasonable to accept. The value stock selector can't do this for you! It only identifies relative value based on current amounts entered. You still have to determine your personal value perspectives!

The value stock selector narrows your search to a few stocks, but this is only the start to finding undervalued companies. There are value calculators in chapter 5.4 to help you project future values and then decide whether these stocks are intrinsically undervalued.

The Dow 30 stock selection is at the discretion of the Wall Street Journal's editors. GM is still considered a blue-chip Dow 30 company, but arguably does not currently meet all of the 10 advantages listed on page 116. The important point is that Dow 30 stock selection has changed over the years, with newer established companies replacing others that have not continued growing with the times.

GM could simply be dropped from the Dow 30 if it does not turn its business around at some point. For example Sears is no longer a Dow 30 stock, but Wal-Mart now is. Intel and Microsoft are in, while Kodak and International Paper are out. In this way, the Dow 30 will always be an elite group of company stocks with occasional changes over time.

GM caught my eye, but on further investigation I decided to pass on the stock. However I still wondered if perhaps the auto group in general was in trouble, or just GM? I noticed that the S&P 70 stock selector had Ford, symbol F, scored as the top stock.

F was trading around $8 and dipped under $7 in early 2006. The dividend yield on F was higher, after GM cut their 2006 dividend in half. I noticed on the long-term charts that GM traded up to around $90 in 2000 and F traded up to around $35. At their 2006 lows, both stocks were trading at around 1/5th or 20% of their past highs.

Notwithstanding fundamental company values, this may indicate that their stock prices have a relationship and trade in sympathy. This only makes sense, as both are American based auto companies with similar businesses, product mixes and financial structures.

Ford was still profitable up until 2006, when it too went into the red. They have similar debt, credit rating, pension and union costs issues. I like the currently lower than $7 stock price as a speculation only, on a future value turnaround. F still gets an F value grade, for now!

Most industry sectors often trade in sympathy, such as the drugs, banking and auto group etc. Finding a company that continues to do extremely well in an industry that has been marked down in price by the stock market often presents the best of both value worlds.

Companies like Toyota, symbol TM, offer a product mix of smaller, less gas guzzling cars and trucks than their American competitors. Their sales, market share and earnings were all going up at the same time GM and Ford's were going down.

TM sold off with the rest of the market between 2000 and 2001. It later soared from 2003 to 2006 at the same time oil prices were climbing. Hindsight is 20/20; TM is not an S&P 100 stock and is trading at all time highs at over $100. Interesting, but I'll pass!

Toyota also doesn't seem to have the same debt, pension and labour problems the others are having. It's strange how history often repeats, because this all seems the same that Chrysler experienced in the late 1970's and 1980's when oil prices last soared.

Chrysler is now Daimler Chrysler, symbol DCX, and was a great stock to own in the 1990's. Lee Iacocca turned the company around from near bankruptcy at the time. Could history be repeating itself with GM and F? Is this indicating value or speculation?

It's still speculation until forecasted plans turn into profits. However you should now have a good feel for a value investors thought process when assessing value information.

Value investing starts with comparing numbers. If these numbers work out, investment decisions are then based on common sense expectations. In other words how reliable do you believe the company will be in executing its business plan, reducing costs, developing new technologies and products, growing sales, earnings, dividends and other shareholder value.

I'm a contrarian value investor at heart. I like to gradually buy beaten up, out of favour or ignored quality stocks, in anticipation of them coming back into favour over the next few years. This is a patient and often-lonely way to invest, which some brokers describe as catching falling daggers – because these stocks tend to hurt for a while longer as they go even lower in the short-term.

In the long-term this tends to work out lovely. I only buy stocks that I think have the possibility to at least double over the next 3 years. I prefer stocks that may possibly be at least 10-year holdings. My goal is for a long-term average rate of return of at least 15%.

There is no point going over every Dow 30 stock in detail. You probably know them as well as the next investor. Here are some of my thoughts on how I watch these stocks. This is really just my common sense opinion, and you may agree or disagree.

Late in 2005 and early 2006 the drug stocks fell out of favour. MRK Merck, PFE Pfizer and JNJ Johnson & Johnson all bounced around within the value stock selector's top 10. I still haven't bought any of them and MRK has since recovered from the mid $20's to mid $30's, with all those thousands of Vioxx lawsuits yet to be settled.

PFE bounced off of $20 to the mid $20's. I like its lower price, meaning more shares leverage potential. However this leverage isn't as great when you consider that Pfizer and JNJ are tied as the biggest drug companies, which may limit their upside.

This is because a hot new drug has a larger percentage of earnings impact on a smaller company's value. Drug companies need to keep up their pipeline of new drugs to replace older drugs with expiring patents. They need to be big, but biggest isn't always best!

I noticed over the past decades these companies go back and forth as the biggest drug company; based mainly on new drug approvals, patent extensions and sales expectations. I generally look for the second, third or fourth large cap and still safe drug company, that will keep up with drug group returns, and may exceed this as they pursue the top spot.

I noticed on the S&P 70 that BMY Bristol Myers was priced low at around $20 like PFE, had the highest dividend yield at over 5% within the group, and was less than $1/3^{rd}$ the market cap company size compared to Pfizer.

In 1999 and 2000 BMY traded as high as $70, close to MRK's high and higher than PFE or JNJ has ever traded. BMY's $40+ billion market cap, versus PFE and JNJ's $170+ billion market cap, really attracts me to BMY also as a possible buyout candidate!

BMY seems really attractive as a value stock, currently around $22. Its P/E is less than 14, dividend yield is 5%, and dividend coverage is 1.44, all favourable in both absolute and relative value terms. Its price is low and is trading near its 52-week low.

BMY is one of the big drug companies, but small enough that growth is levered if they hit on a new drug. Alternatively another drug company may want to buy BMY as part of its own growth plans. Perhaps I'm missing something, but BMY seems undervalued!

When MSFT Microsoft fell below $24 it advanced within the value stock selector's top 5. The same happened for INTC Intel as it fell below $22. These both used to be high tech growth stocks with triple digit earnings multiples but today are out of favour.

MSFT at $22 now offers more than a 1.60% dividend and at $18 INTC's dividend is over 2%. MSFT has a P/E multiple of 18 and INTC has a P/E of only 14. Both are mature companies instead of pure growth plays, but they both spin-off billions of cash in earnings and are still leaders in their businesses.

Look out as MSFT's new 64-bit Vista operating system and INTC's new chips hit the market next year. Will this cause a new PC and mobile chip upgrade cycle, with sales and earnings growth rates like in the 1990's? In any event, for now there seems to be value!

I think I missed the easy money in oil stocks, but XOM Exxon Mobil now at $60 does still have some appeal on a value basis. XOM's dividend yield is attractive at over 2% and especially with its very low 10 P/E.

Nobody knows exactly where oil prices are going and I can see reasons why they should go higher or lower. With an eye on potential geopolitical conflicts and Peak Oil supply shortage scenarios, I'm leaning on the higher side but passing on the bet for now. If I wanted to buy an oil stock I would probably buy CVX Chevron at $57 instead, which currently pays an even higher 3.5% dividend and has an even lower 8 P/E.

CAT Caterpillar and BA Boeing get the lowest scores and have already made terrific price runs. Nobody knows for sure when these cyclical stocks will finally correct. I'm not buying, as I believe the easy money has been made. Momentum traders would say these are the best Dow stocks to own right now. It takes all kinds to make a market – a good thing, as all trades need both a buyer and a seller.

I see value in DD Du Pont and DOW Dow Chemical, both now under $40. Again look at their comparatively low P/E, high dividend yield and low trading range. High oil prices, hurricane damage etc hurt earnings, but these companies have great product brands in demand that should only take some extra time to adjust prices, margins and lift earnings again.

Two of the top rated value stocks are $32 VZ Verizon and $26 T AT&T. I'm hoping VZ eases back to $28 again, putting its dividend near 6%, and P/E at only 11. These utility stocks usually have lower growth rates, but are safer havens if the stock market craps out for a while. I can handle 6% as I wait for the economy and stock market to boom again.

Banks seem undervalued on paper, like $46 C Citigroup and $40 JPM JP Morgan Chase. Both have more than doubled from their post 9/11 lows, but this doesn't concern me as much as higher interest rates, which negatively affects loan demand, defaults and earnings. However, banks now depend as much on fees as mortgage spreads, insulating their earnings from wild swings that higher interest rates used to cause.

My main concern is that highly leveraged low-down, no-down and even no-doc real-estate loans have positioned bank balance sheets like casino bets against a recession ever happening again. Low interest rates plus extra easy mortgage financing created this so-called boom, that to me looks more like a bubble ready to pop. Nobody seems to question higher real-estate prices anymore because lenders can resell mortgages before the ink gets dry, and buyers think they have no skin in the game to lose if house prices ever fall apart.

The odds actually seem stacked in favour of a recession soon if you consider all the negatives related to expected energy costs, government debt and deficits, currency crisis, political conflicts etc. Also bank shares have enjoyed over a decade of ever-higher prices and may be overdue for a major price correction. For all these reasons I see better value holding off buying bank stocks, at least for now!

The value stock selector had AA Alcoa at the top spot at $23, but AA is up almost 50% now at over $31. It was entertaining reading all the analyst's downgrades of AA at $23 versus all their current buy recommendations at $30. If you track enough of these past stock reports, it will seem like analysts prefer to buy high and then sell low!

Analysts do provide interesting value perspectives, detailed breakdown of earnings and even forward estimates to work with. However they are usually wrong in the end! Most analysts have the value stocks mentioned above as sells, usually disguised as a hold.

This is often because they don't usually issue flat-out sell recommendations for a variety of reasons, some which may represent conflicts of interest. For example they may not want to issue a sell if they underwrite the company's stock or bonds, usually representing millions of dollars in fees. I actually get uncomfortable if most analysts agree with me!

MMM 3M hit the top spot around $70 in 2005, now ranked 28th at around $85. KO Coca Cola moves in and out of the top 10 on small price fluctuations it seems. Each time it broke below $40 it made the top 5, but now at over $43 it is down to 21st.

Anyway you get the idea and if you update the Dow 30 blue-cells every weekend and S&P 70 monthly like I do, you will get a good feel how the value stock selector works. Once you have identified the top Dow 30 and S&P 70 stocks worthy of looking into, you then need to consider their future earnings and how this affects your perceived company values and stock prices.

These blue-chip companies often provide reliable earnings guidance, or there are many analysts with opinions of their own forward earnings estimates. The next chapter has tools to help track past earnings and to project future earnings, to estimate intrinsic value.

Chapter 5.4
Value Calculators

Intrinsic Value of Future Earnings - Discounted Cash Flows Method

Actual Earnings Values

Per Year	1996	1997	1998	1999	2000	2001	2002	2003	2004	2005	growth last
Earnings Per Share	$1.00	$1.10	$1.21	$1.33	$1.46	$1.61	$1.77	$1.95	$2.14	$2.36	9
Earnings Growth Rate		10.00%	10.00%	10.00%	10.00%	10.00%	10.00%	10.00%	10.00%	10.00%	years avg =

Discount Rate 11.00%

Projected Earnings Values

2006 - 2015

Growth Rate	2006	2007	2008	2009	2010	2011	2012	2013	2014	2015	10-yr Total
	10.00%	10.00%	10.00%	10.00%	10.00%	10.00%	10.00%	10.00%	10.00%	10.00%	10.00%
Future Value	$2.59	$2.85	$3.14	$3.45	$3.80	$4.18	$4.59	$5.05	$5.56	$6.12	$41.34
Present Value	$2.34	$2.32	$2.29	$2.27	$2.25	$2.23	$2.21	$2.19	$2.17	$2.15	$22.44

11.00%

Growth Rate	2016	2017	2018	2019	2020	2021	2022	2023	2024	2025	20-yr Total
	10.00%	10.00%	10.00%	10.00%	10.00%	10.00%	10.00%	10.00%	10.00%	10.00%	10.00%
Future Value	$6.73	$7.40	$8.14	$8.95	$9.85	$10.83	$11.92	$13.11	$14.42	$15.86	$148.56
Present Value	$2.13	$2.12	$2.10	$2.08	$2.06	$2.04	$2.02	$2.00	$1.99	$1.97	$42.94

11.00%

Growth Rate	2026	2027	2028	2029	2030	2031	2032	2033	2034	2035	30-yr Total
	10.00%	10.00%	10.00%	10.00%	10.00%	10.00%	10.00%	10.00%	10.00%	10.00%	10.00%
Future Value	$17.45	$19.19	$21.11	$23.23	$25.55	$28.10	$30.91	$34.00	$37.40	$41.14	$426.66
Present Value	$1.95	$1.93	$1.91	$1.90	$1.88	$1.86	$1.85	$1.83	$1.81	$1.80	$61.67

11.00%

Growth Rate	2036	2037	2038	2039	2040	2041	2042	2043	2044	2045	40-yr Total
	10.00%	10.00%	10.00%	10.00%	10.00%	10.00%	10.00%	10.00%	10.00%	10.00%	10.00%
Future Value	$45.26	$49.79	$54.76	$60.24	$66.26	$72.89	$80.18	$88.20	$97.02	$106.72	$1,147.97
Present Value	$1.78	$1.77	$1.75	$1.73	$1.72	$1.70	$1.69	$1.67	$1.66	$1.64	$78.78

11.00%

Growth Rate	2046	2047	2048	2049	2050	2051	2052	2053	2054	2055	50-yr Total
	10.00%	10.00%	10.00%	10.00%	10.00%	10.00%	10.00%	10.00%	10.00%	10.00%	10.00%
Future Value	$117.39	$129.13	$142.04	$156.25	$171.87	$189.06	$207.97	$228.76	$251.64	$276.80	$3,018.88
Present Value	$1.63	$1.61	$1.60	$1.58	$1.57	$1.56	$1.54	$1.53	$1.51	$1.50	$94.40

Growth rate & P/E multiple		DCF, Graham, Buffett & Lynch - Fair Value		
current stock Price	$94.40	sum of Disc. Cash Flows	$94.40	stock price
actual Earnings last yr.	$2.36	DCF's / last yr. earnings	40.04	DCF P / E
exp. Earnings this yr.	$2.59	DCF's / this yr. earnings	36.40	DCF P / E
Growth rate this yr.	10.00%	50 Yr. Graham	44.00	P / E est.
trailing P/E ratio	40.04	5% Buffet like	$92.79	stock price
leading P/E ratio	36.40	Peter Lynch PEG ratio	3.640	if P/E/G =1

Rule of 72 - int. % or years to double money		Compound time is money	
enter interest rate	10.000 %	semi-ann.	2
Rule of 72 years est.	7.200 yrs. approx.	principal	$ 100,000
compounded annually	7.273 exact years	int. % rate	8.50%
compounded monthly	6.960 exact years	# of months	240
you want $ doubled in	5.000 yrs. approx.	total repaid	$ 528,497
Rule of 72 int. rate est.	14.400 % approx.	APY total	$ 511,205

Retirement Savings, Annuity Payments & Estate Plan			
Pre-Retirement		**In-Retirement**	
starting RSP value	$ 10,000	RSP value	$ 151,888
yearly RSP contrib's.	$ 1,000	payout yrs.	20
years to retirement	20	growth rate	7.50%
growth rate expected	11.00%	estate value	$ -
retirement RSP value	$ 151,888	yrly income	$ 13,860
total contributions	$ 30,000	total value	$ 277,192

Bond Calculator - Yield to Maturity, Present Value & Duration			
buy date (dd/mm/yyyy)	7/19/2006	all coupons per year	$ 65.00
maturity (dd/mm/yyyy)	7/19/2016	current interest yield	6.842%
term to maturity in yrs.	10.000	annual yield to maturity	7.219%
current bond price	$ 950.00	semi-annual coupons	$ 32.50
bond's face or par value	$1,000.00	effective yld. to maturity	7.340%
coupon rate of interest	6.500%	required annual return	7.250%
coupon pays per year	2	present value of bond	$947.30
Macaulay's duration	7.417 years,	modified duration	7.155

It is reasonable to assume that if you had to choose between doing something the easy way or the hard way, you would choose the easy way. However this presumes the end result, the straight-line shortest distance between two points, is the same either way!

I like easy as much as the next person, but the saying I prefer to live by is that anything worth doing is worth doing well! Just because it worked in the past doesn't necessarily mean it will work again in the future. There must be a logical reason for it to work again.

In any event we need to understand how it worked, factoring in as much relevant information as is reasonably possible, before we assume that it will work again. This whole book is about understanding value and applying this knowledge through simple but powerful excel tools to reasonably and predictably achieve wealth goals!

The value stock selector tries to keep things simple, while at the same time factoring in the most important value indicators. Stock prices are affected by these known current values, but also unknown expected future values plus a whole range of other factors.

The absolute value of a stock's high dividend yield, high dividend coverage and low P/E may indicate the margin of safety for a stock's known values. The relative value of a stock's high dividend, high dividend coverage and low P/E may be the best indicator of how undervalued or overvalued a stock is compared to others, based on known values.

In other words a stock may be overvalued even if it is cheap compared to others, or undervalued even if it is expensive compared to others. Timing the market doesn't work, so the best we can do is to regularly buy relatively undervalued quality stocks with an adequate margin of safety, regardless of the stock market's overall value.

Unknown expected future values are future earnings, the economy and stock market performance in general, and anything else that is unpredictable or unreliable that may affect investors perception of a stock's value. There is no easy way to deal with this!

The value stock selector tries to resolve unknown expected future values by betting against the stock market's popular perception. This contrarian approach assumes the stock market sells-off or bids-up stocks based to a large extent on uncertain expectations.

Future values are uncertain; therefore it may be reasonable that there is a higher margin of safety in stocks with low expectations built into the price, with the opposite also true. You may also reason that if future results turn out better than expected, the percentage gain in price or leverage value may be more for stocks with low expectations.

This is the purpose of the value stock selector's contrarian momentum and low price lever, while maintaining our quick and easy theme. Various value indicators are broken out, but it is only the overall score and rank that determines a stock's relative value.

There are even quicker and easier formulas to attempt to determine undervalued quality stocks. They tend to factor-in only some of the known values and none of the unknown values. They usually reason that high dividends, or low P/E's, or low stock prices are enough to value a stock, and that this one value alone is all you need to know.

Dividend yields alone are directly determined by a stock's price and dividend, but do not directly factor-in earnings. However the Dogs of the Dow approach reasons that safety of earnings is implied for companies that can afford to pay dividends.

The value stock selector values earnings separately because a company may pay a dividend even if it loses money. In this way dividend value is set-off or enhanced by earnings values. Earnings effectively determine the reliability and quality of dividends.

For example, late in 2005 GM at $25 was the highest dividend yielding DJIA stock, at 8.00%. This alone would have made it a Dogs of Dow top stock, with its high dividend implying value and a high margin of safety. However GM continued to lose money, with its dividend being cut in half only a couple of months later, on the way to $18 a share!

One could argue GM's dividend yield was unreasonably high, and its value needs to factor-in an expected dividend cut. The value stock selector effectively did this for you, as GM's +3 dividend and +3 contrarian price value was fully offset by its −3 earnings and −3 relative P/E value. The only value left over was GM's +3 low price lever value.

Both investment strategies have similarities and agree that only quality DJIA stocks offer the best risk versus reward opportunity value. However the value stock selector also considers other S&P 100 stocks as alternatives, if their scores qualify. The differences are subtle but important, and only time will tell which approach works better in the future long-term.

In any event the Dogs of the Dow approach has produced impressive past results. From 1957 to 2003 they outperformed the Dow by over 3%, averaging 14.3% compared to 11% for the DJIA. From 1973 to 1996 the Dow averaged 15.80% while the Dogs of the Dow averaged 20.31%.

Variations of the Dogs of the Dow are as follows:

Back-Tested Average Returns 1973-1996		Value Investment Strategy
DJIA Index	15.80%	the 30 Dow Jones Industrial Avg. stocks
Dogs of the Dow 10	20.31%	10 highest dividend yielding out of Dow 30
Dogs of the Dow 5	23.40%	5 lowest priced out of Dogs of the Dow 10
Dogs of the Dow 4	26.41%	4 highest priced out of Dogs of the Dow 5
Foolish Dogs of the Dow 4	28.03%	40% in lowest, 20% in the other 3 - Dow 4

Several large-scale stock scandals over the past few years were a result of financial statements being manipulated to exaggerate revenues, expenses and earnings. Regulators are now more closely scrutinizing accounting practices, and Wall Street analysts are starting to emphasize cash flow and the "quality" of earnings in its recommendations.

DCF Discounted Cash Flow analysis is the most effective way to determine a company's Intrinsic Value based on expected future cash flows. Analysts estimate future free cash flows over time, which are then discounted to present values that are added together.

These forecasted future free cash flows are based on a company's expected operating profit, plus non-cash expenses such as depreciation, amortization and goodwill, less all capital expenses, taxes and working capital changes. Free cash flow offers a more transparent way to value earnings than P/E ratios and is less likely to be manipulated.

DCF intrinsic value models provide a clearer picture of expected growth, efficiencies, structure and costs. In short this extra work reveals a company's "real" earnings value. DCF analysis effectively values long-term growth rates, which impacts share prices the most.

Interest rates also have a big impact on company and share values. They affect the costs of capital, demand for products and services, and the economy in general. Lower risk interest rate investments also compete with stocks for investor capital.

Interest rate changes are effectively factored into DCF values. In the calculation of present values of future cash flows, a discount rate is applied. If interest rates are going higher, this discount rate may need to be adjusted higher, lowering DCF stock values.

The discount rate should be set at a reasonable rate compared to similar investments. For example the long-term return rate of the stock market has been 11%, therefore an 11% discount rate may be reasonable as one stock competes with investment returns of others.

If a company is in a new and untested high growth business, it may be reasonable to use a higher discount rate to factor in higher risks associated with unproven growth rates. On the other hand discount rates may be a bit lower for a proven stable growth company.

Companies are usually expected to be in business for a long time, potentially forever. DCF is a reasonable method to put a present value on all expected future cash flows. The sum of all these present values should equal the company's intrinsic value.

Forever is a long time to estimate future cash flows. Also the further you go out into the future, the less reliable your predictions become. It is more reasonable to predict growth rates over a few years, and then assume earnings will naturally plateau from then on.

Present Value calculations discount future cash flows because a dollar received today is worth more than a dollar received tomorrow. The further into the future, the less valuable it is now. In this way, cash flows expected far into the future have significantly less impact on overall stock values today, compared to cash flows expected over the next few years.

Analysts typically use DCF intrinsic value models to factor-in earnings growth predictions for five or ten years at most. After this reasonable expected growth period, earnings are then assumed to grow at a very low rate or 0% from then on.

Assuming your predictions come true, DCF is the best way to factor-in time and comparable returns against expected growth, to calculate fair value. DCF works well for any investment, business, stock, life annuity etc., with a series of future cash flows.

As cash flows are expected to plateau over a few years, going far out into the future does not materially change the DCF intrinsic value. This is why DCF models typically only need to calculate the present value of future cash flows over the next 10 to 20 years.

***

On your wealth plan excel workbook, click the sixth tab at the bottom called 'Value Calculators'. This spreadsheet is yet another powerful wealth planning tool that is easy to use, designed to help you further identify the intrinsic value of an investment.

The main table is called 'Intrinsic Value of Future Earnings – Discounted Cash Flows Method'. There are also six other tables that tie into each other, called 'Growth rate & P/E multiple', 'DCF, Graham, Buffett & Lynch – Fair Value', 'Rule of 72 – int. % or years to double money', 'Compound time is money', 'Retirement Savings, Annuity Payments & Estate Plan', and 'Bond Calculator – Yield to Maturity, Present Value & Duration'.

The DCF table is detailed and flexible. It starts by determining an average growth rate, based on previous years known actual earnings.

These known values are then used to project the Growth Rate, Future Value and Present Value of future earnings.

Future values of earnings or growth rates may be updated further for any given year. Present values should not be changed, but you may change the Discount Rate for any ten-year period, which is then factored into present values for all years in that decade.

The top section of the DCF table tracks reported earnings over the last 10 years. In the 'Per Year:' blue-cell, enter the current year minus 10. All green-cells for the remaining 59 years in the DCF table will then auto-update based on that year value.

Next, enter per year known actual blue-cell 'Earnings Per Share' for the past 10 years. If you don't know all 10-years earnings, a few sequential past year earnings may still work. However, starting with the previous year, going back in time, no years should be skipped.

Your blue-cell past actual earnings per share entered will auto-fill the 'Earnings Growth Rate' green-cells for each year. For example if you enter the last 6-years earnings, you will see that each of the last 5-years have an earnings growth rate compared to the previous year.

Erratic and negative earnings produce messy growth rates! For example, if earnings last year were $1.00 but this year they are $0.00, the growth rate is –100%. If the company had negative earnings instead, the growth rate is worse, but is still –100%. Similarly, if negative or no earnings last year, you cannot calculate a growth rate for this year.

Very large fluctuations in earnings may produce meaningless growth rates. If you enter earnings as .01 the first year, then $1 the second year, then back to .01 again the third year, repeatedly over 10-years, this produces an average growth rate of 5456%, useless for future growth predictions. You should see this as another example why quality companies produce more reliable results!

Applying expected growth rates to current earnings is the preferred way to project future values. However the DCF table allows you to overcome the problem of meaningless blue-cell growth rates by entering green-cell future value earnings if more reliable.

The last column shows the 'growth last' years involved in calculating a 'years avg. =' blended growth rate, which auto-fills into their respective green-cells. This average growth rate is auto-filled into future growth rates over the next 50-years, for now!

An average growth rate based on 10-year known past earnings is usually best to work with, when conservatively estimating future growth rates. However there are exceptions if you believe it more practical to only consider the past few years' earnings.

For example, if a company's business changed 3 or 5-years ago, resulting in material changes to its earnings and growth rates, that are still applicable going forward, then it may be more practical to apply 3 or 5-year instead of 10-year average growth rates.

One of the best examples I can think of is when AAPL Apple Computer starting selling the iPod. This new product changed the outlook of the whole company. The iPod significantly increased sales and earnings, and also enhanced the value of the Apple brand and sales of its other products.

How long Apple's current growth trend will last is unknown. The important question to ask is whether to apply 3, 5 or 10-year past growth rates to future earnings projections!

You could extend this argument to companies that are expected to grow at a faster rate than their past known earnings indicate. However this is what usually gets you into hot water, when analysts' future expected earnings don't turn out as expected.

Looking at past actual results versus past guidance may also indicate the accuracy or reliability of future guidance. The point is you may change future earnings and growth rates as desired, just try and balance future value guesses against known past values!

For effect, the DCF table starts in 1996 with $1.00 in earnings, growing at 10% each year until 50 years into the future at 2055. You should notice that the present value of future earnings decline each year, even though earnings continue growing at a constant rate.

The 2006 future value of earnings is projected to be $2.59, and the present value of this is $2.34. For 2055 the future value is $276.80 but the present value of this is only $1.50. In other words $2.59 in 2006 is worth more than $276.80 in 2055, when discounted at 11%.

If you change the first discount rate to 0%, you will see how present values factor-in the effect of time, as present values will no longer be discounted and will equal future values. The long-term return of the stock market is 11%, a reasonable discount rate to apply.

Notice that the last column's '2006 – 2015 10-yr Total' of earnings is $41.34 and $22.44. This is simply the first forward 10-years projected earnings, or present value of these earnings, added together. For 20 to 50 year totals, these values are cumulative from 2006.

Notice that the future value totals for each decade go up dramatically, but the present value totals only increase marginally. Future value totals range from $41.34 to $3,018.88, while present value totals range from only $22.44 to $94.40.

$94.40 is the estimated 50-year DCF intrinsic value or fair price for this investment. This assumes a 10% constant earnings growth rate for 50-years, discounted against an 11% comparable rate of return, starting with last year's earnings of $2.36. In other words the present value of $3,018.88 earned over 50-years may be worth $94.40 today!

It should be apparent that this scenario is unreasonable, because it is impossible to predict a company's fortunes for the next 50-years! Let's assume instead that you believe, based on a combination of past results, forward company guidance and analyst predictions, that a 10% growth rate may be reasonable for the next 3-years.

You also believe the growth rate will then slow down to 5% for the next 3-years. After 6-years the growth rate is unpredictable, so you drop this further to 0% from then on. For 2009 change the blue-cell 'Growth Rate' to 5% and change the 2012 growth rate to 0%.

You will notice the dark-green-cell 50-year DCF intrinsic value has now dropped from $94.40 to $30.50. You should also notice that the 40-year present value is only 33 cents lower and even the 20-year present value is only 12.7% lower at $26.68.

I put the DCF fair value of this investment somewhere between $27 and $30 per share under this scenario. This example effectively demonstrates that a 50-year DCF model does not produce an intrinsic value significantly different than a 20-year DCF model, which also shows why you really don't have to project DCF values to infinity!

For stocks you own or are interested in, start researching actual past earnings and forward estimates to plug into the DCF table. If you are really ambitious you may even want to dig deeper into financial statements to apply free cash flows instead of earnings values.

I usually don't go this far as DJIA quality stocks tend to report reliable earnings that are usually a reasonable indicator of future growth rates. One thing I do like to do is to use a DCF table to predict growth rates that are needed to justify current share prices!

You do this by entering near-term green-cell 'Future Value' earnings expectations that seem reasonable based on past performance. You then consider reasonable scenarios by adjusting future years' growth rates until the intrinsic value equals the current share price.

Low growth rates mean that low expectations are built into the share price. This may imply a higher margin of safety, or even leverage value if results work out better than expected. Similarly, high growth rates may imply more risk and downside leverage.

DCF does have shortcomings, as intrinsic values often do not align with market expectations. DCF is not appropriate for short-term investments, and long-term estimates may be off or interest rates can change. In any event you may wait too long and miss out!

**

Your DCF table values are also used in the 'Growth rate & P/E multiple' table. This table now shows 'current stock Price' $30.59, 'actual Earnings last yr.' $2.36 and 'exp. Earnings this yr.' $2.59. These blue-cell values can be changed as desired.

Based on the blue-cells price and earnings, the 'Growth rate this yr.' 10.00%, 'trailing P/E ratio' 12.97 and 'leading P/E ratio' 11.79 green-cells auto-update. The expected growth rate this year, G, is calculated by subtracting last year's actual earnings from this year's expected earnings, divided into last year's actual earnings, times 100.

P/E ratios are calculated by dividing the current stock price by earnings. The trailing P/E ratio shows the current stock price is 12.97 times last year's actual earnings. The leading P/E ratio shows the current stock price is 11.79 times expected earnings this year.

Notice that the price is based on DCF values, which suggests a fair DCF P/E is 12 to 13! This assumes an 11% discount rate applied in present value DCF calculations. However, a 12 to 13 P/E ratio does seem a bit low compared to the current average DJIA P/E of around 21. This is the main reason why the value stock selector emphasizes relative stock values.

The P/E ratio is an important metric to consider because, as Peter Lynch puts it, "the P/E ratio of any company that is fairly priced will equal its growth rate". In other words P/E = G, where P/E is a stock's P/E ratio and G is its earnings growth rate.

The next table is called 'DCF, Graham, Buffett & Lynch – Fair Value'. Changing blue-cell values in this table and the previous table will auto-update this table's green-cell values. This table summarizes four different value perspectives on a stock's fair value.

The 'sum of Disc. Cash Flows' $30.59 is the DCF table's 'stock price' fair value. The 'DCF's / last yr. Earnings' 12.97 and 'DCF's / this yr. Earnings' 11.79 are the 'DCF P/E' fair values based on last year's actual and this year's expected earnings.

The next three fair value indicators are based on Benjamin Graham, Warren Buffett and Peter Lynch's value investing perspectives. Benjamin Graham wrote the Intelligent Investor and is known as the father of value investing. Graham taught at Columbia, where he mentored Warren Buffett who is known as the greatest value investor of all time. Peter Lynch is a value investor, known as the most successful mutual fund manager in history.

Investing tips from these famous value investors are discussed at the end of this chapter!

Graham's fair value formula is E x (2G + 8.5) x 4/Y. E is the current earnings per share, G is the expected earnings growth rate and Y is the yield of a triple-A rated bond. This simple formula is how Graham estimated the fair value of stock prices.

Graham's even easier P/E formula is 2G + 8.5, dropping the E and 4/Y. This works fine as long as bond yields remain low. If bond yields change significantly from 4%, then 4/Y needs to be factored-in again. Remember that rising safe interest rates imply that riskier stocks may need to be priced lower to maintain their value attractiveness.

Multiplying by 4/Y adjusts both the fair P/E and stock price to factor-in interest rates. For example, if AAA bond yields drop from 4% to 2%, 4/Y equals 2, which may result in fair P/E's and stock prices doubling. On the other hand if AAA bond yields rise from 4% to 8%, 4/Y equals 0.50, which may result in fair P/E's and stock prices being cut in half.

The stock market's historic rate of return is around 11%. Therefore a company with no growth prospects, but will maintain current earnings, implies a P/E of 1 / 11 x 100 = 9.09. Graham must have based his 8.5 on then rates of return of 1 / 8.5 x 100 = 11.7%.

To easily confirm this, change the DCF discount rates to 11.7% and growth rates to 0%, which produces a $20.07 DCF 50-year present value. Notice the 'Growth rate & P/E multiple' table now shows a $20.07 share price, $2.36 for earnings and P/E ratios of 8.51.

Graham's formula values the growth rate times 2, but only if growth rates are expected for 7 to 10 years. Shorter-term growth may not be worth the trouble and longer-term growth is totally discounted as unreliable. I agree, but also believe this may be too rigid.

Graham's fair value P/E aligns well with normal DCF scenarios, but seems high at other times. The 'DCF, Graham, Buffett & Lynch – Fair Value' table modifies Graham's fair value P/E estimate to 9 + (G multiplied by a growth time factor). This scales the fair value P/E and stock price higher or lower, based on expected growth length of time.

If growth is expected to last less than 3-years, the growth time factor is 0. The others are: < 9-years = 0.5, < 15-years = 1.0, < 21-years

= 1.5, < 28-years = 2, < 36-years = 2.5, < 43-years = 3, > 42-years = 3.5. Long-term growth is worth more than short-term growth, within reason. The growth time factor tries to allow for this and is not up to Graham's 2.0 until after 20-years of growth is expected!

To keep things simple, AAA bond yields are assumed to be 4%. Therefore 4/Y equals 1, so this was left out of the calculation. For demonstration purposes, just change the DCF discount rate back to 11%, and the two 3-year growth rates to 10% and 5% as before.

The 50 'Yr. Graham' 44.00 'P / E est.' fair value now needs to be updated. The blue-cell represents 50-years expected growth, which again is not reasonable. It should be between 3 and 6 years, as we now assume 3-years of growth at 10%, 3-years at 5%, and 0% thereafter.

Change the blue-cell to 3 or 6, and its corresponding growth time factor of 0.5 is then multiplied by next year's expected growth rate of 10%. The modified Graham fair value P/E green-cell changes to 9 + (10% x 0.5) = 14.00.

Leave the growth rate at 10%. Just know that if you instead had used an average 6-year growth rate of (10% + 5%) / 2 = 7.50%, and changed the 'Growth rate this yr.' to 7.50%, the modified Graham fair value P/E would have changed to 9 + (7.50% x 0.5) = 12.75.

This is very close to the fair value DCF P/E of 12.97. If you multiply this P/E by actual earnings of $2.36, the DCF fair stock price is $30.59. The modified Graham approach indicates a P/E of 12.75 to 14.00, and a fair stock price of $30.09 to $33.04 per share.

Buffett uses a somewhat different approach, but his exact intrinsic fair value P/E or stock price formula has not been published. The formula is apparently quick and easy to calculate in your head, without relying on a calculator or computer spreadsheet.

Estimated future earnings are somehow multiplied by a confidence factor between 0% and 100%. The more likely he believes these earnings will occur, the higher the percentage. I assume past results play a big part in Buffett's confidence factor!

These probable earnings are then discounted against a U.S. treasury yield, which Buffett has 100% confidence in. This value perspective forces you to carefully value earnings. If you are not very confident in a stock's yield advantage, buy government bonds instead!

The 'DCF, Graham, Buffett & Lynch – Fair Value' table shows a 'Buffett like' approach. It uses the 'Yr. Graham' blue-cell value as its number of years of expected earnings growth. Continuing with the last example, this should be between 3 and 6 years.

To keep things simple, this Buffett like formula assumes the U.S. treasury yield is 5%. The P/E multiple of a 5% yield is 1 / 5 = .20 x 100 = 20. Put another way, if an investment costs $100 and provides no growth opportunity other than safe 5% interest, then you are paying 20 times the $5.00 to be received in yearly interest.

Buffett somehow values actual earnings differently than expected growth, adding these values together for his fair stock price. To value a stock's actual earnings, I assume he multiplies this by a 20 P/E as a base stock value. In other words current earnings are more reliable and may be worth 20 times this amount, similar to treasury yields.

You then need to value expected earnings growth, which is the tricky part. This growth value should factor-in the expected growth rate and how long this growth is expected to last. It should also be discounted to a present value using our safe 5% treasury yield.

The base stock value and value of expected earnings growth are then added together and discounted further, multiplied by your confidence factor. This Buffett like formula works well with normal values, meant to provide a feel for how Buffett's intrinsic value works.

However it can't be Buffett's actual formula as exponentials are used to factor-in time and a 5% treasury yield discount rate, into the expected earnings growth rate. This can't be done in your head, but hopefully helps you understand Buffett's value perspective.

One thing I like about a Buffett like formula is that it may indicate your margin of safety. If you work backwards, varying the confidence factor until you get a fair stock price close to DCF values, this gives you a feel of how much of your expected growth has already been priced into the stock.

For example, change the 'Yr. Graham' blue-cell to 3 and the 'Buffett like' blue-cell to 55%. The result is a $30.92 Buffett like fair value stock price. This seems reasonable, with your expected growth rates priced into the stock somewhere in the middle.

If this percentage is very low, the stock may be undervalued at your higher expected growth rates or higher confidence factor. Similarly, if this percentage is 100% or more, the stock may be overvalued compared to your expected growth rates or confidence.

Change the 'Yr. Graham' blue-cell from 3 to 6. The Buffett like fair value stock price updates from $30.92 to $40.44. The extra 3-years of expected growth is worth more!

Now change the 'Buffett like' blue-cell to 42%. The Buffett like fair value stock price updates to $30.88, close enough to the $30.59 DCF fair value stock price. If you expect an extra 3-years growth, then you only need to be 42% confident to justify a $30.88 stock price. This shows longer-term growth tends to provide a higher margin of safety!

The bottom line of the 'DCF, Graham, Buffett & Lynch – Fair Value' table calculates the 'Peter Lynch PEG ratio'. Peter Lynch believes that P/E ratios should reflect a company's growth rate. For example a 20 P/E is justified for a company growing long-term at 20%.

The PEG ratio is a simple tool to help determine if stocks are overvalued or undervalued. It factors in the stock price and expected earnings, against the earnings growth rate. This provides a snapshot of how much of earnings expectations are already built into prices.

The PEG ratio is calculated as the stock price divided by expected earnings per share, divided by the earnings growth rate. In other words the leading P/E ratio divided by G, or P/E/G. If the PEG ratio equals 1, the stock price fully reflects earnings per share growth.

If the PEG ratio is less than 1, this may indicate the stock is undervalued or that the market does not expect the company to meet past growth rates. Value investors prefer a PEG ratio of less than 1, as long as expected earnings growth is reasonably achievable.

If the PEG ratio is more than 1, this may indicate the stock is overvalued or that the market expects the company to exceed past growth rates. Growth stocks typically have a PEG ratio greater than one, as growth investors are willing to pay more for rapid growth. Higher prices as a result of growth at any price is unreasonable and represents added risk!

Continuing with the same DCF earnings and growth scenario, The 'Peter Lynch PEG ratio' equals 1.179. The formula uses the 'Growth rate & P/E multiple' table's 'current stock Price' $30.59, 'leading P/E ratio' 11.79 and 'Growth rate this yr.' 10.00%. The calculation is simply P/E / G = 11.79 / 10.00 = 1.179.

A PEG ratio of 1.179 is slightly higher than 1.00, but close enough that I would still consider the DCF $30.59, or around $30.00, the fair value stock price. If you play around with the 'current stock Price' to get a PEG of 1, this suggests $25.95 is the fair price.

It is helpful to compare a stock's PEG ratio to similar industry stocks and even stock index PEG ratios. This will give you a quick feel if your stock is considered a growth company compared to its peers or the stock market in general.

Low or relatively low PEG ratios may indicate a higher margin of safety, with the opposite also true. The higher the PEG ratio, the more certain you should be about your earnings growth expectations. Value investors avoid stocks with high PEG ratios!

PEG ratios are important, but need to be weighed against your other value indicators. From my value perspective, I take extra care to look beyond dividends, earnings and price when the PEG ratio is higher than 2 or the DJIA PEG ratio, whichever is lower.

Compare trailing PEG ratios over past years to the leading PEG ratio as an indication of the reliability of expected growth rates. Stock prices that have higher than reasonable growth built in are susceptible to fall hard if premium earnings targets miss their mark!

***

The 'Rule of 72 – int. % or years to double money' table calculates the approximate interest rate or the number of years it will take for invested money to double. This is simple enough to do in your head.

The rule of 72 says that to calculate the approximate number of years to double money at a given interest rate; simply divide 72 by the interest rate. The 'enter interest rate' 10% blue-cell results in approximately 7.2 years to double money at 10% interest.

The rule of 72 also says that to calculate the approximate interest rate to double money over a given number of years; simply divide 72 by the number of years. The 'you want $ doubled in' 5 'yrs. approx.' blue-cell results in approximately 14.40% interest rate.

This is a neat trick! However the rule of 72 assumes interest is always compounded annually. This table shows 10% 'compounded annually' in 7.273 and 'compounded monthly' in 6.960 'exact years'. Do you understand why they are not the same?

The compounding frequency determines how many times interest is added per year. It is important to realize that all interest rates are not compounded the same way and this can have a significant impact on overall investment returns or loan costs! More frequent compounding works for investors and against borrowers.

For a $10,000 one-year loan or investment, 10% interest compounded annually simply adds 10% once to the principal balance, or $10,000 x .10 = $1,000 + $10,000 = $11,000. However, a 10% semi-annual rate adds 10% / 2 = 5% to the ongoing balance twice per year, or $10,000 x .05 = $500 + $10,000 = $10,500 x .05 = $525 + $10,500 = $11,025.

If you don't read the light coloured very small print on your loan agreement, such as how interest is compounded, you probably wouldn't know that 10% is effectively 10.25% and your bank just made an extra $25! A wealthy mindset knows and understands details!

Interest investments usually compound monthly, however most bonds compound semi-annually. Mortgages usually compound semi-annually in Canada or monthly in the U.S. Auto loans and leases usually compound monthly, but credit cards often compound daily!

Everyone understands that finance companies and credit cards charge very high interest rates! However many consumers still don't know that effective interest rates are boosted even higher by compounding as frequently as possible! This is why regulations now require better disclosure of EIR, APR or APY interest rates.

If annual compounding were the same as monthly compounding, the exact number of years to double money would have been the same. Monthly compounding doubles money in less time, therefore its EIR Effective Interest Rate, APR Annual Percentage Rate or APY Annual Percentage Yield is higher than 10% compounded annually.

The 'Compound time is money' table effectively demonstrates how values change when applying various types of interest rate compounding. Use this table to enhance your understanding of the value perspective "Time Is Money"!

Blue-cell values are: 'semi-ann.' 2, 'principal' $100,000, 'int. % rate' 8.50%, '# of months' 240. In other words a $100,000 loan or investment, compounded at 8.50% semi-annually (twice per year), over 240 months (20-years). Green-cells values result in: 'total repaid' $528,497, versus 'APY total' $511,205.

Compounded semi-annually, compared to simple annual interest, affects overall value by an extra $17,292. Change the first blue-cell to 12, which applies a monthly interest compounding instead. The total is now $544,124, or $32,919 more than the APY rate. Change it to 365, daily compounding, resulting in $547,286 or $36,081 more than APY.

As you change the blue-cell compounding frequency, the yellow-cell description updates to indicate which type of compounding you are using. Play around with all the blue-cell values to reflect different compounding scenarios as desired.

The most common compounding frequencies per year are: annually=1, semi-annually=2, monthly=12, weekly=52 and daily=365. However some loans or investments compound: quarterly=4, bi-monthly=6, semi-monthly=24 or bi-weekly=26. Daily compounding is based on either 360 or 365 days per year and there is even continuous compounding.

When making investment or loan decisions, find out the EIR, APR, APY or annually compounded equivalent interest rate to make sure you are comparing apples to apples! Perhaps we might change our credit habits if we knew that a 19.99% 365-daily compounded credit card works out to over 22% APY, and that 29.99% is almost 35% APY!

***

The 'Retirement Savings, Annuity Payments & Estate Plan' is a simple way to plan for retirement cash flows before and during retirement. The pre-retirement plan does not add-in tax refunds, or allow you to view or change each year's interest rate or contribution. It is not as flexible as the RSP wealth on steroids table, but essentially does the same thing.

Pre-retirement blue-cells are: 'starting RSP value' $10,000, 'yearly RSP contributions' $1,000, 'years to retirement' 20 and 'growth rate expected' 11.00%. The green-cell results are: 'retirement RSP value' $151,888 and 'total contributions' $30,000.

This is straightforward so just change the blue-cell amounts as desired to your pre-retirement scenarios, or mouse-over comments if help is needed. The importance of this table is to show the cash flow effects after you are in-retirement!

During pre-retirement you only have to plan how much to add to your RSP each year and how to reasonably invest it, in order to reach your long-term retirement goal. In other words you are just dealing with RSP cash inflows, and time and compounding.

However, it is just as important to consider needs during retirement, which has both cash inflows and outflows, with less flexible time value and therefore less risk tolerance! The in-retirement RSP value blue-cell auto-fills based on the pre-retirement RSP value, which should be updated to your more accurate RSP wealth on steroids results!

In-retirement blue-cells are: 'RSP value' $151,888, 'payout yrs.' 20, 'growth rate' 7.50% and 'estate value' -. The green-cell results are: 'yearly income' $13,860 and 'total value' $277,192. This scenario provides $13,860 per year for 20-years, with $0 left over!

The first important point is to estimate the number of payout years that your RSP is expected to make cash outflows. This is essentially predicting how long you believe you will live after retirement, so that you can maintain your standard of living and don't outlive your investment income. You need to pad this a bit, in case you live longer!

The second important point is that interest rates in-retirement is usually lower than pre-retirement. In-retirement cash outflows need to be reliably less risky, and predictably on time. You also need to allow for various taxes or other costs that have to be paid.

The third important point is that you may need to build in an estate value to cover costs such as funeral and burial costs. You may also want to leave an estate for someone, or to charity, in which case you may need to consider inheritance taxes and probate costs.

The in-retirement table calculates your expected life annuity. This is essentially the same as an insurance annuity, which may also factor into yield various actuarial life data. For this scenario, $13,860 in yearly income is surely not enough to meet all these needs!

Don't forget that $13,860 is not your in-retirement yearly take home pay! This is before RSP withdrawal taxes that are deducted as you receive this income and later adjusted further after you file your then next tax return.

The green-cell total value is simply the total of all yearly income plus any estate value. In this scenario $13,860 is actually $13,859.58 in yearly income x 20 payout years = $277,191.67. This is displayed as $277,192 because cell values are formatted in dollars.

Also don't forget to allow a margin of safety and adjust values for inflation! If you change the payout years to 30 and enter an estate value of $25,000 to leave some money and cover various costs, your yearly income drops to only $9,994 per year, before taxes!

The cost of inflation table, at your wealth plan's time and compounding tab, will calculate how much yearly income you will need while in-retirement. For example, if you plan to retire after 20-years and you want to receive yearly pre-tax income equivalent to

$30,000 today, then assuming 2.5% to 3.0% inflation, this shows $49,000 to $54,000 per year will be needed.

Assuming 11% pre-retirement returns for 20-years and 7.50% in-retirement returns for the next 20-years, adjust the yearly RSP contribution amount and you will see that yearly contributions need to be increased to between $6,404 or $7,173, to achieve $49k to $54k per year income at retirement! With an estate value of $25,000, yearly contributions need to increase to $6,755 or $7,524!

Most of us have savings affordability limits, balanced against our current expense needs. $1,000 may be the maximum you can afford to contribute each year. However, if you can afford to contribute more, you need to know the optimal amounts. The point is to keep on track financially by knowing where you are at all times in your overall wealth plan!

***

The 'Bond Calculator - Yield to Maturity, Present Value & Duration' table is an excellent tool for calculating bond values and to understand how they really work!

The value of a bond seems straightforward as they pay regular interest and a lump sum at maturity. However, valuing bonds are more involved than this. The important values to an investor's rate of return are a bond's Safety, Effective Yield to Maturity and Duration.

Bond safety is simply the issuer's ability to repay. Bonds are typically used to generate dependable interest income, and to balance out the inherent risks of stocks, real estate and other investments. Bonds are usually the safest component of a diversified portfolio!

Bond rating agencies such as Moody's and Standard & Poors qualify a bond's safety from investment grade down to junk bonds. Government bonds tend to rate the highest as they have the ability to raise taxes, implying added safety. Corporate bonds tend to rate lower depending on their financial situation and the company's outlook.

Bonds compete with various other investments and are valued in relation to prevailing interest rates. Bonds also compete with other bonds, with higher rated bonds being valued more than lower rated bonds, because they represent less investment risk.

In other words, low quality bonds have to offer potential higher returns to investors than high quality bonds. If bonds represent the safest investment component of your portfolio, then a bond's rating must be high. Only Investment Grade Bonds are considered safe!

Bonds are priced to reflect an effective yield to maturity. This changes constantly according to the bond market's current: bond ratings, interest rates and prices that investors are willing to pay. Bond prices and yields move in opposite directions, with a bond's price moving up as its yield moves down, with the opposite also true.

The effective YTM is a safe bond's actual return on investment, if held to maturity. This factors in the bond's premium or discount price as compared to its face or par value, all coupon interest payments until maturity, and the interest payment frequency.

Bond prices and yields always move in opposite directions! When comparing the effective YTM of a bond to its discount or premium price, the coupon interest rate and the current interest yield, the following are always true:

If a bond's price, compared to its face or par value, sells at a:

❏　　**Discount:** the coupon rate is less than the current yield, which is less than the YTM.

❏　　**Premium:** the coupon rate is more than the current yield, which is more than the YTM.

❏　　**Face Value:** then the coupon rate equals the current yield, which equals the YTM.

Bond market prices fluctuate every day, and if a bond is sold prior to maturity, the return on investment is determined by the current sale price plus all coupon interest payments received. In short, bonds that are traded may have gains or losses!

Duration is a measure of a bond's price sensitivity to changes in yield. In other words, if the yield changes by a given amount, duration predicts the impact on the bond's price. Duration factors-in YTM, term to maturity, the payment frequency and coupon rate.

Duration is simply multiplied by the percentage change in the effective YTM to predict the bond's price change. For example, if a bond's duration is 5.50 and the effective YTM moves up 1.75%, we should expect the bond's price to move down 5.50 x 1.75 = 9.625%.

Short, near and long-term interest rate expectations need to be considered when planning a long-term bond portfolio with a variety of maturities. Each bond has its own duration and an average duration can be calculated for a portfolio of bonds.

Average duration effectively measures the weighted average term to maturity of a bond portfolio's cash flows. When analysts predict changes in interest rates and recommend shortening or extending bonds, it is the average duration they are referring to.

This seems complicated but doesn't have to be. Rather than trading bonds, a simple approach is to invest in a variety of quality bond maturities between one to ten years. As short-term bonds mature, reinvest in short, near or long-term bonds to lengthen or shorten your bond portfolio's average duration.

Be careful buying bonds! For stock trades, you know the price and added commission you are paying. For bond trades, your broker's fee is in basis points of yield, carved into the buy or sell price of the bond. The longer the bond's maturity, the more your broker makes for the same basis point charge. Know a bond's yield before fees are calculated!

A simple alternative, or for bond portfolios less than $25,000, is to invest in a quality bond mutual fund. Bond funds manage average duration for you and tend to have lower fees than stock funds. Be careful to choose bond funds that only hold investment grade bonds, as some focus on trading junk bonds or may deploy a variety of higher risk strategies.

Frederick Macaulay introduced this fixed income value concept and its somewhat complicated formula. Many analysts prefer to use a Modified Duration formula that adjusts Macaulay's Duration to also factor-in the frequency of coupon interest payments.

The compound time is money table shows how value is significantly affected by how often interest compounds. Bond coupon interest is not compounded, but the frequency of payments determines when interest is reinvested, which changes the effective YTM.

The 'Bond Calculator - Yield to Maturity, Present Value & Duration' main table blue-cells are: 'buy date (dd/mm/yyyy)' 7/19/2006, 'maturity (dd/mm/yyyy)' 7/19/2016, 'current bond price' $950.00, 'bond's face or par value' $1,000.00, 'coupon rate of interest' 6.500%, 'coupon pays per year' 2.

The green-cell results are: 'term to maturity in years' 10.000, 'all coupons per year' $65.00, 'current interest yield' 6.842%, 'annual yield to maturity' 7.219%, 'semi-annual coupons' $32.50, 'effective yield to maturity' 7.340%, '

The buy and sell dates are entered in day/month/year format, that automatically changes to month/day/year format. Only the months and years are used to calculate the bonds term to maturity, displayed in years and after the decimal any parts of a year.

The bond example shows a current price of $950.00, which is priced at a 5% or $50 discount to the shown $1,000.00 face or par value received at maturity. The coupon rate of interest is 6.500%, multiplied by the face value, equals $65.00 per year. However the bond coupons are paid semi-annually, equalling $32.50 in interest paid twice per year.

The current interest yield does not factor-in payment frequency and simply divides the yearly interest by the bond's price, or $65.00 / $950.00 x 100 = 6.8421%. This shows the interest only yield compared to other investments, but doesn't factor-in bond face values.

The 7.219% annual yield to maturity uses the excel Rate function to factor in the bond's 10-year term to maturity, $65.00 in coupons per year, the bond's $950.00 price and $1,000.00 face value. The annual yield to maturity is then adjusted to an effective YTM of 7.340%, calculated by adjusting this Rate function and using exponentials to instead factor-in $32.50 semi-annual coupon payments instead of annual coupons.

If you change the coupon pays per year to 1, the annual YTM and effective YTM is the same. As the pay frequency increases, the effective YTM also increases. Also note that the semi-annual coupons yellow-cell description changes to 'annual coupon payment'.

Next is a tool to estimate bond prices. Under this scenario, the 'required annual return' 7.250% blue-cell works out to approximately $947.93 'present value of a bond'. If you change the current bond price blue-cell, the annual yield to maturity becomes 7.259%.

Using our original 10-year bond scenario and $950.00 price, the 'Macaulay's duration' is 7.417 'years' and the 'modified duration' is 7.155 years. This 10-year bond's price is less sensitive to interest rates and yield changes than a bond with a 10-year duration.

As you go deeper into fixed income liability planning, there are a myriad of complex derivative duration functions that use parabolas and polynomials to better match or factor-in a bond's convexity or bond curve tendencies. However, predicting interest rates is as much art as science and is not usually worth all this effort.

Using modified duration to adjust a bond portfolio's effective maturity, to take advantage of expected interest rate swings, is not even practical for most brokers. The purpose of all this is to understand how bonds really work. This may help you to make short, near or long-term bond value decisions with more than just the quoted yield factored-in.

Active individual investors often have a good feel for the direction of interest rates based on everyday economic events they read about. If you believe interest rates are going up, simply buy quality short-term bonds. As these bonds mature, if you then believe interest rates are going down, start buying longer-term quality bonds.

As interest rates go down, you may then decide to sell some bonds to lock in gains. This makes sense if your asset allocation changes to a higher percentage of your investment capital for stocks or real estate, which usually benefit from lower interest rates.

The simplest and most practical way to manage bonds is to allocate bond interest and principal payments to the most appropriate investments as funds become available. In other words hold bonds until maturity and either rollover bond returns or invest them in something else. In this way, duration doesn't matter, only the effective YTM!

Now you know as much about bonds as most brokers! In the end, the best way to manage bonds is the easy way – buy only quality bonds, with maturities spread out over several years, and just manage the interest payments as you receive them.

For stocks, the best way to achieve superior returns is to invest in undervalued companies. The value stock selector is an easy way to help you identify relatively undervalued quality stocks. The best way to determine intrinsic value is to compare various value indicators such as the sum of discounted cash flows, P/E multiples, PEG ratios etc.

***

We can all learn from the value perspectives of Graham, Buffett and Lynch. These exceptional value investors have articulated common sense investing principles that help guide and focus average investors, towards outperforming even the so-called experts.

Benjamin Graham is known as the father of value investing as he literally wrote the books on financial analysis during the early and mid 20th century. His books Security Analysis and The Intelligent Investor are considered the bibles of value investing.

Before then, valuing stocks was more art than science. Graham focused investors on tangible value indicators such as dividends, earnings, assets and debt values.

Graham's value investing principals are:

1. Invest in big companies with big sales. Big companies can deal with economic downturns, while small companies often can't. Big companies are less risky!

2. Determine a stocks intrinsic value. Graham preferred stocks that trade at less than $2/3^{rd}$ of its NCAV net current asset value, after subtracting all liabilities.

3. You need a margin of safety. If you are paying more than $2/3^{rds}$ of NCAV you don't have an adequate margin of safety and may lose even if the company does well.

4. Invest in stocks that pay dividends. A long history of dividends is a key sign of profitability and provides a return when stock prices are not performing well.

5. Invest in financially strong companies. Strong cash balances and low debt levels represent less risk. A company's total debt should be less than its tangible book value.

6. Invest in companies that are growing. Look for consistent earnings growth trends, doubling earnings over the last decade, while avoiding significant declines in any year.

7. Invest in stocks with relatively low P/E ratios. Graham preferred companies when they were trading below their historic average P/E ratio.

8. Pay attention to book values. Don't pay more than 20% to 33% over a stock's book value, all assets minus all liabilities. Invest at least 25% in bonds and 25% in stocks.

✓ $10,000 invested with Graham in 1948 would be worth around $30 million in 1996!

Warren Buffett is the world's second richest man and is known as the Oracle of Omaha. Buffett's business interest developed early in life when he ran a paper route, collected golf balls, operated pinball machines and sold Coca-Cola.

Graham was Buffett's mentor at Columbia University, when some of Buffett's key value perspectives were formed. Buffett's publicly traded holding company Berkshire Hathaway owns many private companies and holds significant stock in large public companies such as Coca-Cola, American Express and The Washington Post.

Buffett's value investing principals are:

1. Invest in companies with a long history of profits. Buffett values the return on invested capital of profitable companies with low debt. He also believes that earnings should double every 10-years, P/E ratios should be low, and PEG ratios should be less than 1.

2. Invest in companies with high profit margins. Net income after expenses, but before tax, is divided into sales. Companies with higher profit margins represent pricing power, with a built in margin of safety. Strong brands usually command higher prices!

3. Invest in companies that are well managed. Divide net income by the number of employees to value the efficiency of management. Great management is a must!

4. Invest in companies with low debt. Current assets should be worth at least double current liabilities and total debt should be less than shareholder equity.

5. Invest in companies with strong cash flows. Free cash flow adds depreciation, amortization and other non-cash expenses back into earnings, but deducts capital expenses. Buffett values the efficiency of earnings in building shareholder equity.

✓ $10,000 invested with Buffett in 1965 would be worth around $50 million in 2005!

Peter Lynch managed Fidelity's Magellan mutual fund from 1977 to 1990. The fund had only $20-million in assets as Lynch took over, but grew to become the world's largest and highest rated equity fund with around $15-billion in assets under management as Lynch retired.

Lynch's average annual return was around 29%! He believes average investors can pick stocks better than most professionals. An individual investor is not subject to committee or trustee approval and is usually quick to identify, research and act on investments.

Lynch's value investing principals are:

1. Invest in companies you are familiar with. Boring companies that consistently produce great products are usually great investments. Focus on new products that will drive sales.

2. Invest in companies with a long history of earnings. Consistent and stable earnings are preferred, while avoiding Initial Public Offerings and new companies.

3. Invest in companies that grow fast, within reason. Earnings growth of over 20% but less than 30% is preferred. Too much growth is unreliable and attracts competition.

4. Inventory levels are a value indicator. If inventories are growing faster than sales, this may be an earnings warning. The other way around may indicate potential shortages.

5. Invest in companies with low debt. Equity of 75% versus debt of 25% is acceptable.

6. Invest in stocks with relatively low P/E ratios. P/E ratios of half the historic average are attractive. If double, avoid the stock. Add the dividend yield to the growth rate when calculating PEG ratios. A PEG of less than 1 is undervalued and 0.50 is attractive.

7. Invest in stocks that reliably pay dividends. Prefer stocks with a long history of rising dividends, through good times and bad. High dividend coverage, or low percentage payout of earnings, indicates safety and the ability to raise future dividends.

✓ $10,000 invested with Lynch in 1977 would be worth around $300,000 in 1990!

Graham, Buffett and Lynch have unique value perspectives and rely on different stock value formulas. However there are many similarities and they seem to agree on the most important value indicators.

Here is a summarized list of the investment value perspectives above:

1. **Big companies**
2. **Intrinsic value**
3. **Margin of safety**
4. **Reliable dividends**
5. **Financially strong**
6. **Relatively low P/E ratios**
7. **Book values**

8. Long history of profits

9. High profit margins

10. Great management

11. Low debt

12. Strong cash flows

13. Familiarity

14. Fast growth, within reason

15. Inventory levels

Now you have all the components to develop your personal wealth plan, like a company prepares a business plan. As your plan and wealthy mindset is put into action, you are wealthy from that point forward. When the income generated from your savings and investments alone meet your foreseeable needs, you are then independently wealthy!

Investing is all about capitalizing on expected future values! A wealthy mindset understands this and tries to appreciate the wealth effects of current behaviour and trends, and to learn from history. The next chapter discusses global value perspectives.

Chapter 6
Global Value Perspectives

The wealth of a nation has similarities to individual wealth. A nation receives income, in the form of taxes, and has debt that drains wealth and future consumption. Governments consume in the form of operating costs, infrastructure, education, defence, health care and various other agency services, plus debt repayment.

Persistent government deficits, if not corrected at some point, will lead to credit being denied, or at best will cost more in taxes as credit worthiness is graded lower resulting in higher interest rates. In short, governments have to spend within their means or they too may go bankrupt. If this ever happens you need to know what wealth value remains.

The American economy has changed! Its growth value was once based on the industrial production of things sold to the world, resulting in trade surpluses. It is now based on its remaining credit and purchasing power available to spend and consume. The result is huge debt measured in trillions of dollars, with growing trade deficits measured in many billions of dollars per month, both unsustainable by any reasonable economic measure.

The American economy is heavily dependent on its citizens' abilities to continue growing consumption at any cost. Similarly, American citizens are heavily dependent on the government to continue supporting consumption addiction with low interest rates and money supply growth. Government and citizen debt are both close to their limits!

The growing availability of credit and creative new ways to borrow against equity has accelerated this trend. A few years ago most people, if they qualified, had one credit card with $1,000 available. The balance owing was usually paid off by the deadline each month, so that high cost interest wouldn't be charged. This single credit card was mainly used for small purchases, emergencies or when required to make travel reservations.

Today people are solicited everywhere to sign-up for new credit cards offering competitive perks or points, often regardless of credit worthiness. People are induced with introductory short-term low interest rates into an endless cycle of new cards, now used to pay down existing long-term debts and high cost interest on other credit cards.

Most people have credit cards from several banks and retailers, offering credit lines of tens of thousands of dollars to impulse buy or get a cash advance at any time, for almost anything imaginable. Wealth needs have simply been replaced with consumption wants, resulting in out of control personal finances. Once the exception is now the norm.

Consumers find themselves in a credit trap, with the reasonable need for one credit card replaced by more and more cards just to pay off the old cards. Banks and regulators have made it far too easy to substitute good financial judgement with additional high cost credit. All debt has limits and if not repaid sometime, the banking system breaks down!

Bank growth now relies more on service charges and high interest rate spreads from credit cards, than from traditional loans and mortgages. You might think a competitive business such as credit card lending would result in lower interest rate spreads, but this has not happened and shows no signs of changing.

Far too often the result is an unmanageable monthly expense. Very high interest rate payments are assessed, with only the minimum payment required, reducing the principal loan balance by an insignificant amount. Unreasonably high credit card debt is essentially encouraged to be carried forward indefinitely, instead of being paid off monthly.

Credit cards are simply unsecured loans. Issuers are willing to carry balances because unreasonably high interest rate returns far exceed loan default costs, so far! It should not be surprising that many banks and retailers make more profit from interest and service charges on credit cards than from the other goods and services they are known for.

The end result is an economy addicted to consumer debt, with credit cards as the drug of choice and issuers as willing pushers. The percentage of income saved today is at all-time lows at the same time that levels of consumption and personal debt are at all-time highs.

Personal bankruptcies, often blamed on too much credit card debt, are out of control and at record levels. Lenders and regulators created this gluttonous credit environment, but also see the dangers to the banking system. Unfortunately political policy is influenced more by special interest lobby groups than common sense concern for average citizens.

Reasonable spending and lending is needed and should be encouraged, to reduce debt and increase savings. A simple solution is to raise the required percentage of credit card principal repaid each month. This allows you to pay balances off faster, as a short-term loan should work. However this only helps if balances are not charged up again!

The only real solution is to lower credit card debt to reasonable levels. If credit card interest rate spreads were regulated lowered, at least for people with a history of good credit practices, issuers would then have to reign in how much and to whom they lend, to protect their profit margins. Lower profit margins force issuers to lend responsibly!

Instead laws have been changed in a band-aid approach to simply make it more difficult to declare bankruptcy just to avoid paying off credit cards. This makes it harder to get away from credit card debt and for now keeps a consumer based economy rolling along.

Credit card lending is now saturated at its upper limits. Many are at the point where they can't afford even the minimum monthly payment on additional cards. The solution should be to lower spending and pay down debt. Instead the response is to find more creative ways to borrow against any remaining equity not already fully collateralized.

We all need a place to live and for homeowners, your house used to be like a forced savings plan that you left alone. Today we are constantly being encouraged to borrow against home equity, the only remaining form of purchasing power most have left.

Home equity loans have turned our so-called financial castles into just another piggy bank! Like any loan, borrowing against the equity in your home reduces your savings and increases your interest expenses. More importantly it extends the time to pay off your home, effectively changing you from a homeowner to a home renter.

The same lender who pushed credit cards to expand your personal consumption, are now also pushing lower-cost home equity loans to help you repay high-cost credit cards that you can no longer afford. This actually makes sense, but only if you use home equity as a short-term loan to pay off and cancel some credit cards, and not to expand consumption.

Your lender seldom requires your credit cards to be cancelled. They don't want to lose this high return business, even if you are stretched financially and may charge-up credit cards again. Wealth is surrendered in return for temporary debt relief, under this scenario.

Lenders encourage more debt, longer loan terms and smaller payments instead of less debt, shorter loan terms and bigger payments. The illusion is this makes it easier for you to pay each month, but the reality is that their interests are better served this way. The point is that it is your responsibility to take control of your financial interests and wealth plan!

This all comes back to our definition of wealth as a store of value to meet your foreseeable needs. A wealthy mindset is reasonable and disciplined, and the problem today is that excess consumption has replaced the desire to save or live within our means.

Basic economics and history provide the certain eventual consequences for individuals and nations that continue irresponsible wealth management. The result is not a matter of if but when; if consumption and debt behaviour is not changed before it is too late.

America needs to look to the histories of Great Britain and even Rome, as the emperor may soon have no clothes! There is a major transfer of wealth upon us to nations such as China and India, and it appears to me that China will become the wealthiest nation in the world within one generation if major changes in wealth management don't occur soon.

Top economic minds around the world grapple how to deal with global trade imbalances. Avoiding a global economic crisis will not be easy as a result of trade imbalances and debt per person growing for years to unrecoverable levels. Economies have good and bad cycles, but it is our ability to cope with the next downturn that is most at risk!

Very low interest rates have accelerated the trend of excess consumption by some nations, while at the same time provided booming exports for other nations. Growing U.S trade deficits and Chinese trade surpluses act like two sides of the same wealth coin.

At all personal and government levels, we continue to deplete our savings and borrow against any remaining equity to increase consumption and acquire depreciating assets. On the other hand China's savings, wealth and economic power accelerates at all levels.

U.S federal debt has risen from around $540 billion in 1975 to $8.4 trillion today, with the legal debt ceiling again being raised recently to $9 trillion. Debt has increased from under 35% to now above 60% of Gross Domestic Product.

It's obvious that most of this debt growth wasn't invested, as consumer spending is now at a record 71% of GDP. Your bank would deny or call-in your loan if your personal finances operated the same way as the nation's high-risk debt service ratio.

This debt works out to over $28,000 for every man woman and child. Who's picking up this check as our workforce tax base continues to age, with Baby Boomers starting to retire en-masse in 2008?

The really bad news is that total debt, with Medicare, social security and other under-funded federal, state and municipal liabilities is anyone's guess. Some put this at over $60 trillion - over $500,000 per US household!

China's average income is still low by North American standards, with GDP at around $6,800 per person. However China's debt is under $250 billion, which works out to less than $200 per person. Public debt is less than 30% of GDP and they now have over $1 trillion USD in reserves, while the U.S. current account deficit is around $800 billion.

The U.S. economy averaged 3.16% real GDP growth, after inflation, since 1975. At the same time, real GDP growth in China has averaged almost 10% per year. The U.S. continues to raise interest rates to cool down current inflation of over 3%, while China's consumer prices inflation currently averages only 1.9%.

China has had inflation concerns as well, but these are after inflation real GDP growth rates and they are expected to continue. If the U.S maintains 3% net growth while China's net growth is 10%, it is only a matter of time and compounding until China's economy is larger.

It's true that China needs to trade with the U.S., as exports drive their surpluses, growth and overall wealth. China's largest exports are to: Japan 16.8%, Taiwan 11.4%, South Korea 11.1%, with the U.S. ranked only fourth at 8%. However, with over 1.3 billion people, their economy will quickly become self-reliant as standards of living continue to catch-up to western standards.

On the other hand, the U.S. government borrows billions of dollars each month from China to support its growing debt and deficits. China's financial and therefore political leverage with the U.S. is growing as well. Who really depends on whom?

If someday China decides to invest surpluses at home instead of abroad, or if political push comes to shove, we need to ask how willing China will be to continue buying or even holding U.S. debt. This may be a matter of when, not if!

This scenario may apply to other nations holding U.S. debt, however militarily we must remember China is a nuclear power with ICBM long-range delivery capability. China's military spending commitment for equipment and technology, for new nuclear submarines for example, is ambitious beyond even U.S. standards. Some suggest future wars over trade and oil is inevitable; I'm only suggesting that military influence leverage is neutral.

The real wealth position driver is that Chinese citizens live within their means, generate surpluses and accumulate investment savings. As China's standard of living improves, its consumption grows as well. Emerging Chinese manufacturing companies, or ones already located there, will benefit the most.

Soon China may be at the point where they make up both sides of their supply and demand equation and will no longer have to rely heavily on external trade. On the other hand, the U.S. cannot compete with labour rates in China, India etc., and therefore we will have no rational choice but to continue importing, unless we want to pay more.

The U.S. still has technological advantages, but for how long? Remember when Japan mainly exported shoddy basic goods, but by the 1980's became the leaders of quality consumer electronics. Look at the U.S. versus the Japanese auto industry today!

Perhaps future American growth will depend on how many Wal-Marts, McDonalds or Starbucks open in China or how many Coca-Cola's are sold there. Will they still want American entertainment as their movie and music industries develop Chinese celebrities?

Will the Chinese Yuan, also called the Renminbi, or the Euro eventually replace the U.S. dollar as the world's reserve currency? Before you say no, ask which nations will want wealth values based on a risky currency that is steadily dropping in purchasing power.

Most currencies are based on the amount of U.S. dollars held, or at least tied to the value of the dollar in some way. If the U.S. financial situation gets bad enough, confidence in any government to manage debt may be put to the test. Currency is only paper if we lose confidence in its promised value and perhaps gold will return as the main store of value!

Rising gold prices present a unique set of problems for dollar based currencies. Gold is priced in U.S. dollars and competes with currencies as a store of value. Gold has historically been one of the few dependable safe haven investments during times of crisis.

However gold, which traded around $252 an ounce just a few years ago, has not been a good investment for the past two decades. In 1980 gold was over $850 an ounce as a result of all-time high $40 per barrel oil prices, high interest and inflation rates, the Iran hostage crisis and Russia invading Afghanistan. As oil prices fell under $20 per barrel, with inflation and interest rates normalizing lower after the Cold War ended, gold lost its lustre.

Over the past decade, central banks around the world sold significant amounts of their currency backed gold reserves to instead hold other paper currencies, mainly dollars. This added supply depressed gold prices further. More importantly, most paper currencies are now based more on other paper currencies than on tangible hard asset values like gold.

Gold has industrial value as a soft, ductile and malleable metal. Gold is a good conductor of heat and electricity and has unique reflective and corrosive properties. However gold's real value, back to ancient times, is based on its rarity and beauty, as the metal of choice for dentistry, coins, ornaments and especially jewellery.

During times of crisis such as war, hyperinflation, political corruption, economic chaos or currency collapse, gold is accumulated and hoarded as a safe haven store of wealth value. China and India are rapidly developing their economies and lifestyles to western like standards, however most citizens remember times of crisis experienced not that long ago.

The value and safety of gold to Indian society is entrenched for political and religious reasons and it is the traditional marital dowry. They also don't trust financial vehicles such as mutual funds for their investment savings.

India was the world's largest gold market until the 1962 Indo-China war. Due to reserve losses, India's Gold Control Act prohibited holding gold bars or coins. Gold had to be converted into jewellery and declared, resulting in a huge cash black market for gold.

In 1992 India's Gold Control Act was abolished and gold purchases were liberalized subject to paying a duty. Not surprisingly, India is again the world's largest gold consumer, even though they are still a poor country.

Since 2001 India has been buying over 800 tonnes, over 25% of the world's demand for gold, per year. It is estimated that India holds over 11,000 tons of gold!

China is not that far behind India. Gold is valuable to Chinese people as a traditional symbol of wealth and good fortune. Today, gold is especially valuable to China as a hedge against a depreciating U.S. dollar, and rising commodities prices such as oil.

On the other hand, western nations have discouraged holding gold as an investment. Until recently it was difficult to even buy gold. Today we have various gold and silver ETF's Exchange Traded Funds, valued directly by the amount of gold or silver held. ETF's trade like a stock, without the disadvantages or advantages of holding bullion.

In 1933 the U.S. dropped the gold standard for all but international trade. In 1971 the U.S. totally left the gold standard due to a diminishing gold supply and growing deficits.

I am not suggesting we return to the gold standard, as it does not provide enough flexibility for a nation to efficiently adjust the money supply as needed. Adjusting interest rates and currency levels have been effective mechanisms to stimulate economic growth, avoid unemployment and recessions, or to cool down the economy to avoid inflation.

Applied Keynesian economics seem to have also done a good job avoiding depressions and bank runs, last experienced when most nations were still on the gold standard. However today's fiat monetary system has limits and must behave like a value backed fiduciary trust. Otherwise confidence will be lost in the value of a nation's currency.

Again this requires reasonable limits of debt and deficits, or a fiat monetary system breaks down. Meaningfully backing currency values with gold or some other rare store of value, as a check and balance, helps avoid a government's tendency to overspend.

The U.S. still holds the most gold in the world, however its proportions of debt, deficits and currency in circulation compared to the amount of gold held is way out of whack. A currency note is simply a promise to pay, which only has value to the holder as long as you believe the promise will be upheld.

Reports indicate that China is buying gold, to diversify the risks of holding foreign currencies. China's foreign exchange reserves have grown from around $200 billion in 2001 to over $800 billion today, with a very significant percentage in U.S. treasuries.

China's asset allocation policies for how its huge and growing reserves are invested, to back the value of the Yuan, may have a dramatic impact on future currency and gold values. If just 1% of China's reserves are invested in gold, this equals 498 tonnes or 12% of global gold consumption at $500 an ounce.

If China allocates 5% into gold, this works out to around 2,500 tonnes or 60% of global gold consumption. At 10% this works out to 120% of global gold consumption!

The demand for gold and other precious metals ultimately drives their value. If gold prices appreciate for the long-term, this may result in the largest transfer of wealth ever, relative to each currency's buying power, based again on the amount of gold held.

The Roman Empire lasted nearly 500 years and the British Empire lasted over 350 years. Many believe we have had an American Empire for the past 60 years since World War II and don't see the world's status quo changing much in the foreseeable future.

However, empires usually grow or decline based on their military and financial fortunes. The golden rule may again be that those who own the most gold will make the rules!

Over the past 50 years, gold and oil prices generally move together, with an 80% price correlation at a ratio of around 15 barrels of oil per ounce of gold. In 1980 gold was around $850 an ounce, and oil was around $40 a barrel. In other words the value of one ounce of gold was even higher at over 21 barrels of oil.

Today, gold has increased 2.5 times from $250 a few years ago to around $625 an ounce. At the same time oil has increased 3.5 times from $20 to $70 a barrel. This works out to only 8.5 barrels of oil per ounce of gold. At the normal 15 to 1 ratio, this may suggest gold now has room to appreciate to around $1,000 an ounce.

Some experts predict oil demand may push oil prices to $100 a barrel or higher over the next two years. This suggests gold could be worth around $1,500 an ounce. At the 1980 gold versus oil ratio, $100 per barrel of oil would equal over $2,100 per ounce of gold!

Similarly, the gold and silver ratio has varied between 16 to 100 ounces of silver per ounce of gold. Some experts expect this ratio to normalize between 40 and 50, working out to around $30 to $40 an ounce of silver at $1,500 gold.

If silver again priced in a 16 to 1 ratio to gold, like it did in the early 1980's during the Hunt silver crisis, this works out to almost $100 an ounce or 10 times the current price!

Some consider this pure speculation, believing that oil and gold prices are simply cyclical. They believe commodity prices will again subside, perhaps to less than half their highs, like they did for the past two decades. They suggest that even if oil goes to $100 a barrel, the inflationary impact on the price of everything will hurt the economy to the point that demand will fall materially, which in itself reduces oil prices.

However, even if we assume this all to be true, the supply and demand equation for oil has changed today, probably forever. Oil is consumed energy and is not renewable. Oil reserves do not replenish, which the world is depleting at an annual rate of 6% per year. Unless new reserves are found, this suggests there are only 16 years of oil left.

China now makes up 22% of the world's population and consumes almost 7-million barrels of oil per day. China's oil imports have doubled over the past 5-years to 60% of their total current needs. China was a net exporter of oil until a few years ago, but in 14-years oil reserves in China are expected to deplete.

The U.S. is 5% of the world's population, but consumes 25% of global oil production at over 20-million barrels of oil per day. Imagine China's oil and gas demand as standards of living improve, as millions of bicycles are replaced yearly with motorcycles and cars!

China now accounts for 1/3 of global oil demand growth, up 40% in the first half of 2004 alone, and is expected to grow at 7.5% per year. China ranks second in global oil consumption, now ahead of Japan, and is expected to equal the U.S. within 20-years. China didn't need to import oil during the 1980 oil crisis, but from now on its oil import demand is only expected to keep growing.

Yearly world oil demand grows 2% and reserves need to increase by 8%, just to keep at par with 6% rates of oil reserve depletion. However only one new barrel of oil is being discovered for every four consumed. To make matters worse, the oil consumption growth rate is expected to triple over the next 20-years. High oil prices are here to stay, unless we discover another abundant form of low cost energy quickly!

Another perspective on oil and gold prices is to simply factor-in inflation. Use the time and compounding table to project $40 oil over 25-years. Using 3.0%, 3.5% and 4.0% inflation, this results in $84, $95 and $107 oil. This is close to oil price predictions, and does not factor in higher demand and lower reserves today than in 1980!

If you apply these same rates of inflation to $850 gold, this works out to $1,780, $2,009 and $2,266 per ounce today. However all gold, unlike oil, still exists and is recoverable and recyclable in some way. In other words gold has rareness value, but is not consumed and competes with other rare precious metals and even gemstones such as diamonds.

Islamic law forbids accepting a promise to pay. Religious fundamentalists are gaining more support as the U.S. dollar has lost 33% of its investment value since 2001. Several oil-producing nations are considering pricing oil in Euros, instead of or in addition to U.S. dollars, which would significantly affect the global demand for dollars.

Gold prices rise as the value of the dollar falls and it would not be the first time if oil-producing nations started demanding gold payments for oil. To some extent this vote of non-confidence may result in non-oil-exporting nations also divesting out of dollars or from accepting more dollars for trade.

The point is that oil, gold and the U.S. dollar has a close value relationship to each other. Higher oil prices will cause price inflation, as there is an energy component in practically everything we consume. So far we have only realized this effect at the gas pump or when heating our homes. Eventually all businesses will have to pass along these higher energy costs.

The U.S. economy has proven to be diverse and resilient enough to absorb change in the past. However, if oil prices continue to rise, you have to wonder how the nation will adjust this time, when individual and government debt service costs are so high.

The U.S. seems in denial and unwilling to lower consumption within its means, but there may be no choice as the debt tap gets turned off. The U.S. does have one advantage as its debt is based in its own currency, which means the government can pay it back by printing huge amounts of dollars. This would also severely damage confidence value.

This is like shooting the patient to kill a disease, as resulting rampant inflation could end up destroying the economy. The U.S. could try political leverage and threaten to cut-off trade with China for example, to force them to let their currency freely float up in value.

An increase in the value of the Yuan makes Chinese goods more expensive versus comparable goods from other countries. However, if a more valuable Yuan doesn't materially increase our exports to China, while also lowering their exports to us, we would just end up paying more for the same goods, increasing China's wealth further.

In any event China has surpluses, and a more valuable Yuan simply increases their buying power worldwide. Also the risks of forcing their hand on increasing the value of the Yuan are many, and the willingness and leverage to do this is losing ground quickly.

The only solution is to realize how extreme the situation is now, and to change financial management behaviour before it's too late. In the near-term gold and silver may be good investments, but in the long-term only reasonable debt and expenses at all levels will ensure prosperity for future generations.

The economic empire status of the U.S. was built over the past century by capitalizing on cheap and abundant oil energy. Some believe that new technologies, efficiencies and the resulting growth will again save the day. It is paramount that the U.S. faces the reality that cheap oil is done, and the only solution is to develop new forms of energy now!

We are already seeing hybrid-fuelled cars, and wind, solar, geothermal, hydroelectric and other environmentally safe power is again coming back into focus. The U.S. Department of Energy is working with partners to accelerate the development and successful market introduction of these technologies.

Hydrogen fuel cells power completely emission-free electric motors with few moving parts, and insignificant amounts of water and heat as by-products. Hydrogen fuel cells are lighter, take up less space, and deliver 60% energy efficiency or three times that of combustion engines. Hydrogen already achieves 2.4 times as many miles per gallon as gas!

Hydrogen works well in colder climates and has a similar driving range compared to gas powered cars. New hydrogen storage technologies that use carbon adsorption materials and refrigerated, pressurized tanks may be able to store 7-gallons of hydrogen in a single gram. If developed, one tank of hydrogen may be needed to travel almost 5,000 miles!

Hydrogen is produced using fossil fuels, nuclear and renewable energy technologies. Infrastructure costs for hydrogen production, storage, transportation and dispensing did not make economic sense in the past with $20 oil. It does make economic sense today!

Hydrogen is the most abundant element in the universe, found in water, fossil fuels and all plants and animals. The world is mostly covered in water, comprised of H2O or two-hydrogen and one-oxygen atoms. Hydrogen from renewable and inexhaustible water reserves, after removing salt, has the potential to cost effectively satisfy all energy needs forever, and at the same time replace burning environmentally unsafe hydrocarbons.

Hydrogen is a fuel that can burn or explode like gasoline. However hydrogen is less of a hazard as it disperses and evaporates much faster than gasoline and other fossil fuels. Demanding tests have shown that if hydrogen tanks are engulfed in flames, pierced or squeezed, the hydrogen gas will leak out or burn instead of exploding.

Hydrogen is wrongly perceived as very explosive due to the tragic 1937 Hindenburg fire in New Jersey. This resulted in 62 survivors and 35 deaths, 27 of which resulted from jumping out of the airship. The other 8-deaths resulted from injuries caused by burning diesel fuel. The cause of the Hindenburg fire was its aluminum-cellulose fabric covering, which is chemically similar to rocket fuel. Hydrogen actually played no part in this fire!

The benefits are many, but there are several issues limiting full-scale commercialization of hydrogen fuels such as cost, availability, reliability, durability and safety. Overcoming these issues should be a top priority for all nations, and especially the U.S. that depends so heavily on imported oil. If we will it, hydrogen may become the perfect fuel!

The prospects of hydrogen as the world's future fuel are compelling. This may represent long-term investment opportunities for companies like BLDP Ballard Power and to even revive the U.S. automotive industry for companies like GM General Motors and F Ford.

There will always be demand for some oil as it is used in countless products. However, replacing our dependency on oil energy is a major problem, and also our biggest growth opportunity. Everyone stands to benefit immensely, except oil producers.

Economic leadership status may be enhanced if the U.S. decides to embrace and develop hydrogen fuel technologies on a commercial scale soon! This may also be an argument against long-term investments in gold or oil, or for investing in the U.S. dollar again.

However, in the near-term it doesn't appear the will to change has arrived yet! Perhaps this is an argument better saved for when oil prices are $100 per barrel, gold is $1500 an ounce and all levels of the economy are finally realizing the cost effects.

The issues are many and complex but really come back to the premise of this whole book. The keys to value and wealth, for an individual or a nation, are to regularly generate surplus savings and the time and compounding effects of value investments towards meeting your foreseeable needs!

Chapter 7
My Value Perspectives

At this point you already have a good feel for my value perspectives. My path in life, like yours, was affected by where I live, friends, family, work and education etc. I often reflect about choices I made and how things could have turned out if I had taken a different path.

I believe that if you stay within life's reasonable limits, and develop a wealthy mindset, that anyone can be wealthy. You need a minimum level of income, health and education, and you need to stay within the law, have a good work ethic and manage your resources.

Wealth is not luck, a wish, or a dream! It is simply a defined and balanced plan put into action. Most people have the basic common sense means to become wealthy, however most people don't become wealthy because they don't practice wealthy habits.

I am wealthy, and have been since my late twenties. I am not saying that I'm rich, but that I live within my means. I have no debt whatsoever and my investment savings should provide my family's reasonable needs for the foreseeable future.

I had a plan, stuck with it as best as possible and was in position to take advantage of opportunities as they presented themselves. I have also had setbacks, made mistakes and missed opportunities, but luckily I was prepared to deal with them.

You may have noticed throughout this book, the saturation of words like: wealth, value, education, reasonable, practical, tangible, effective, efficient, budget, taxes, debt, balance, amortization, savings, tax sheltered, investment, time & compounding, value investing, stocks, bonds, real-estate, capital, margin of safety, risk, leverage and value perspectives. These words were spoon-fed to me by my father at an early age. Sometimes these exact words were used, but more often they were presented through examples or anecdotes that I as a child could more easily understand and better relate to.

Long before I was born, dad owned and operated various businesses and invested his savings. He had farms, one as an Inn, an apartment building and invested in stocks and bonds regularly. He was not rich either, but was wealthy in many ways.

Dad grew up during the depression and learned at an early age the value of wealth. He was close to being a doctor, but had to drop out of pharmacy school to earn money driving a truck, to support his mother and younger brother after his father died suddenly.

I have five sisters and one brother. I grew up with my three younger sisters from dad's second marriage. My two older sisters and brother are from dad's first marriage. My mother and younger sisters now live in the U.S., while the rest of us still live in Canada.

Dad worked for the government as collector of customs in our area. Since I could first stand we would go for walks to his office after supper, when simple comments were made for me to think about. To keep me content until his work was done, he would make me a cup of hot chocolate, always measured carefully saying *waste not, want not*.

I didn't fully understand the meaning then, as I always wanted more hot chocolate, and it would never have gone to waste. However if I could have had all I wanted, I'd probably get sick or make a mess and I'd be bouncing off the walls from all the sugar.

The point he was making is don't waste your resources, or you won't get what you want. Maybe it means you can meet all your needs if you don't waste time on unreasonable wants. Perhaps dad was just making sure there was enough hot chocolate for the staff and our future visits. Anyway I always got a 2-scoop hot chocolate, which was great!

Even as a child I knew a penny wasn't worth much, but if dad noticed one on the sidewalk he would stop and point to it. When I asked if I should throw it over my shoulder for good luck, he would just laugh and say that only brings luck to the next person who finds it. As you can imagine, we didn't throw coins into wishing wells either.

The amount is irrelevant; the point is that *large amounts of wealth start with small amounts of savings*, and that *easy and sure opportunities should not be squandered*. Also *every journey, no matter how long, has a starting point!*

I'm not suggesting the solution to our financial problems is to become penny-picking misers; just that you have to be aware of every cent you save and spend. However I can't tell you how many times my good luck habit of picking up pennies helps me make exact change, instead of breaking a bill into coin that would just get lost in the sofa!

Dad also used to say that *if you take care of the pennies, the dollars take care of themselves*. Perhaps we should be saying to our kids that if you take care of the dollars, the millions take care of themselves, adjusting for inflation!

We lived in a middle-class neighbourhood in Sydney, Cape Breton, Nova Scotia, one of the poorest areas of Canada. My friends had the best clothes and toys, and money given to them, which was always spent at the local dairy store on junk food.

These friends seemed rich to me, and I didn't appreciate dad's point that they lived in apartments or the smallest houses and many didn't have a car. In other words, *if you are given everything you want, you won't learn how to get what you really need*. In any event I wanted some too, and was fascinated with how to make money at an early age.

Dad told me to *turn lemons into lemonade*, which I must have taken literally. I preferred a Kool-Aid stand, which worked out great as mom supplied the dollar for the flavour packets, plus the sugar, containers and glasses. She showed me how to mix it with ice and water, and she and my sisters were my first customers. That $1 became $5 in no time!

I promptly spent this on junk food and learned my first lesson in cash flow management at age six. I went back to mom for another $1, but my line of credit was getting cut-off after the next batch of Kool-Aid. From then on I had to manage my own ins and outs!

I think I ended up with only $2 left over after buying more sugar and flavour packets for my third batch. To solve this dilemma I doubled my prices and learned another point the hard way. I sat on my front step for a day before realizing there are limits people will pay.

When I was eight I helped a kid up the road with his paper route. He seemed to be rolling in money and I knew it was time to stake my own claim. I had to convince the Cape Breton Post circulation manager that I could handle the job, as I wasn't the minimum age.

My mother was concerned that it was too much responsibility and that I wasn't big enough. She cautiously agreed, shortened my paper bag straps with safety pins so the papers wouldn't drag on the ground and made sure I had a raincoat on when needed.

The work wasn't complicated, but did present some challenges and opportunities that I didn't expect. Every weekday I delivered papers after school and on Saturday, rain, shine or snow. Dad actually had a much bigger paper-route in North Sydney as a boy and immediately supported the idea as *learning comes from doing*.

I swapped my route with a kid down the road as his route was in my neighbourhood and mine was in his. We haggled over the houses in the middle, netting me a few extra customers. I learned early on the importance of dad's *persuasive negotiation, little extras add up over time and people prefer to do business with people they like* comments.

I thought it would be easy to collect the $1.80 payment every two-weeks, but I often had to go back at night and carry some customers for months. The dilemma was that cutting their paper off might cost me a customer; otherwise I would have to pay for their papers until they eventually paid me. Plus I didn't want to do anything to jeopardize my usual .20 tips!

I had my first cash flow problem as a result of customers not paying on time. I also had no profit to show and had to borrow from my parents to pay my newspaper supplier bills. Other times I had extra money as people caught up their payments.

Dad's *easier said than done* started to make sense and sink in. This is a common problem for most businesses, as overdue receivables, working capital shortfalls and cash flow management problems are the top reasons why even good businesses can fail.

Dad used to say if you push against a brick wall all day you will build up a nice sweat, but you won't get anything done. In other words, *you need to work smart!* Dad told me to **break the problem down, think about it while putting yourself in the other guy's shoes and act only when you have a solution**. I thought people wanted to stiff me, but I eventually realized they were just not home at certain times.

I worked out a system of leaving notes and had a list of times I knew people would be at home. With tips, I was raking in over $20 profit every two weeks. Most customers gave me an extra $2, $5 or candy as a Christmas present, and I even had side-jobs lined up walking dogs and shovelling snow. It was a lot of work, but the cash was flowing!

Dad would say *it's not how much you make, but how much you save that makes you wealthy* and reminded me that I wanted a paper route to have $2 a week to spend. He suggested I keep $5 on collection days, but the rest I needed to *save for a rainy day*. On our next walk I opened my first savings account at the bank located next to his office.

Every collection day I looked forward to the teller updating my bankbook. My money was safe, and they even paid me a little extra to hold onto it for me. I worked for and saved most of my money, and it was earning interest. $1,000 at 10-years old was pretty cool back then! I understood what dad meant by *a penny saved is a penny earned*.

***

As soon as my two sons were old enough to realize that money buys things, I walked them to the bank to setup their own accounts. Some banks have no-fee junior savings program, which was a great surprise to my youngest son Alex after the bank doubled his first $5 deposit.

Kids naturally don't fully understand the point of saving small amounts. I tell my kids what dad told me, *if you save today, you will have what you need tomorrow*. To encourage them, I doubled their savings deposits until they hit their first $1,000.

It is as important for kids to understand the process as it is for them to save. Make after-school bank appointments so they can be there with you. Again the amounts are not that important, *kids just need to experience, to appreciate and develop wealthy habits*.

As my kids' savings grew over time, usually after birthdays and Christmas, they started buying savings bonds with each $100, like I used to buy at their age. My oldest son Matthew bought his first mutual fund when he could afford the minimum $500 purchase. Alex always wants to keep up with his older brother and got his first mutual fund the next year.

Matt just became a teenager and we sometimes discuss his value perspectives on hot new video games. We enjoy looking these companies up online to research if they are publicly traded. He's starting to understand how investment growth works.

It takes time, patience and persistence to teach kids and especially teenagers, the difference between needs and wants and how to manage limited resources. However most families need two incomes today, with limited time and energy available. Our educational system needs to pick up the slack and be the equalizer in teaching wealth values!

Our educational system up to university level seriously lacks focus compared to schools in Germany, Japan and other parts of Europe and Asia. Curriculum needs to better prepare kids for vocational skills that a service and technology based economy needs.

Schools need to encourage achievement standards, instead of just preparing high school students for not much more than minimum wage dead-end jobs. Low achievers need to be encouraged to improve, instead of high achievers being neglected and effectively told to just blend in. At the very least, *kids need to learn about money*!

Money management needs to be focused on, before kids become adults. They need to learn how to prioritize consumption decisions within limited means. They need to know the value of budgeting for savings and investment, and the real costs of carrying debt such as credit cards. They need to know how to plan for wealth, and that this is not just a dream!

Wealth is passed on to kids not by the transfer of money, but through educating kids about the value of money management! Kids today learn about the value of money from their peers, their parents and the media. They are only learning how to spend!

If we want a society where everyone has an opportunity to succeed, our high school education system needs to level the field on wealth understanding. If kids realize they have choices and opportunities, then innovation, entrepreneurial desire and empowerment goals naturally develop. Otherwise current wealth trends just get repeated!

Even at the university level, young adults often graduate without the skills needed to manage wealth. They often end up with debts that set them back for decades, with only part-time or entry-level positions to cover the interest payments on accumulated loans.

My wife and I setup educational savings plans for both our sons, soon after they were born. Instead of the minimum over 18-years, we bit the bullet and fully funded their RESPs in 8-years. This will cover all of their tuition and books, and we are discussing whether we should add more or let them cover their own residence and living costs.

***

Dad retired in 1978, bought his dream home and moved us to the Annapolis Valley, just before I started grade seven. This was an adjustment but also presented opportunities as high school students can always find part-time work in a farming community.

I always had money and continued to build savings with after-school jobs such as: installing tree guards, picking apples, pruning trees, picking up dead chickens, ear tagging cows, picking various fruits and vegetables and tobacco, weeding gardens, chopping firewood, separating chicken parts, various canning plant jobs, barn construction, driveway sealing etc. Name a job; I did it at one time!

I had higher money aspirations than any of these jobs offered, but I value the skills I received and how complex the means of production is at various levels. Each job was a challenge and learning experience that inspired me further to succeed, if for no other reason than to make sure that I wouldn't be stuck doing these hard-work jobs forever.

I wasn't connected locally to get a cushy retail job, but I was determined to leave farming for an easier way to make money. However I do remember dad asking what my specific goals were after high school and replying that I would shovel manure for $80,000 a year. I didn't agree then but now appreciate mom's **money isn't everything** response.

I had a thousand moneymaking ideas and still do. Dad would caution that **if you start something, you should be prepared to finish it**. I eventually learned that success is not impulsive, but only comes from focus and commitment to one project, one step at a time!

I applied for after school jobs at retail stores and fast food restaurants, but nobody was hiring. You sometimes have to be creative and invest time to achieve tangible goals. Dad told me to **think outside the box** if I had enough of farming related part-time jobs.

My favourite fast food was KFC and I told the manager I would work for fried chicken until they could fit me in. He liked my initiative but his boss passed on the idea, worried about how the labour board might react to them accepting free labour.

The colonel's secret recipe remained safe, so I offered my enthusiasm to a local businessman who ran a pizza joint. He was not hiring either, but he was more than happy to change his mind when I offered to work for free!

It was summertime and they had no ventilation. I worked hard until around 2AM each night, when they closed. The owner and his wife only trusted me at first to push a mop, cut vegetables and fold pizza boxes. They were busy and didn't realize they needed help, but within a week I cooked pizzas, donairs and subs, and ran the till.

I did that for almost a month to prove myself, but then decided to call it quits. They finally realized they needed help and offered to pay me if I stayed on. I essentially created my job, as planned, and worked there for the next two summers. The real bonus was that I learned all their recipes, which especially became valuable a few years later!

The only investments I knew of until then were bank interest and Canada Savings Bonds. I had spent $108 of my savings on an 8" black and white television for my room, and paid $400 to buy a used motorbike from my best friend. Then I discovered silver again!

Coins had hidden value at one time, based on their gold and silver content. Dad used to point out older coins that still contain silver, worth substantially more than a coin's face value. I saved old silver coins from my paper route and had a trucker's wallet full of them, until my sisters found them one-day on-route to the nearest corner store.

In 1980 I was in grade nine. Dad put me in contact with a broker in hopes that I would become interested in investing again, before I could waste the rest of my savings. The broker encouraged me to buy gold, but I couldn't afford the minimum gold purchase.

Instead I invested in 50 ounces of silver bullion from a local bank. My younger sisters would find and play with the shiny ingots, so I swapped them for a silver certificate. Silver traded at $8 an ounce then, and I decided to up my ante to $2,400, or 300 ounces.

I didn't understand what value investing was back then. I watched the local TV news each night for the silver quote that was usually up or down a few pennies. Every dime meant $30 to me, which was my first exposure to the good and bad effects of leverage.

Over the next two years I watched my silver rocket to $52 an ounce, an increase of 650% to $15,000. This resulted from Nelson and Bunker Hunt and some Arabs cornering the silver market, buying over 200 million ounces as an inflation hedge. Gold was also a good investment and got all of the attention, but only doubled over the same time.

I received a call from the broker I spoke with occasionally, who told me to get out of my silver, fast! I called my bank to sell, but the price wasn't set until they received my signature. We were in the middle of a bad snowstorm and I couldn't get to the bank for 3-days. It took 2-years for silver to go from $8 to $52, but only 3-days to go back to $16.

In high school I was addicted to video games and personal computers, which were a new fad at the time. I had lots of ideas and was convinced I could write a million dollar computer video game, like other teenagers I read about.

I actually had offers to publish the code for two of my programs, but decided to hold out for bigger offers that never came. Dad used to say; *giving people what they want sometimes gives you what you need* and that *the first offer is usually the best one*.

One of my programs was a video game called Sea Sniper, which manipulated a text screen into a graphical game screen. The other was called Hobo the Clown, a variation of the game Hangman using the 600 vocabulary words we had to learn in grades 10, 11 and 12.

I also developed a multiple-choice vocabulary test program that used all of these words and four incorrect alternate answers. I did this at the request of my grade-10 English teacher for extra credit to pass English that year.

I was an honour student up to grade ten, but after being denied the Consumer Civics award the previous year I decided to do the minimum to pass that year. I had almost a perfect mark and almost 10% higher than the award winner, but my 80+ after school detentions must have played into the vice-principal's decision to deny me the award.

My personal identity values were a bit mixed-up back in grade ten. Schoolwork was easy but I was barely passing, on purpose! My parents probably would have assumed this was just a teenage phase if it wasn't for my math teacher pointing out that I was getting 60% because I was deliberately completing only the first two-thirds of his tests.

I guess you could say I was a rebel without a cause. I hung around equally with the computer geeks, the smokers and other clicks. The only value I put in school was to barely pass so that a grade didn't have to be repeated. I knew I had to pull up my marks again in grades 11 and 12 for college considerations, but also should have realized that *discipline and self-control needs to overcome reckless impulses*.

After not attending a mandatory grading day awards presentation, I returned to tell my homeroom teacher that another student had already handed out our report cards. I saw my marks and had passed all courses, but the teacher who was also my English teacher told me that I had now failed English. My impatience in receiving my report card put me into summer school. *Success is not always fair; you need to know how to play the game*.

After almost failing grade-10 English I needed marks again, but still had the wrong attitude about the real values of education. I wanted shortcuts instead of recognizing the value of cooperation with those in power, namely my teachers.

For example, I chose home economics for an easy grade, instead of chemistry, which I have always regretted. I even received a bad grade in that course after embarrassing the teacher by asking what the heck our 2-hour final exam could be based on with only two-pages of notes for the entire year.

In grade-12 I barely passed English again after telling my teacher Shakespeare was full of crap. Perhaps I shouldn't have taken him literally and shown more restraint as he insisted we participate or tell him if we thought this was full of crap. In any event my English mark somehow dropped from an A first-term to barely passing the year.

I also commented the only courses of value in high school were typing and sociology. I explained that Typing provides a work related skill, and that Sociology teaches you to think outside the box by debating how things really are versus consensus beliefs.

I was immature with a know-it-all attitude and only valued things that would earn money in the real world. I should have known better than to criticize other people's value perspectives and opinions, as dad used to say *you don't know what you don't know*.

More restraint and focus on what I was good at could have gone a long way as AAPL Apple Computer and MSFT Microsoft were emerging growth companies when I was in high school. There are always opportunities and if I had realized the value of these growth stocks, and not just using their products, I would have been much wealthier today.

After high school my parents paid for my first year tuition and books to attend the local university. I lived at home and traveled everyday in my 6-year old Honda civic that they bought for me as a high school graduation gift.

I owned cars before then, bought with various jobs I had throughout high school. My friends nicknamed my Chevy Nova as the pig, because it was a faded red color and accelerated on its own. The pig was traded in for a paint job on my $800 1978 civic.

You can tell I put very little value in cars, beyond the means needed to efficiently travel from point A to B. Whether you buy new or used, automobiles should never be thought of as an investment. Like dad said, *I've never owned a car that has gone up in value*.

Actually I did have one car that I sold for a profit. When I was fifteen I paid $300 for an 8-cylinder clunker, driving it for one hour to my home without a driver's license or insurance. The car barely made it and remained sunk into our driveway like a rusty monument. It was pure luck when someone with the same car needing that specific engine offered me $700. I didn't haggle as my parents were calling the junkyard to tow it away if it was still there at the end of the week. Forget money, this was far too risky!

I also learned from the six American and four Japanese cars that I owned. Japanese cars are better made to take a beating, while American cars are money pits for repairs. I don't fully understand why this is true even today, but I expect it has to do with quality controls and how Japanese focus on long-term growth and value instead of short-term lower price.

***

After my first year at university, I wanted to move out on my own. My parents did not believe this was practical with us living so close to the university. I insisted and they gave me a choice, stay home or pay all your own expenses, books, tuition and living costs.

This was a tough decision and I didn't want to get into debt. My social agenda won in the end, so I chose to move out and start a business. I also held myself to completing my four-year computer science degree on schedule.

Computer Science was in vogue but wasn't easy. My first-year classes of 120 students pared down to 10 or less by my third year. I was usually one of two or three students that spoke English and most of the professors knew English mainly as a second language.

I actually knew after my first year that I wasn't destined to be a code warrior, but when I start something I finish it. Instead of switching programs, I planned to instead complete my 4-year B.C.Sc. degree in 3-years, which was somewhat foolish in hindsight.

My first plan was to take a full course load, plus at least three summer courses each year. The problem was that I could fill-up some of my elective courses, but none of my mandatory courses were offered over the summer.

My next plan was to take yearly course overloads. To do this I needed some easy bird courses to offset my harder core computer science courses. Luckily I knew of a tenured sociology professor who liked to think outside the box as far as university policy.

I told him straight up I wanted to complete my 4-year degree in 3-years, but everyone tells me I can't do it. A full course load was five, but I wanted to take seven courses a year. I wanted all four of his sociology courses and didn't have any of the prerequisites.

To further complicate this, all of his classes were at times that conflicted with my other courses. I told him this shouldn't be a problem if it was true that nobody attends his classes. A risky statement but luckily he laughed and replied there were no classes, and that anyone who goes automatically fails because this would mean he had to attend class.

He loved the idea, eagerly signed and wished me luck. I thought my plan worked, but unfortunately the admin lady keyed in my courses and informed me the maximum overload the computer would even accept was six courses. I was stuck at 4-years.

During the spring semester I researched business opportunities. The problem was I spent most of my savings and didn't have any working capital to invest. Also commercial landlords are very reluctant to sign a lease with a legal minor without collateral.

I lucked into a government business loan program called YES or Youth Entrepreneurial Skills loan. YES allowed me to borrow up to $5,000 interest free for one year. My focus was on starting a retail business, and eventually I found a landlord willing to rent to me.

He offered a 5-year lease at $800 a month, for 800 square feet. The building was not maintained well after its bowling alley, Laundromat and restaurant days a decade earlier. It was empty except for a daycare on the other end from where my business would be.

Even back in 1985, $5k didn't get you far when you had to plan leaseholds, equipment, inventory, marketing and operating expenses. I took some economics, accounting and other business courses as electives, so at least I had an idea how to do a business plan.

I only needed to make enough money to pay for my school and living expenses, so I didn't need to reinvent the wheel. This was only a 3-year project in my mind, and I decided the best I could do with such limited resources was a simple convenience store.

In hindsight this was not a practical plan! The town's population was only around 3,000, with five other convenience stores, plus a full-size grocery store. One of these stores was very close, at a better corner location that they owned, and were in business for 20-years.

I later met other entrepreneurial-minded students who started businesses in university. They rented mini-fridges, sold a line of cool reversible shorts, or had fix-and-flip rental properties. These were all more creative, practical and needed business ideas.

My plan was to align my store with a grocery wholesale group and use their name for instant recognition. I could not buy from competitors, but they offered the best prices anyway. They gave me a 24' lit sign, which saved me $3k, and even paid me to install it.

They had generous product rebate programs and arranged 3-pages of grand opening advertising. They paid for the lead advertorial and solicited my other suppliers for congratulatory ads. This impressed me considering I had not purchased any inventory yet.

Coke and Pepsi rented coolers, but my competitors had a big advantage as I opened after a government-imposed moratorium on free or even rented dairy equipment. The problem was that no matter how much corner cutting I did, I could not open my store for under $10k.

Banks do not lend to 18-year olds, especially with no income or credit history. They shy away from new business loans and didn't want to accept my low quality collateral. They would not lend me the other $5,000 I needed, unless I had an acceptable loan guarantor.

Dad would not co-sign the loan because I was too young and should stay at home and focus on completing my degree. He owned a store at one time and told me how tough retail is, especially while in school, and that *a business is like a marriage*. I was persistent and mom agreed to co-sign my bank business loan for another $5,000.

I worked from 9am to midnight seven days a week, or 105 hours per week. With no air conditioning, I kept everything that could melt in what little refrigeration I had. As I turned 19 that summer, my friends had social lives while I lost money every day.

Loyal customers of the store around the corner frankly told me I had no chance of surviving. I knew they were probably right and questioned myself continually. Many times I thought about giving up and walking away. I wasn't prepared, but would finish this!

I couldn't cut my labour costs, as I didn't have any. I spent all of my credit on inventory and used equipment. One of my freezers was so old that I constantly had to scrape a foot of ice around the sides, and it shocked customers because it wasn't grounded properly.

Everyone had a regular routine of where they bought their daily milk, bread and cigarettes. I couldn't compete on price, because my wholesale prices were close to grocery stores retail prices. I had to find a competitive edge, fast!

The only customers I had at first were kids. My quiet little store, except for the roar of the compressor in that old zapper freezer, must have been an adventure for them. I had lots of time on my hands and would often spend half an hour before ringing in literally a nickel.

Kids would tell me the lady at the other store was mean, and chased them away because she was busy with "real" customers. The kids liked me and started telling their parents to go to my store instead. My first glimmer of hope came as I realized that *decision makers are the most valuable customers, even more than the person paying*.

Low margin grocery items were just collecting dust, so I instead put every cent I had left into candy. On my next order I bought every type of sweet or sour candy you can imagine that retailed for under $1. My little C-store became the mother of all sugar shacks.

Traffic attracts attention and curious adults started to wander in. However I lost many sales because I didn't have much selection. I couldn't afford any dead inventory, so I instead asked customers what they wanted and promised to have it on their next visit.

I had some success making subs and sandwiches, and turning a backroom into a small video arcade. Competitors and their customers started noticing my ads offering 2-litre milk at cost. The retail profit margin was next to nothing anyway, plus the 18% milk rebate and traffic draw were the real incentives to grab a bigger milk market share.

However it was renting movies that really turned my business around. I started with 50 movies on a 50:50 profit share, with a vendor I still know today. I'm a little embarrassed to admit that it was actually x-rated movie rentals that really turned things around. I didn't want to include them but my movie vendor insisted that I needed them.

I started with five x-rated out of the fifty movies and sure enough he was right. I had waiting lists for those five movies, hidden in the back, while the other 45 movies out front gathered dust at first. Eventually my movie selection would grow to thousands, with the x-rated movies representing a more wholesome 2% of my store's rental inventory.

I returned to school in the fall and needed two part-time employees. My store was barely profitable, but I discovered a government program that paid part of a qualified person's salary. They sent me candidates to choose from, who were otherwise not employable.

I focused on controlling customer theft, which I later realized is insignificant compared to the challenges of finding good employees. The costs in terms of employee theft and unreliability far outweigh the financial incentives of these programs. However my best and longest-term employee came from this government program.

I struggled but aggressively paid back both of my loans within the first year. The YES program manager was surprised when I brought him the check. He told me I was the first person he knew of to pay back one of these loans on time, or at all for that matter.

My bank manager was very sceptical of my business plan at first, but he lived near my store and became a regular customer. I'm guessing he also noticed that my bank deposits were growing, when he offered me a line of credit as I told him I needed to expand.

Dad used to say **banks don't lend when you need money, only when you have money**. When I was a boy dad told me about his bank problems with his apartment building. Half way through construction he was over budget and his contractors wouldn't continue until they got paid. His bank wouldn't advance more funds until the work was done and threatened to call-in his loans.

Instead of restructuring all his loans at his bank's mercy, dad would instead borrow from bank B to pay back bank A in full. Bank A would then promptly offer any further loans needed. Dad would instead borrow from bank C to pay back bank B in full. Banks A and B were eager to offer more loans and the lowest cost loan went to pay off the contractors.

If either bank asked if there were any loan problems, the third bank was ready and willing to loan again. Dad juggled bank loans around for almost a year, using one bank to pay off another in full, to buy enough time to complete his apartment building.

Banks share information more readily today and with computers and online real-time connectivity this probably would not be possible anymore. Dad told me this because you can often **turn weaknesses into strengths**. The building was a good investment and our family lived in the bottom apartment my first few years.

I employed a similar technique at different times of cash flow stress at my store. I grew inventory aggressively, relying on supplier credit to carry my growth. Whenever an accounts receivable manager would call to ask if there was a problem, or to threaten to cut me off, I would find a way to pay the entire balance off instead of just the minimum.

Just as dad predicted, they not only provided credit again, they would extend my line of credit each time. To them I didn't need credit and was worthy of more if I could pay off my bill in one lump sum. In reality I was robbing one supplier payment to make another.

I wouldn't have qualified for a credit card then, when I needed one. I have one now, for reservations and to help track expenses, but I keep the monthly balance paid in full to avoid interest charges. I find it ironic that now that I have a card and don't need any more, I probably receive three offers by mail and two phone solicitations per week from credit card companies. They won't give up no matter how many times I ask them to stop.

**

Over the next two years I grew my store, balancing supplier credit while reinvesting profits. I am always cautious about bank debt, but eventually I needed a $40,000 loan to expand further. My plan was to relocate within the building to a larger space of triple the size, and at the same time purchase the pizza restaurant next door for $30,000.

During my lease negotiations I discovered the building had just been sold. My new landlord became my, and a lot of people's, worst nightmare. He insisted that if I wanted to move my store, I had to keep renting my old location as well. He said I could do anything I wanted in my old store space except a daycare or pizza restaurant, as these were other tenants in the building.

The problems started literally from the day after we signed the lease. He came to my store and in front of customers insisted we change the rent terms. The deal was done and I suggested we call our lawyers to discuss any remaining issues.

My plans were in place and I didn't want to start renegotiating an already difficult process to that point. He wouldn't leave and asked to see my signed copy of the lease. I showed it to him with one hand on it, but told him I needed to call my lawyer for advice.

He literally ripped the lease from my hand and left the store, and I followed. He then threw the lease in his car trunk, slammed it close and drove away. The university paid a first year lawyer to help students with legal issues, and I used this service during my lease negotiations. She advised me to call the police to retrieve the lease.

The police got my statement and then talked to my lawyer who was on the phone with me when the lease was stolen. They approached the landlord for the return of the lease, which my landlord denied stealing and said a lease was never signed.

I was in the right and my lawyer told me he would be charged with theft of information. My plans were on hold and I was in jeopardy with only an old lease that ended soon. I also couldn't complete my plans as I didn't have possession of my new signed lease, and at the same time my landlord could produce this lease and hold me to it at any time.

A few months later he was convicted with theft of information, but there was no penalty or damages as the courts are very lenient on civil matters. I did at least have a lease then, but should have realized this situation was not going to work out. Dad used to say that **contracts are valuable only when both parties are reasonably happy with the terms**.

I naively thought that the law and the courts would protect me, as I was in the right. This slumlord also owned hundreds of apartments, and had dozens of lawsuits pending from almost everyone he ever did business with. Time and time again the courts did nothing.

My landlord did not apply normal business practices. He mocked our laws, the police and the courts regularly. Whenever I asked him to do something required under the lease, he would just hold out his hands like a handcuffed person and say, "take me to court".

I moved my store and purchased Angelino's pizza next door. I decided the only viable use for my old store space was a Laundromat, which the town needed. The space once had a Laundromat years ago, with the water, electrical and drainage lines still in place.

I gutted and rebuilt Angelino's completely. I replaced the various house appliances with commercial units and redesigned the kitchen to work more like an assembly line. All I really bought for my $30k were some excellent recipes, a pizza oven and a mixer.

I streamlined the business from prep to cleanup. During peak times, pizza pans were used instead of making pizzas one at a time on a board. Extra phone lines were added, plus an easier to remember phone number. I had a logo developed for my pizza boxes, of a character throwing pizzas in the air that looked like Mario from Nintendo.

Flyers were printed with a new menu that I completely revamped. Food was tax free under $4 then, and my $3.99 pepperoni and cheese 9" pizzas flew out the door like Frisbees. College students would call for five, delivered, and we knew what they meant. The oven held 15 small pizzas and we often had them out the door before the call ended.

Business value was created but there was an important problem; the pizza tasted different and people started noticing. I thought this had something to do with my switching to pizza pans, not realizing that pans had to be blackened first so the pizzas wouldn't stick.

The previous owner didn't provide his secret recipes, the main value I had purchased. Luckily, his disgruntled cook called one day to inform me that it wasn't right that his boss gave me the wrong recipes, because he was waiting for me to fail so that he could take over again. The cook told me the missing pizza sauce ingredient, and when I added it I could immediately taste the difference.

Also luckily, I still knew the recipes from my old high school summers pizza shop job. As soon as the recipes were modified, all was good for a while. I expanded the menu with chicken wings, fish and pasta and developed a local eat-in market to ease slow delivery periods.

Two months later I was offered almost triple my $30,000 investment to sell the business. However my landlord, who tried to stop me from buying because he didn't believe I could run a pizza business, now decided he wouldn't let me sell it either.

He couldn't really stop me legally as there was a transfer clause in the lease, but the buyer, who was also my accounting professor, then didn't want this idiot as his landlord. I considered legal action and later had no other choice, as things got much worse!

Angelino's prepared sandwiches during slow times for my store, which I also expanded with 40' of energy efficient refrigeration and over 200' feet of grocery shelving. My store was known for the best movies and video game selection, with over 4000 now owned rental units plus a dozen VCRs. Angelino's was hopping and my store doubled its sales in no time.

I had signs placed in the store and the restaurant that my Laundromat was opening soon. This was no secret and customer feedback was very positive. My landlord and his just as crazy wife were poking in and around all the time. I gave them a pizza one evening as a peace offering and thought the worst was behind me.

My next challenge came when my plumber tried to turn the water on for the Laundromat. The landlord decided then he didn't want this and wouldn't allow the water turned on. He owned five buildings with 120 apartments across the street and the last building had just three washers and three dryers. My lawyer told him I had rights. His reply, "take-me-to-court!"

To make matters worse, the wall between my store and restaurant was not built to code. I had to replace it or both my businesses would be shut down by the fire marshal. This was the landlord's responsibility but that take-me-to-court response cost me almost $8,000.

His slum-empire expanded with apartments out back, overloading our building's water and drainage systems. Floor drains regularly backed up and flooded both my store and restaurant. Mopping, disinfecting and deodorizing were regular staff duties, and to help customers avoid stepping in or smelling sewage as they ordered food or rented a movie.

Heat was included in my rent as the whole building had one boiler and connected HVAC system. The landlord advised one winter day that the compressors in my store's coolers and freezers, and my restaurant's pizza oven provide enough heat for my businesses. From then on he refused to supply oil or allow access to the furnace room.

This not only upset customers, half of my staff of fifteen refused to work under these conditions. It was so cold that you could see your breath, we wore gloves in between making pizzas, the dough didn't rise properly and our eat-in business disappeared.

The snow in the driveway, parking lots and entrances were never cleared adequately, on time or sometimes at all. My insurance could have been cancelled for building safety violations and the health department threatened to cancel my food shop license after a hole developed in the roof after a storm. Good thing they didn't stop by during a sewage backup!

Each time the law treated this as a civil matter. My only solution was to sue. To make a long story shorter, after my landlord exhausted every possible delay with six different lawyers, I eventually got my week in court 10-years later. Even this comedy of legal errors was to be repeated when the judge died suddenly after the first trial, but before delivering his decision.

In the end I won a judgement against his company, not worth the paper it is written on. His banks eventually foreclosed on all his properties throughout the province. I also received a personal judgement against him and was awarded rare punitive damages. However I can't collect on this either, as he no longer buys anything in his own name.

He's still a slumlord and up to his old tricks even today. I occasionally read about various tenant complaints and even arson investigations around some of his properties. I've concluded *the legal system is inept in enforcing business contracts*, as it can't control even the most extreme offenders! The time, energy and legal costs are just not worth it!

My renovated Laundromat without water access never did open. My lawyer had advised me to keep paying rent on the space, and I would get this back at trial. However after two years and my landlord's third or fourth court delay, I couldn't afford to keep paying this rent.

After this he seized my restaurant equipment illegally because I was suing him, against both my lawyer and his lawyer's frantic advice. Eventually I was vindicated at trial, but it was worth nothing of value. Like dad said, *avoid doing business with unreasonable people*.

Often one party to a contract has leverage over the other party. Unless you hold this leverage you must be especially careful, as words on paper may not mean much to an unreasonable person who is holding all the cards.

When a contract says that someone owes you money, or work, or something else of value, you need to look beyond these terms to specifically what the consequences are if they don't pay or perform. *Contracts are like paper money, simply a promise to pay*.

All of the above landlord issues are examples of how time and time again I naively believed that the courts would make me whole again. I was always proven right and awarded damages, but this meant nothing of value and I was powerless to prevent it.

Dad used to say **the power is where the money is**. This is similar to the golden rule, **he who has the gold, makes all the rules**. My wants for a business blinded reason and I should have known better. I should have simply chosen not to do business with him!

A business broker I knew had buyers for my store, restaurant and Laundromat for $250,000 if the Laundromat had opened. In the end I met my goals, graduated debt free and on time. A few years later I sold my store for $108,000, which is still open today. Ironically the store around the corner actually ended up changing into a Laundromat.

I could write another book on the mishaps and adventures of my various past retail businesses and the ineptness of the legal system. I've endured dozens of regular break-ins, mostly by the same young offender; when every three months the police would warn me of his next correctional centre release date. The important point is that **businesses can build wealth value, but only if the terms are reasonable and you are totally committed!**

I started with a vision of how my business would provide for my wants, but under estimated how much physical and mental energy and commitment was needed. Even today when I see an empty retail space, I start analyzing what business would work there.

I also didn't fully appreciate the various time costs and risks involved. Dad would say, **there is an easy and a hard way to do things** and *think long and hard before acting on your impulses*. I learned by doing and finished what I started, but usually the hard way!

By my early twenties I started and operated several convenience stores, video stores, a video arcade, french-fry wagon and security alarm business. I met my wife Barbara at university, who worked in my businesses and experienced all the ups and downs with me.

I did not plan for any of these businesses to be more than a financial stepping-stone to a more lucrative career after graduating in 1988. My businesses and school load was intense, while at the same time I partied as hard as any other student. In a three steps forward two steps back fashion, I built wealth and experience without any real focus.

University years represent the freedom of adulthood, without real adult responsibilities. After graduation the future becomes now, as reality sinks in and you have to seriously consider career, marriage and family directions. The value of family became even more real as dad passed away a year later in the fall of 1989.

Dad was a pillar of strength and wisdom to me. I wanted to make him proud and I know that he valued me as his son. Words can't express how much I miss him!

***

Everything was changing and I had to figure out what I was doing with my life. I thought I was ahead of the wealth curve until then, but I knew I needed to focus. A booming stock market, the movie Wall Street and the excitement and wealth potential of my earlier silver experience initially attracted me to the stock brokerage industry.

In 1988 I signed up for the Canadian Securities Course, required to become a licensed stockbroker. After passing the CSC I approached brokerage firms in Halifax, but as luck would have it most were firing instead of hiring, a result of the 1987 stock market crash.

Retail brokerage sales didn't interest me as much as financial management, company research and building wealth by investing in stocks and bonds. I believed my computer, math and business background were better suited to manage a mutual fund. I approached a few fund companies but they said they only hired experienced brokers.

I continued to operate my businesses and in the spring of 1991 decided that the timing might be right to approach the same brokerage firms once again. This time two of them called back for interviews after going over my resume.

The manager of a French Canadian brokerage firm remembered my 3-year earlier visit and entrepreneurial background. After completing some personality and aptitude tests he offered me a job. I then needed to just pass the Registered Representatives Manual Exam.

My manager took an interest in me and I thought I had found a mentor. I did learn a lot from him, but never received any formal sales training. The CSC and RR Manual Exam teach the vocabulary of investing, how financial ratios are calculated and how to write a stock or bond sales ticket to become a licensed broker, but you don't learn how to invest!

My first task as a broker was to develop a list of 200 friends, relatives and anyone I knew that may want to open an account. I eventually realized that my business background was not a hiring point because of my experience, but because I had many business contacts.

As my manager said, *dialling for dollars is the name of the game*, and when it came to IPO's *just smile and put some lipstick on this pig*. Once he gave me a list of employees to call, of a company with a secondary stock offering. The idea was good, but the company had never made a profit and even our analyst didn't like it. This didn't matter; employees want to own a piece of their employer, regardless of the stock's value.

Stockbrokers are not good money mangers! Clients see their portfolios as a means to grow wealth over time, while brokers and their firms see client portfolios as assets to derive commission streams. They get paid when they do trades, whether you win or lose!

Stockbrokers are under various pressures to produce results that may conflict with your wealth goals. Client's value brokers as personal wealth managers, but firm's value them only as salesmen, asset gatherers and distributors of financial products.

Firms want brokers to focus on making contacts and opening accounts. They also want brokers to leave stock picking and portfolio management to analysts or mutual funds for liability reasons, so that they get sued less often when trades don't work out.

It is more time efficient for a broker to have a list of analyst-approved stocks that all clients should own, instead of developing individual portfolios. *Brokers have to find a home for cold stock issues to have any real chance of receiving hot IPO's*. Hot new issues are few and far between, but are generally regarded as great bait to open new accounts.

I know of several stockbrokers and financial planners that are considered top performers by their firms and colleagues, based only on assets under administration, number of accounts, and of course gross commissions generated. However I would not trust any one of them to manage a dime of my money!

There are many so-called experts who have ruined clients financially with a great system to gather and place assets, but with no idea how to then choose wise investments or manage them. Assets under administration grow through perfecting a sales system, creating another conflict as brokers lose touch with client needs.

My manager would say *it's just a numbers game*. He was referring to numbers of prospecting calls for new clients, not existing client performance. A broker is actually better off keeping his pipeline of prospective new clients full, than catering to existing clients.

Brokers are concerned about losing you money, but only because you might transfer your account to another broker or sue! Reckless brokers *churn-em and burn-em* while efficient brokers know that *you can sheer a sheep for life, but you can only skin it once*.

People often choose financial planners based on looks, personality and presentation, rather than education, experience, performance and individual attention. Two of the top producers I know of proudly admit they don't know the first thing about investing and wouldn't dare invest their own money. Their formula for picking mutual funds is simple; whichever one pays the highest commission load and ongoing trailer fees!

Most firms have perks in the form of cash bonuses or trips to motivate brokers to raise the bar. I made our firm's presidents club requirements two years in a row, and would have made it three years but for an admin error that was corrected too late.

The first year I qualified based on the number of new accounts opened. The second year was based on growth of total assets under administration, transferred-in that year. The third year was based on gross commissions generated. These were the only prerequisite conditions to make the firm's president club each year!

The point I am making is that *customer service, satisfaction and portfolio performance is irrelevant; as long as new accounts, deposits, transfers and commissions keep rolling along.* Out performing the stock or bond markets was never mentioned, but we did get a pat on the back if a client transferred in another account or referred a new client!

I know of brokers that became heavy hitters as a result of exposing clients to extreme risks and leverage. Not only were risky securities recommended, clients were encouraged to borrow against home equity and retirement nest eggs, to then leverage this further through margin loan accounts. Some brokers even exercised discretionary trading without client permission, or worse securities violations, often overlooked by their firm's compliance department depending on the broker's commission production.

Even the luckiest brokers eventually hit a cold streak. As client losses and legal threats mount, *high rolling superstar brokers become unemployed liabilities in a heartbeat*. Firms only remember a broker's last trade and what they did for them lately.

Our manager held Monday morning meetings to review our commissions and present our in-house rankings. The most active trading day of the month was usually the cut-off day to make our next pay check. This was when brokers had one last chance to size-up any remaining client cash positions at month's end, for trade opportunities to maintain their ranking.

Every year it seemed that one broker was fired out of the blue some Friday afternoon. They had 5-minutes to say goodbye and pack a banker's box of personal belongings, that was searched to make sure clients contact info wasn't taken.

Minutes later the manager called a meeting to divvy up accounts, keeping the best ones for himself. We had to contact our new clients immediately about the broker change, to gain their confidence and pre-empt account transfers before the broker was hired by another firm. We all wanted to avoid a lower ranking and a surprise Friday meeting.

As my commissions and ranking moved higher, this put pressure on brokers above and below me. It was not uncommon for a broker that was behind that month to sandbag their trades. They would simply hold off and put through a flurry of trades in the last hour of the last trading day of the month, to ensure they maintained their commission standing.

My employer was as established, recognized and reputable as any other bank owned brokerage firm. I actually had more lucrative offers with a minimum pay guarantee from so-called bucket shops, boiler rooms and boutique firms that I luckily avoided.

I accepted less pay to work for a quality firm, receiving a $2,000 per month draw that I had to repay. My businesses were generating more than this and I had to agree to get rid of them all as soon as possible. I was committed and thought of brokers as professionals, but in the end I was just a suited salesman of investments, instead of movies or pizza.

I thought of my profession as a win-win-win! I would help people grow their wealth, get paid well in the process and at the same time grow my own wealth through investing. However stockbrokers are usually the worst managers of their own wealth, as you cannot be objective when you are that close to every news event, rumour and stock tick. I know of brokers who churn client accounts, their own accounts or their family's accounts just to make their monthly commission nut.

***

Before I knew how to invest like a professional stockbroker, I bought PCA Petro-Canada and RY Royal Bank shares. Both are blue-chip companies that are trading at about 10-times what I paid in 1991, plus dividends!

The third stock investment I purchased was a new mutual fund that my manager said had a dynamic way of valuing stocks. His decades of experience must know better than a rookie like myself, who only saw value in boring old oil and bank shares. Thinking that my new clients and I now had an inside shortcut to wealth, I lapped up all the wisdom I could get and eagerly switched into the Polymetric Performance Fund with his blessing.

Perhaps Polymetric is another word for investment skydiving. Long story short, regretful brokers and clients started referring to that mutual fund as the Poly Poop fund, as it never did turn around and no longer exists. I wish I had known back then that this fund company had trading accounts with my manager.

My manager called all the brokers into his office one afternoon with a revelation. He claimed that Central Guarantee Trust at $9 a share was cheap, now trading below book value. Trust companies were losing money, but would be gobbled up by the banks for two times book. He said this represented a double upside with no real downside for clients.

My other manager was a cranky old fellow, who I initially avoided but respect to this day. He would not allow clients to take unreasonable risks, and his occasional phone yelling fits were to prevent clients from destroying wealth on foolish stock tips or faddish IPO's.

He absolutely hated the trust company idea and told us to stay clear! Company risks are many and the industry is losing money hand over fist with no turnaround in sight. The trusts are going out of business and the banks will scoop them up for pennies on the dollar. He said common shareholders are screwed and will end up with nothing!

This was a dilemma for me that I should have decided to just do nothing. Instead I reasoned that my more refined manager, who relied on various financial statements, must know better than my cranky manager who often didn't turn on his computer.

Now I had a rock solid chance to recover from the opportunity costs given up when I sold my safe RY and PCA stock to buy the money losing Poly Poop Fund. I also had more business money built-up, plus a personal injury car accident settlement to invest.

Newly licensed brokers are on close supervision for good reason, and all my trade tickets had to be initialled by one of my managers. My clients bought some CGA shares and were diversified; however I had losses to make up, so I ploughed about half of my savings into CGA at $9 a share. Licensed brokers are pros and this was easy money!

About a month later my clients complained and wanted to sell. I went to my manager with pink sell tickets to be initialled at $7 per CGA share. He said I should double up instead, which I did but only for myself.

Long story short some clients demanded I sell their shares, while others transferred their accounts. He eventually agreed to sign my sales ticket at 13 cents a share to lock in a tax loss at the time. As my cranky manager predicted, the common shareholders ended up with virtually no value. However bank shareholders won big time as most of the trust companies client accounts became amalgamated into the banks.

As I got to know my cranky manager, he explained the importance of trust in maintaining client relationships, to survive in this business. There are many temptations and if a client still wants to speculate after you explain the risks, you have to put your foot down. The ones that stay will thank you later, and the ones that leave will blow their accounts up anyway. I eventually realized the wisdom of his ways.

He also showed me how to use options safely to enhance returns. He said *the only investment value of options is writing slightly out of the money covered-calls*. He would only allow his risk adverse clientele to buy blue-chip bank and utility stocks, but he would also sell covered-calls to generate extra income and enhance their returns safely.

Each call option represents 100 shares. If you own 500 shares you can write or sell 5 calls, receiving 500 times the call premium. If the stock remained lower than the call exercise strike price, it would expire worthless and new calls could be sold. If the stock was above the strike price your stock might be called away at a profit, plus the call premium, plus any dividends paid while you held the stock.

This worked especially well during flat markets. He would write slightly out of the money covered-calls over and over again for years on the same stocks. While most bank shareholders received only 3% dividends, his clients were receiving an extra 15% return.

When the stock market eventually turns around, you may decide to stop writing covered calls and just let your stock run. He would stick mainly to bank calls because they are among the most actively traded options. Other than covered calls, he described the options market as an illiquid pro market that is rigged against investors.

The person who buys an option is simply making a bet on the future price of a stock, bond, index or other security. The time window is very small, the spread between the bid and ask is often wide and option premiums and commissions are high, all adding to risk.

Option buyers, mostly individual speculators, lose about 80% of the time! On the other hand option sellers, mostly market makers, can reasonably play these percentages all day by trading naked or uncovered options, with wide spreads built in their favour. However market makers can move faster because they are better equipped, and they don't pay commissions!

Individual investors can't do this safely; but if they are covered, by owning the underlying stock, they can reasonably participate. The downside to covered calls is that you give-up your stock's upside. You also have to hold onto the stock in case you get called. *Covered calls should only be done on quality stocks you would hold anyway*.

Futures are an obligation to buy or sell an underlying commodity. They function like an option, with even more leveraged risks. Margin is used to control very large amounts, with only small amounts of capital that can be wiped out in an instant. Over 90% of futures contracts are closed out before expiry. *Futures are simply a crapshoot that investors should avoid!*

***

At that time Barbara and I were married about a year and she was close to going on maternity leave from her teaching job. I had sold most of my businesses and was still fighting a costly landlord lawsuit. As a result of buying CGA, my investment practice income suffered a setback and at the same time my savings were almost wiped out! All that I had worked for up until then, to stay ahead of the curve, had disappeared. I was in a very tight corner and realized that I was wealthier when I was 8-years old, through high school and in college than I was now with my struggling new professional career.

As your resources and options become limited, and future opportunities seem less predictable, anxiety and stress build. I was still young, tough and battle ready, but I felt vulnerable and needed some direction and focus if I was going to turn this around.

To make matters worse, I was neglecting my health. Smoking was cool when I was in high school, and I am so glad for my kids that it is not today. When I started at my firm almost everyone smoked, but a few years later I was the only smoker there.

I consumed over a pack a day, plus eight cups of coffee. Every second of my time was spent either making money or worrying about it. Stress adds weight and my ego slumped further as I gained around 30-pounds over time.

In high school I played intramural sports such as curling, soccer and basketball. A few times a week I went on 3-mile runs around where I lived, and ran on our school track team. After all my farm work was done, I usually lifted weights or swam every day.

As a broker the only exercise I was getting was running to the food court at lunchtime to woof down the cheapest and fastest food. As a stress reliever after work, I gambled at bar VLTs on the way to my car's parking lot. Not uncommon for business owners with control issues, I wasn't very good at turning these problems off after work.

Discipline and focus had become depression, and none of this helped my family life.

I needed to have hope again, so I put together a business plan. Luckily I was raised to avoid debt, and other than my mortgage payment our monthly living cash burn rate was relatively low. My savings were fried in CGA, but out of respect for my dad I had used the $10,000 I inherited as a down payment on the semi-detached starter home we lived in.

The stock market was flat, the economy in recession, but I could not afford to wait. In a moment of desperate clarity, I developed a 3-point plan to turn weakness into strength. First I would educate myself how to invest properly, to better build, keep and serve my retail clients and at the same time demonstrate to my firm how committed I was.

Second, I would go after some institutional bond accounts. These were hard to come by, with long established broker relationships. I had developed an interest in bonds and my math skills gave me an edge that I thought I could work to win over these accounts.

Third, I discovered that my first store's movie vendor actively traded mining and technology penny stocks. He also had four friends who day traded. The five of them would transfer their accounts if I would let them watch every stock tick on my quote terminal during fast markets. I also had to match their discount broker's commissions.

These five traders alone could represent as much as $10,000 a month in commissions. They bought volatile high-risk stocks and would tie up my office computer a few hours each day, but their trades were marked unsolicited which represented no liability to the firm.

Over the next two years I completed the options and futures courses to expand my broker's license and knowledge base. I also was one of the youngest brokers in the country to complete the Certified Investment Manager program, which also conferred the designation of FCSI or Fellow of the Canadian Securities Institute.

Other than becoming a full CFA Certified Financial Analyst, I had every credential and license possible. Most clients didn't perceive value in the BCSc. CIM or FCSI on my business card, but it may have provided some extra credibility with institutional clients.

Unlike accountants or lawyers, brokers don't get paid based on credentials, experience or billable hours. Brokers don't even get paid for producing good client returns. Their value is based on sales and marketing, such as public speaking skills, expensive suits or age. When my hair started turning grey, probably from stress, my wife wanted to color it but I decided to keep it that way. My manager said that grey hairs offer an older looking credibility edge.

My eventual goal was to build a retail book of two hundred clients with around $20 million in assets under administration. I estimated that this would produce on average around 1% or $200,000 a year in sustainable long-term commissions.

However the economy was still in the toilet and retail investors remained gun shy from the 1987 stock market crash. My plan anticipated making up for retail commission slack with my traders, and by landing some institutional accounts in between RSP seasons. I presented the plan to my manager, which he thought was excellent!

After getting to know our bond desk and inventory, I approached several institutions about our firm's advantages. We were the low man on the totem pole of the bank owned brokerage firms, but if you dug into our limited bond inventory you could still find a few undervalued bond gems. *The bond game is all about investment safety and yield!*

I approached various private and government pension funds even though I was told this was a waste of time. My manger said I wouldn't get past their dragons, meaning my detailed bond opportunity letters and phone calls would be screened and never returned.

He approved my plan but thought my time was better spent dialling for retail client dollars. His system had me making 60 cold calls a day, resulting in three appointments and maybe one new account per week. This usually produced a $10,000 mutual fund buy-ticket worth $200 in commission, of which less than half went to me. I couldn't cover my repayable draw this way and realized I was making more than this back in grade seven.

It took a few months but I discovered a niche market with several hospitals that regularly rolled over millions in bonds. I tracked all their maturities, and built a relationship with our bond desk so that I could offer a superior yield when the time came.

On a regular basis I was writing millions in safe government bond orders before my first coffee, and generating more commission than from my retail client book some months. My traders stopped by just before the market opened to place bets for the day and put on a few hundred more in commissions. Late morning and early afternoon I focused on retail client trades and in the afternoon on appointments or prospecting new contacts.

In addition to the hospitals, I was bidding on bonds for the Interprovincial Lottery Commission, various pension funds and our province's general operating account. The orders were in the millions per ticket and I was just scratching the surface. I knew that as I continued to find the best yield, it was only a matter of time to become a major player.

Things were starting to work out as planned, and then more good luck. Dad used to say that *good and bad luck runs in threes*. I never understood why, but this has always proven true for me. I think he was referring to the tendency for things to get even worse during bad times, and for things to get even better during good times.

Dad would say that *you must always be prepared for the unexpected* and that *you need to position yourself to protect your upside just as much as your downside*. Dad would also say *don't assume anything*, as this usually makes an ASS out of yoU or ME.

Our provincially owned power utility was going public and everyone would want to own a piece of the company. There was also an instalment receipt exclusively offered to provincial residents as a further incentive. This was an excellent opportunity for small investors, creating thousands of new accounts and millions in commissions we were told.

The icing on the cake was that brokers would receive $20 an hour for their time. Imagine getting paid on top of your stock commission, and having new clients call to immediately open an account to buy stock, instead of hanging up on you for bothering them.

The conditions were that we had to work out of the power company's assigned broker room and take the time to answer questions and explain the details before accepting orders. Locals could buy up to 5,000 instalment receipts per family resident at $6 per share, with the other $7 instalment due a year later. A no-brainer for investors and brokers couldn't lose!

I soon realized the broker room was really just a high-class boiler room. The stock was a solid investment but most brokers abused the terms put in place to help new investors. I received a lot of heat from my manager to pull up my socks and sell, as I was way behind most other brokers. My career with the firm hung on the outcome!

This didn't make any sense to me as I had signed up for every hour in the broker room I could get. In the end I was logging more hours than any other broker in the province and should have been receiving the most orders, but I wasn't even close.

About 10-days before the selling period ended, I happened to meet the broker who remembered me from my silver conversations in high school. I explained the problem to him and he smiled and told me what was really going on.

He asked if I was getting a lot of minimum 50 or 100 share orders from little old ladies who wanted to know everything, like what a dividend was and when they would get their $20 checks. They are upset when you can't split a minimum 50-share order for each of their five grandchildren. After an hour the best you end up with is a 50-share order that you won't get a payout on by most brokerage firms if the order is less than 200 shares.

I agreed and said that's what we are getting paid by the hour for. He informed me that I was the only broker doing it right, but *the right way doesn't work in this business*. He told me to listen to how the other brokers field their calls and I would figure it out.

I assumed he meant I wasn't a good salesman, but this wasn't his point at all. The reason I was getting only small time-consuming orders was because brokers would first ask how many shares the caller was interested in. For orders of less than 200 shares, some brokers had higher minimum orders, an excuse was given why the customer had to call back.

Calls were distributed and they knew someone like me would be taking the next call. Brokers would take names and numbers, for unlicensed assistants to call back later and fill-in account details, so their phone lines stayed open. This was all clever but conflicted with the rules, but I had no choice in order to keep my job but to play the same game.

As soon as I started filtering orders, I too started receiving 5,000 share orders with a maximum broker payout, times several family members, on a call that took only a few minutes. First time small investors were left out as usual, while some brokers joked about buying stock for pets when a wealthy client ran out of relatives names to use.

Only Nova Scotia citizens could be issued the instalment receipts, but they somehow found their way into institutional accounts and mutual funds. Some high profile brokers lost their jobs as the press and the securities commission eventually caught wind of this.

I scraped up enough to buy 5000 instalment receipts for myself. I was then told to write orders in my wife and child's name. I would receive the sales commission even though I couldn't pay for these shares, that would be transferred somewhere before settlement.

I played the game and went from worst to first in our firm based on the number of shares sold, all within the last ten days. I even anticipated the other brokers sandbagging their orders, and I knew to hold back half of my orders for the last day.

The whole experience was a valuable lesson about our industry and how things really work. It was also a great payday that saved my job. The broker who came in last at our firm on selling that new issue had his farewell Friday meeting a few months later!

I opened over 200 retail accounts, although half of these were only for 50-share orders from early in the campaign. Some accounts would develop over time; while others I advised to take share delivery to avoid a $25 inactive account fee. I also opened 50 new self-directed RSP accounts, a requirement for presidents club, as clients contributed their NSP shares – for the tax break and tax-free compounding.

My commissions were building in all three areas according to plan. My traders were trading and my institutions were transferring in millions in quality bond assets with regular big-ticket trades. I also had a base of retail clients and referrals to build on.

***

My plan would be complete if I could figure out a way to get back the savings that I had lost on CGA. I realized that my manager didn't have the answers as he was a terrible stock picker and I heard he had lost most of his own savings a few years earlier.

I was more educated and experienced then I was as a rookie and knew there must be a big stock score I could ferret out for myself. I had already lost 90% of my hard earned business savings, so I didn't care about the risks of losing what little remained.

My portfolio had gone from solid oil and bank stocks, to poly poop, to a bankrupt trust company, when I would have been happy with a 10% return. Instead of higher yield, my savings capital grubstake had vanished from over a hundred thousand to under $5,000 on supposedly low-risk investments.

I was upset but determined that my savings were going back to six digits, or zero! I wanted to bet it all and go for either broke or the brass ring. I thought there was no risk difference between a value investment and a penny stock, when I should have realized a common mistake, that *speculations are perceived as investments when greed and fear overcome rational thinking and recognizing real business value*.

In the pursuit of maximum leverage I bought several cheap warrants and out of the money call options, but lost on almost every trade. Even the option trades that started working out I usually pressed my bet, which then fell apart before the option expiry date.

I gave up on options and started paying more attention to my five traders who were making tens of thousands, and losing similar amounts, in a matter of hours. They each had their own style, quirks and routines to trade highly leveraged low-priced stocks.

Trader number one was a government employee who also owned apartment buildings. He considered himself an investor as he only bought stocks over $5. These were so-called real-stocks he said, however watching paint dry would have been more exciting.

He would spend hours reading financial statements, Value Line and press releases and his philosophy on growth stocks seemed reasonable. However his trades were during a bear market and I don't believe he had any successful trades.

His picks may have worked better in the dot com years to follow, but buying growth stocks in a bear market, just because they are trading at 52-week lows, is sometimes referred to as catching falling daggers, as prices often go even lower. Trader number one failed to realize that *for short-term profits, you should never fight the tape*.

Trader number two was a retired sea captain. He would stare at my screen for hours in silence rubbing his beard and twisting his facial expressions as the handful of stocks he watched traded. He was cranky or rude as the world conspired against his bad trades, but boasted joyfully about obvious good trades that only he could recognize.

His philosophy is that the screen, how the stock trades, tells you everything you need to know. He referred to stocks only by their symbol, never the company's name, and didn't care what was driving the stock price up or down, only that it was moving.

He believed that if a stock is going up or down in price, with above average volume, you need to trade before the reason for this market action becomes public knowledge. Most of the time this doesn't work out, but he was very nimble at cutting losses and leveraging his wins that were often big enough to make up for the losses.

Market makers love momentum traders and take opposite positions. They wait for the trading volume to settle down and the price action to reverse, when their short trades can be unwound and covered profitably. Market makers simply bet against the herd!

Charts and technical trading patterns give important clues to a stocks short-term direction, helpful just before timing a stock trade, but have nothing to do with the long-term intrinsic value of an investment. However traders are only interested in the short-term trend and are often paranoid. Trader number two would say that *insider trading affects all stocks and if you are not inside, you are outside*.

Current stock prices try to predict future events. This is especially true for thinly traded small caps! However if you look at stock charts of any large cap stock before a major announcement, you will almost always notice a run-up or run-down preceding the news. In short, *rules are broken and short-term prices are unreliable, while recognizing long-term value is the safest way to make investment decisions*.

Over the course of a week trader two would typically buy 10,000 shares at every .05 interval from .50 to $1. He would double-up or unload it all based on the next few up or down ticks. He gazed into my computer screen like a fortune-teller into a crystal ball. After a dozen trades he would then ask me the company's name, or what they did.

The only fundamentals that mattered to him are how the stock traded at that moment. He traded like a general in the heat of battle; strategically deploying troops of buy and sell tickets in reaction to the last trade. His trading instincts were very good, but he would usually give back gains over the summer, not recognizing the usual seasonality of small caps.

If he had only traded over the winter, he would have made a killing. However he failed to recognize that *small cap stocks tend to run from January to April, hence the saying sell in May and go away* until late next fall.

The third trader also worked for the government and was the most active of the five. He was the most consistently profitable trader of the group and was also a screen watcher. His trading style used daily trading information to ultimately trigger his buy and sell decisions, however he also valued digging into the story behind the play as well.

By scanning the most-active daily trading lists, he could spot stocks usually between $0.25 and $2 that were building momentum. He would read press releases, contact the company and its investor relations and promoters to find out the scoop. He also looked at where recent private placements were priced at and when future funding was expected.

He would then *put all these pieces of the puzzle together like a story*. This story stock play had a beginning, middle and an end. The beginning started usually with the history of the company, current share structure, who was running the play and their other stock successes. It showed how much funding was raised early on, the mining rights or technology acquired and the near-term news flow expected by the company.

Late in the beginning or early in the middle of the story is when trader number three bought in. This is when the promotion and investor relation team starts touting the new play and press releases start churning out exciting developments. With private placements placed and insider options set, the push is on to move the stock higher.

Trader number three would take large stock positions as the promo team starts up, but before the stock advanced too far. Paying a reasonable premium over the price that insiders and private placements received was ok, but not too high or insiders might already be selling. In other words, *small cap stock plays are attractive only when the story is still in the early stages and the promotion cycle hasn't ended*.

The trick is that you will never know when the insiders have unloaded and the company will never say when the promotion has ended. For this you need to look to the trading volume and price movement for clues to act on first and ask questions later. *Stock prices rise with expectations of positive news, plus above average trading volume. However it only takes a lack of news, or low trading volume, for prices to fall!*

Trader number three knew not to confuse fundamentals with a stock play story. In other words, *for small cap stocks there is no fundamental value other than the public value perception of the story*. If the story is a business sector or area-play on gold, diamonds, oil, dot coms or whatever, you should only be in while the market still likes the story.

After trader three builds a substantial six-digit share position, the other traders are let-in on the story. Short-term traders are inherently paranoid and it was not unusual for trader three to be touting a stock to another trader just before I was instructed to sell his entire position. *Small cap stocks are simply promotions as insiders, tout sheets and other shareholders often say buy at the same time they are selling or shorting stock to you*.

Trader number three built positions and then became a promoter of his holdings to anyone who might buy into the stock after him. This increased his odds of success, knowing the story would soon end. He knew that *small cap stocks are musical chairs that almost always get pulled from under you as the promotion cycle ends*.

The fourth trader ran his own business and traded the same stocks as the other traders. As some trades won, he became more active until losses started hitting. Actually all five traders traded somewhat in a boom, bust and rebuild cycle every year. Not surprisingly my monthly commissions ran up from January to May and fell off over the summer.

The fourth trader didn't have as much time to watch stocks all day, unlike the third trader at his government office computer. He traded short-term but also looked for plays to develop over a few years, usually holding longer than the second and third trader.

As you might expect, this sometimes worked out to bigger wins but also bigger losses. Trader number four occasionally had major home runs, usually followed by major strikeouts that evened out his year.

The fifth trader was younger than the others, with a property management job for a nation wide insurance company. He had a good educational investment background and saw penny stocks for what they are, high-risk speculation. He generally followed the lead of the other traders who all shared ideas and opinions and touted their plays to each other.

Being closer to my age and with a securities educational background, I could relate well to his investment philosophy. Small cap stocks were a way to place leveraged bets, and if you were lucky enough to hit big, then you would invest this money and never put it back into small caps.

After taking hundreds of orders for all five traders, I started to develop a feel for each of their trading styles. Trader number three always had the best overall batting average. *For low-quality high-risk small caps, analyzing the story, buying low and avoiding losses are the key values to overall and consistent trading performance*. However, *small cap stock trading is gambling, driven by greed and fear* which their yearly returns reflected.

Win streaks and pressed bets were usually followed by panic selling and losses, with emotional highs and lows after stock halts resumed trading. Experienced traders know to get out of a stock before the news and promotion cycle ends, hence the saying, *buy on mystery and sell on history*.

None of them had the answer I was looking for, until one day I decided to make a bet on a stock play that four of my traders started buying at the same time. All but trader number one, who only bought stocks over $5, were buying a 40-cent stock called Bre-X Minerals.

News releases indicated the company had raised a few hundred thousand and would be exploring for gold in Indonesia soon. The stock was the right price for leverage, but the market trading action barely had a pulse and Indonesia was far from any hot area play.

For traders who typically trade on short-term market action only and don't believe in long-term fundamentals, it was strange that they were buying such a quiet stock. Supposedly the manager of a nearby brokerage firm, who knew one of the company's key geologists with local family roots, told my traders that this stock was going to fly.

My traders were paranoid and usually didn't trade on rumours unless the screen backed this up with above average trading volume. There must have been something more hush-hush compelling about the story because they all started buying anyway. I wasn't in on the real scoop, but my gut said to bet my last savings and buy this stock.

With less than $5,000 remaining and after factoring in commission, I bought 10,000 shares of Bre-X at .40. I had a few hundred dollars left over, but wanted to avoid buying any odd-lot shares. I now tend to go for long-term home runs and little did I know how controversial my first penny stock purchase would become!

My manager reviewed all broker trades and came to me later that week with a pink sell ticket for my Bre-X. He claimed that **brokers operate in a fish bowl and should not be buying speculative stocks**. I replied that I was not buying this stock for regular clients and just tagging along with my traders unsolicited buys.

I had lost most of my savings on his advice to switch from large cap bank and oil stocks into the poly poop fund, and then into a bankrupt trust company. Now he was forcing me to sell a leveraged small cap stock just because it might look bad if one of his brokers buys a risky penny stock. This made no sense and it was my money, but I had to sign the sell ticket!

The result was another $400 loss including commission at a sale price of .38. Long story short, my heart sank as Bre-X soared over the next two-years to over $280 per share. At the high, my $4,000 first penny stock speculation not only would have recovered my lost savings, it could have made me a multi-millionaire well before my thirtieth birthday!

Three of my traders made money on Bre-X but sold out long before the stock traded above $2. However trader number five kept his 50,000 shares and parlayed this further into millions.

I question myself as to which points along the way I would have sold some Bre-X. My trading style tends to look for points when the play starts to look tired, when my initial investment should be recovered. I closely followed the play develop and believe I would have sold 1,000 shares between $5 and $10.

I also tend to sift out shares and probably would have sold 100 shares at every $5 peak between $10 and $25. But at around $25 Bre-X became recognized as a potential huge home run, a strong-buy then recommended by several large brokerage firms.

Through $50 a share analysts were calling for Bre-X's Indonesian deposit to be worth billions. At around $200 a share some were calling it the richest gold mine ever found! The press heralded stories of instant millionaires and it seemed that everyone wanted to own some Bre-X. At that point I believe I would have started questioning who didn't already own the stock, as a good rationale to start selling the bulk of my shares.

As the stock breached $250, analysts speculated that the largest gold companies in the world needed to partner with or buyout Bre-X, to avoid losing market share to another major gold miner. Everyone saw dollar signs and wanted to share in the company's good fortune and nobody needed verification how real the dream was!

Legal fights developed as ex presidents and prime ministers were signed up as board members of major gold miners, for the sole purpose of influencing the Indonesian government to politically manoeuvre control of the gold deposit away from Bre-X. Awards were presented to the company for its success, which the company used as a platform to proclaim how big business was trying to cheat small investors.

This was all ironic as confirmation drilling clearly showed that the company's drill results were a complete fraud. In a short period of time the stock dropped to $30 and over the next few months to pennies a share with each successive stock halt and confirmation of further no-gold drill results.

The company continued to claim someone made a mistake and future results would prove the gold was there. Investors became paranoid of a cover-up when they should have realized that *there is never just one cockroach when material errors surface, such as accounting irregularities or fraudulent drill results*.

Investors and even analysts held on to the end that the company was right and that major gold companies were just trying to cheat the little guy out of their fortune. Reality finally did sink in as the head onsite geologist suddenly leapt to his death during a helicopter trip to the drill site, and later Bre-X's president died of a ruptured brain blood vessel.

I believe I would have made around $2 million, as did many other lucky traders, but would have held onto a few shares on the way down, just in case it was a real investment. In the end Bre-X was a wild ride for many and one of the largest stock scams ever!

Perhaps this is a lesson that fortunes can be made and lost through leverage. For investors who need to build wealth safely, it should be seen as an extreme example of how *there are too many reasons why small cap stocks are simply not a reasonable investment!*

It is not advisable, but if you feel the need and can afford to put 5% of your savings into leveraged speculations, you probably won't get into too much trouble. However if you use the time and compounding tables to project reasonable compounded safe investment returns on these funds over time, your yearly results might not be as exciting but your overall long-term results will almost surely be superior.

I would have done just as well if I had stayed in my original boring but safe bank and oil stocks, with accumulated dividends and capital appreciation, that would now be worth over ten times my original investment. In short *the best way to achieve wealth is to avoid losses and compound returns safely*.

Almost anyone with a common sense understanding of real value can outperform most financial experts, especially my old manager! I was told this early in life but had to learn this again the hard way. *Wealth education is as important to value as any other type of education*, my key driver in writing this book.

I learned much from my traders and still wonder where my wealth would be if my manager didn't make me sell my Bre-X stock. I still had less than $5k in savings but at least my investment practice was growing. For the first time since joining the firm I had hope and control over my professional career, instead of feeling like it's a temporary job.

However the pressure around the office never let up. The commission bar not only kept raising, it was always set unreasonably out of reach. My next year business plan was to generate $180,000 in commissions, about 50% higher than the previous year. I was told this had to be raised to $220,000, higher than any broker in the office.

I got to know the other brokers around the office and their situation was not much better. We all realized there would never be a satisfactory sales level. One of my colleagues said this was so they can always fire you for not making your targets.

He was many years my senior and his situation must have been particularly stressful as the bulk of his commissions came from one institutional client. Whenever that client was not investing, he would often jest that any of us could be eating rats by next year.

This all demonstrates the importance of controlling your own destiny. Everything was going to plan but I was still not in control. A year later, after having a slow month while off sick for a week, I returned to find out that our firm just bought another local firm.

The two operations would be merged into a new larger office, with most brokers moved into a bullpen instead of offices. My manager informed me that my trading clients were no longer welcome, and my institutional clients were now with another broker at the firm.

If I didn't like it I could resign, and I was offered no compensation for five years work building up this business. I had an offer to move my clients to another firm and my manager was probably surprised when I didn't choose to resign. The next Friday I was called in for a meeting and let go anyway.

I found out later that my trading clients were more than welcome at my previous firm. I expect that my larger retail and institutional clients ended up with my manager, as was his typical practice when brokers were let go in the past.

I didn't go with the firm that offered me a job because the manager there had an even worse reputation than my current manager. In fact he was the manager who gave my traders the original tip on Bre-X being a good investment.

The firm I did want to work at hired me a month later, but changed their mind before I could start. I found out later as I sued my old firm, that one of the partners at my new firm was a sailing buddy of my old manager. I was in good standing with no blemishes on my record, but it seemed like a nebulous cloud of character bashing was cast to black ball me from taking my clients back.

I then joined a mutual fund firm that had been recognized that year with the prestigious Top 50 Canada Growth companies. They mainly sold mutual funds but just started offering stock and bond investments through another firm as clearing agent.

The firm's manager was the slick presenter I mentioned earlier who bragged he didn't know the first thing about investing and picked mutual funds based only on the commissions paid. I went to the firm's convention a month later and realized most of their reps were more concerned about their golf handicap than client returns.

Actually several brokers I know deliberately golf alone as a targeted prospect marketing technique. A well-placed tip can get you the exclusive attention of an unsuspecting whale investor for several hours. This is usually more than enough time to point out what his other broker is doing wrong, sell him on how successful and conservative you are, and to wear down any other sales objections. Personally I've never had time for the game.

After placing my first hospital bond order of a few hundred thousand dollars, my new manager wanted me to put this into a bond mutual fund instead, for ten times the payday. To him the **know-your-client** rule must have meant know how to best skin your client. I had to get away from that rag-tag situation and wasn't surprised a year later to hear about investor lawsuits and the firm eventually folding.

***

Once again a bad luck run of three left me in a very tough situation. The last of my savings was spent buying computer and office equipment for my final brokerage job. Barb was on maternity leave and close to delivering our second son Alex, and I had no income or prospects as my first firm was doing their best to keep me out of this rat race of a business. I was financially broke at 28, depressed and felt totally defeated.

Luckily I had paid off our mortgage aggressively and the last payment was that month. I knew I didn't have the time or capital to start a new business, but figured that I could make due even if I had to flip burgers for a living.

The spec of pride I had left wouldn't allow to me to consider welfare, although I probably more than qualified. In hindsight, having no debt is the only reason I still controlled my situation, which allowed me the time flexibility to still find a way to turn things around.

I approached mutual fund companies again about managing a fund, now that I had all broker education credentials. The funny thing is, this time they said they don't hire experienced brokers because they have bad habits. They hire fund managers out of Wharton Business School without experience so they can meld them a certain way.

I had a lot to offer but couldn't win no matter which way I turned. Not only were my personal goals at stake, now I had a family that depended on me. I had hit rock bottom and then out of nowhere I experienced a life value from the last place I expected.

I kneeled alone one night in the dark and surrendered to god. This was extremely difficult for me, admitting defeat and no control over my life. I prayed for direction and courage without restrictions. For the first time in my life I admitted that maybe I didn't have what it takes to be successful, and that if I was meant to flip burgers so be it.

Perhaps during all of those years of mom dragging me to church something had actually sunk in. Many times I had argued with mom using lack of proof to disclaim any tangible value of prayer and religion. She patiently would provide personal examples of how faith works, which I would dismiss as not logical.

When mom asked if I prayed regularly, of course I did. I prayed for my stocks to go up, or at least not down anymore. I prayed for my lottery numbers to hit, for a hard eight to roll on the dice or for swinging bells to hit on my VLT. I prayed for a client to walk into my office with a big check. I prayed for health, wealth and wisdom, however happiness to me was just a concept, an illusion that I never really understood the meaning of.

After my religious experience I realized that I had never really prayed before. ***You can't make demands or pray with conditions. The whole point of prayer and faith is accepting that you will receive the help you need, not necessarily what you want.*** As usual I had to do things the hard way and hit rock bottom in order to realize this.

I can't fully explain it, but I woke up the next morning with a drive and clarity that I had never experienced before. I didn't know what was going to happen, but somehow I knew I wasn't alone and that things would be ok. Calm, focus and excitement replaced the previous day's stress, despair and depression.

While surfing for jobs on the internet I realized that I should start a webpage and email list for investors to share ideas and research. I knew there was a need as my traders always complained that nobody provided research on small or micro cap stocks. At that time I was thinking this could be a neat hobby after a hard day of flipping burgers.

The brokerage industry claims they don't follow small cap stocks, as these companies don't have fundamentals to base research on. This is true, but the real reason is that large cap stocks offer more commissions via higher trading volumes and underwriting fees.

Similarly, most of the information about small and micro cap stocks comes from promoters or investor relation firms that are paid by these companies. The information is usually tainted and optimistic to unreasonable at best, or impossible to a lie at worst.

Recommendations and opinions on most stocks have conflicts, both big and small caps. CFA's writing big cap reports exaggerate often and miss badly, but at least they try to use a professionally recognized method to value a company's stock.

However brokerage firms are still settling hundreds of millions of dollars in investor lawsuits and regulator fines over recommendations with conflicts of interest. In the late 1990's, dot com analysts became stock TV celebrities as they trumped one another with higher and higher price targets. The sheep lined up for their eventual slaughter!

In the end trillions of dollars of wealth was created, transferred and evaporated as a result of the dot com bubble and various stock scandals. Over-hyped or conflicted analyst reports only fuelled the flames. As P/E ratios skyrocketed into the hundreds, analysts proclaimed *it's different this time; words that investors should always be wary of*.

This is not unique as *the stock market shell game repeats with every bull market cycle!* Following a stock market crash or correction, brokers clean house, regulators update the rules and players lick their wounds until they forget and feel safe to play again.

New disclosure laws resulted in brokerage firms cutting back or totally getting out of the research business, now that conflicts have to be fully disclosed. Independent research firms with unbiased research may provide investors comfort to get back in the game again. In any event it will reduce the brokerage industry's legal liability next time.

As stocks get overvalued in the next bull market, remember that *bull markets change investor perception, but not intrinsic values*. Everyone from first time investors, brokers, the media to even seasoned analysts will again break the rule *don't confuse brains with a bull market*. In the end *intrinsic value eventually wins and determines a stock's real worth!*

My mission then was to help small cap speculators, including myself. My mission now is to help young people understand what wealth really is, and how to value, obtain and hold onto it. I made and lost millions on small cap stocks, but my wealth was built on common sense values. Trading values have a way of disappearing, while wealth you work for and invest properly has a way of growing. In other words *invest, don't speculate!*

Back then I thought that my professional background and trading experience might be valuable to other small cap traders, and they might in return share information with me. I developed a format to present stock info in a way that most traders were familiar with. This included news, corporate and share structures, trading and funding history, insider reports, project overviews and general info on various small cap mining and tech stocks.

I added a bulletin board as a way to trade information and speculative guesses about various active stocks. In the mid-1990's, before cheerleading stock market TV stations that we have today, investment websites were mainly free grey pages. My small cap website grew almost overnight to the point that I had to put together an email list to keep up with requests for news releases and trading volume stats of stocks that we followed.

The site took on a life of its own and absorbed most of my time. However the information wasn't flowing as freely to me as I was providing it. My email list was growing monthly by the thousands and website hits by the hundreds of thousands. I needed my time back and almost shut everything down, but then got a call from one of the companies I followed.

This mineral exploration company liked the website's balanced approach on following small cap stocks. They wanted us to consider following their progress, in hopes that readers might want to contact the company for more information about their stock. They liked the website's concept, reputation and wanted exposure for their story.

My new full-time hobby was enjoyable and I was good at it, but I needed to defray some costs. I started selling sponsorship banner ads and then I wondered if a business opportunity was right in front of me.

To test the waters, for $3,000 a year I offered to rotate a company's banner ad with a link to their website. As a bonus I would email and post on the website a snapshot of the company's stock structure, project descriptions, trading history and other details. I would not post any stock price targets and there had to be a notice that a fee was paid.

The first company that called me for advertising wanted to go over the offer and price. I hesitantly mentioned $3,000, assuming that he wanted to beat this amount down. Before I could say per year, he replied that $3k a month sounds about right.

When I told him this was for an entire year, he replied ok send me a 12-month contract for $36,000. What the heck I thought, let's go with this new pricing structure!

The second call came a month later as a referral, from where I didn't know. I had to drop the minimum contract time to 3-months, but within half a year I had five to ten contracts at most times.

Not only was the cash tumbling in, these companies started flying me to conventions and corporate functions. I quickly developed an enviable contact network of analysts, financiers, market makers, geologists, promoters and investor relations groups.

The learning curve was fast and steep and I knew some controls were needed. I started to pick and choose clients, which meant turning away business. I developed a corporate filtering system needed to keep bad deals with risky prospects or seedy reputations away.

All small cap stocks are risky, but most don't understand how risky they really are. I wanted to be an advocate for small investors, to at least point out obvious red flags they needed to know. *After following hundreds of small cap stocks, I can count on one hand the plays that have turned into real businesses with long-term value*.

They can be traded profitably, but even if you know what you are doing it is gambling at best. These companies are almost never profitable businesses, or ever will be! Even if they are, common shareholders don't realize any value most of the time. In short, *small cap stocks are funding and trading vehicles, for insiders to unload worthless paper shares*.

From my time commitment and information value perspective on small cap stocks, it is somewhat ironic that the stocks I have made money on did not have the best potential. Like most small cap so-called investors, I held on to promising stocks and traded the less promising stocks for quick profits.

I usually went for investing home runs instead of trading base hits. I've had dozens of ten or more baggers, ten times my investment, that I have let ride and eventually evaporate in value because I believed too much in the company.

I could pick them better than most, but was as guilty as the next guy of not *valuing need over greed, or fear*. Eventually I learned that *for small cap stocks, the deal is more important than value*.

The fundamentals of small cap stocks have more to do with corporate structure, financing and promotion than any underlying business value. No matter how valuable these companies seem, you don't want to be caught holding if the insiders have sold their shares. Similarly I have seen deals that have gone bust, but I knew insiders and promoters were still pregnant with the stock and might want to come up with a plan B.

I have seen good deals go bad due to lack of funding, and bad deals turn good because insiders were connected and could finance a future deal. A mining play in South America turns into a diamond play in Canada or a dot com company, depending on what small cap stock sector or area play is hot and attracting attention at the moment.

When, not if, a deal blows up, if the insiders have distributed most of their stock, they usually roll back or consolidate the share structure to fund the next deal. I've had stocks that have been rolled back and renamed several times, resulting in 1 new share for every 10, 20 or even 100 old shares each time. Others have simply de-listed and are worthless.

Consolidation dilutes shareholder value as the stock price almost always falls again to pennies, where insiders then issue themselves cheap new shares. As private placement funding concludes, the promotion phase then shifts into high gear again, with your new breakeven price now at meteoric heights.

The insider stock distribution phase is the last part of the cycle, when small investors usually buy-in. *Follow what insiders do, not what they say!*

However there are limits on how many times even small cap investors are willing to get burned. Management is everything and past success attracts investor attention and easier funding. *Small cap stocks are not businesses; they are simply stock deals that rarely have any real fundamental investment value.*

To cap my good luck run of three, my personal stock portfolio was growing leaps and bounds - on paper! In addition I was invited to join the board of directors of an African gold and diamond exploration company and also a new dot com company.

The exploration company was an exciting speculation based on past property values. The stock traded from .15 to over $2, but I lost money in the end because I was too close and focused on the wrong values. I believed in the story but reminded the other directors of the importance to secure funding. Unfortunately I did not heed my own advice!

The company had several solid funding options but decided instead to go with our sponsoring brokerage firm after they supposedly guaranteed to raise all the money we needed. The company seemed destined for the big time once this funding was secured.

I warned the other directors to secure the first funding we could get, as we were being heavily shorted on each price and volume increase. They didn't seem concerned because our sponsor promised our money was coming.

To be sure I called the brokerage firm and asked like any investor, how I could get some of that stock they were underwriting. I was shocked when the broker replied that he checked around the firm and nobody had ever heard of a new stock issuance for that company.

I knew this was a serious red flag but continued to hold, believing other financings would still be available. It was not proven but appears that our sponsoring brokerage firm never had any intention to fund the company, as they were who was shorting us all along.

The cancelled funding announcement cut our stock price in half overnight. On every rally higher, the stock exchange would halt trading for a few days, for no other reason than to inquire why it was going up.

The company had to issue news releases that they didn't know why the stock was active, confusing shareholders even more. Long story short it de-listed a year later and we were pretty sure who asked the exchange to keep halting us.

I decided not to join the board of the other company because it had no chance of success. The CEO first approached me with his idea of a pretzel franchise that I knew had no appeal to investors, market makers or for funding. I refused the company as a client and told him to change the name to something dot com and let me know how it worked out.

I never expected to hear from him again, but two weeks later he called back after doing exactly what I suggested. He wanted me to be the new CEO and offered 50% of the company, equal to 50-million shares. This obviously got my attention and I knew of several internet deals that had more potential than most other dot coms out there.

The company had shareholder loans on the books, and the stock's trading volume was dead in water at a nickel a share. There were no assets, cash, staff or even a business plan to build on. The stock had been rolled back and renamed several times already, and I was concerned about potential directors liability from any past skeletons in their closet.

I turned down being a director, so he instead offered to buy my website for the same share consideration. I would still develop and drive their business plan as my profitable dot com website would become their first acquisition. This actually made some sense.

The stock was still a worthless shell, with the deal being far from clean or tight. There were almost 60-million shares issued and my 50-million new shares would increase this to almost 110-million. However the company had over 3,000 shareholders, with his family controlling most of the outstanding stock, and the dot com market was red hot.

Rather than specializing, I suggested a buckshot dot com incubator approach to improve our odds of attracting deals for stock, cash funding and investor attention. The concept might work like it had for other dot coms. I suggested that if we were lucky we could attract some funding if the stock traded up to .25 over the next year.

Before the company had even announced its plans, the stock started trading several hundred thousand shares a day at around .08. The day after the news release, the stock was trading millions of shares at over .50. The market was valuing the company at over $50 million dollars based on only a business plan, before it had raised a dime.

Everything was backwards during the dot com frenzy. Instead of ready-aim-fire, fire-aim-ready worked just as well. Instead of business plan, funding, acquisitions and growth, dot coms could grow, acquire, fund and then put together a business plan. ***Companies and deals were thrown together in days instead of developing over years!***

On the announcement of my site being acquired, the stock shot up to $2. We were a $200 million company and we still had not raised a dime. After the stock settled down close to $1, a barrage of brokerage firms offered to raise millions for us in bought share deals.

Not only was there enough cash to open an office, our stock could be used as currency to attract and acquire other deals. I suggested we kill three birds with one stone by acquiring various dot com businesses for stock, hiring their talented programmers and graphic designers, and announcing each acquisition which represented growth.

The stock received press as another up and coming dot com success, and it seemed like we knew what we were doing. In actuality there was a constant race just to hold things together long enough to announce new deals. For example, the company quietly had to pay someone 50,000 shares to buy back its dot com name to save face as the CEO forgot to register it before announcing the name in a press release.

The company purchased gaming, financial and community forum sites and developed its own meta-search engine. We looked at developing or buying online shopping and auction sites to mass merchandise specialty items. We were negotiating with the agent of a well-known celebrity to be the spokesperson for the company, like other dot coms had done.

Within a couple of months the stock traded from under $2 to over $5 and a few months later to over $6. At the peak the market valued the company at $600 million, with just a few million cash in the treasury and almost no revenue other than share issuances. Employees became paper millionaires and my stock grew to around USD $300 million.

The company had a real shot at a senior stock listing which would attract fund buying and analyst coverage. However the CEO, who could barely turn on a computer, started believing investors and brokers that were saying he was an internet genius.

His ego simply confused brains with a bull market and he lost sight of building business value. Brokers were constantly buttering him up on travel junkets to pitch their services in return for millions of cheap shares. I knew these were players and the stock would just end up immediately back into the market and I strongly advised against it.

I was working at least 16-hours a day driving the business plan, but forgot to fully protect my upside. The CEO went against my advice and issued his new friends millions of cheap shares. I lost faith in our prospects and wanted my shares issued as well, but did not get them. The deal was never real and any value I helped create was in jeopardy.

A lawyer charged me $7,500 to write a demand letter for my shares. I decided not to sue after his second $7,500 bill; realizing legal costs would probably be hundreds of thousands and by the time I won the company wouldn't be worth anything. Been there, done that already!

Sure enough, within months the stock had fallen apart. Various deals unravelled and the team of programmers I had put together quit. The bucket shop brokerage firms probably made millions, while vested employees, average shareholders and I got wiped out. A year later the stock consolidated 1 new for 60 old shares and was renamed again.

The CEO probably made out like a bandit, but doesn't even realize the potential he left on the table. I did ok and chalk this up as another value lesson. I have occasional what-if moments when I think about how well our business plan was working, at a time before Google, eBay and PartyPoker became household names.

In January 2001 I wrote my email list and posted on the website that I was shutting everything down in May. I didn't want to lose the income but honestly I could not see any value in the market for at least the next 4-years. I said that I expected the dot com bubble to burst by May, around when stocks usually tend to sell off after the winter run.

In fact the sell-off happened in March that year, so I was close. I calculated the fair value of the Dow Jones Industrial average at 8,500 at a time when stocks were rocking and the DJIA trading at over 11,000. It actually sold off and touched 8,500 on two occasions since then, and 5-years later the Dow was still around 11,000.

Earnings have caught up over the past 5-years and I calculate the Dow's fair value is now around 10,700. With the current political uncertainty in the world, $75 oil prices, higher inflation and interest rates and a lower expected US dollar all working through the system, I wouldn't be surprised to see the Dow breakdown to 9,500 again.

Cash has been king for me over the last 5-years with money market investments, and some silver, making up the bulk of my portfolio. On an actual return basis and especially risk adjusted, safe yielding cash outperformed the stock and bond markets and still is.

I am starting again to gradually build positions of the value stock selector top 5 stocks during periods of market weakness. If the Dow does sell-off to 9,500, my asset allocation would probably shift quickly from 20% to 80% stocks.

My last email also mentioned to watch for bull markets in oil, gold and industrial metals to lead the way. Commodities usually leg up first for a few years, signalling the next bull stock market, the cycle often ending in recession just before the next presidential change.

This is happening right on queue and as housing prices continue to soften there will be a further shift to metals and then stocks as capital always seeks the best yield. Higher interest rates take 18-months to impact the economy, with the smart money leaving speculative real estate in 2004 and 2005.

Before the Democrats take back the White House, I see oil at over $100 per barrel. If it stays there for a year, gold should trade up to its historic 15:1 ratio or $1,500 an ounce or higher! I also believe silver may move to a 40:1 or at least 50:1 ratio with gold, or $30 to $40 an ounce. However I don't want to fool myself thinking that it's different this time, so I'll hold off on predicting an extended metals bull market beyond 2008 for now.

***

To keep busy between market cycles, in 2001 I bought an area franchise for one of the world's largest business services networks. The cash flow and return at my level and higher levels of the franchise was very good, unfortunately not so good for franchisees.

I now know this is typical for most franchises. Independent business owners and franchisees both risk their savings and loan capital and devote all of their time and effort to build a dream business. However a franchise system may end up costing more in many ways, compared to doing it on your own. *Franchises usually result in surrendering control of your wealth destiny to a system designed to collect royalties and dictate rules*.

Business survival stats for franchises, versus independent businesses, seem impressive. However this can be misleading and doesn't factor in replacement franchisees when the first franchisee goes bust. Franchises come and go and even those considered successful often stay open mainly because new franchisees are available to replace old ones.

People buy franchises to protect their downside. They offer an established business format, easier financing, training and assistance. However the majority of value a franchisee receives is front-loaded, while royalties continue forever. In short *franchises offer the illusion of safety but really just limit your upside, like buying a job*.

Fees, training and royalties are expensive and never end. Franchisees expect economies of scale to produce lower construction, upgrades, equipment, marketing, advertising and supplier costs. Instead *costs are usually higher than independent businesses receive*.

Royalties are an added expense paid every month, based on a percentage of top line gross sales, whether or not the business makes a bottom line profit. From gas stations to fast food, *franchisors make risk free money while franchisees take all the risks*.

Franchisors have almost total control and can change the rules if franchisees somehow start making more than a survival wage. As far as fees, royalties, kickbacks and other costs, *franchisees get hit when they enter, exit and every time in between*.

Like any investment there are good and bad franchises. The point is to not assume anything! At the bottom of your long list of questions to ask any franchisees that feel safe enough to talk to you, make sure you ask if they would do it again!

When I owned and operated independent businesses, I envied franchisees with modern stores, national advertising and customers lined up accordingly. After owning a franchise and an area franchise I now know *the grass is not always greener on the other side*.

Franchisees borrow and pay a relative fortune for a business. Franchisees own the depreciating assets, while the franchisor owns the valuable assets. Rent is often higher than what you might be able to negotiate on your own, while the lease and franchise agreements allow the franchisor to seize control of your investment if royalties or fees are ever late, or for any number of other reasons!

Franchise outlets always look new because franchisors require franchisees to pay the cost of regular brand image upgrades. We changed from yellow to red this year, here's your $120,000 bill and we expect a check or your store keys within 30-days. I'm exaggerating, but this can happen. The point is that *your needs are not valued, just the system's needs*.

Be wary of things already worked out for you! Franchisees usually can't negotiate product costs or who they buy from. Retail prices and profit margins are usually dictated, with hidden franchisor kickbacks often built in. Franchisees don't control procedures or marketing and are not able to take advantage of so-called unapproved opportunities.

The flexibility I had to adapt my businesses and to market changes would not have been available under a uniform franchise system. They do work out most of the bugs that may save you much trial and error frustration, however *make sure that all franchise costs are reasonable and know that simplicity really means loss of flexibility*.

In the end I decided to sell as the franchise was mentally stuck in neutral, which is like reverse in business. Area franchisee cash flow and value was there, but I didn't believe in the franchisor's management methods. Until the franchisor realizes the need for real value to exist at the franchisee level, how could overall system growth plans succeed!

Franchisees pay our returns and are the lifeblood of the system, but the franchisor didn't get this. Good intentions need to translate into tangible franchisee value instead of just lip service; otherwise the trend of high franchisee turnover and just as many franchises closing as opening continues. Instead of these anti-growth trends being perceived as a business model problem, they were simply seen as additional resale fee opportunities.

***

As you can see my personal, business and investment background is varied, providing many different wealth value perspectives. I'm sure you can identify with some of my experiences and hopefully this translates into ideas to refine your own value perspectives towards developing a balanced and focused life wealth plan.

To achieve reasonable wealth goals, a wealth plan is needed. The steps you take along the way are just as important as the destination. My grandmother used to say *the devil is in the details* and in math *showing your work is often more important than having the right answers*. Thomas Edison used to say *genius is 1% inspiration and 99% perspiration*.

I fully believe that kids need to have reasonable responsibilities at an early age, to experience and learn from the ups and downs that are involved. They need to appreciate the input value of work and the output value of rewards for a job well done. Dad often said that *anything worth doing is worth doing well!*

I try and take time to explain to my children the value of planning, saving, investing, paying off debt and why things are done a certain way. I explain the value of hard and especially smart work and that simple responsibilities like cleaning the dishes or their room, yard work and homework help shape their future wealth attitudes and behaviour.

When they want things out of the ordinary, they know I will ask what their value perspective is and why this is needed. They know that *true wealth comes from value, the freedom of being in control and focusing on needs before wants*.

Extravagant wealth is not needed and surplus good fortune offers better value helping others with real needs. We are all fortunate where we live and need to help those who were not born as lucky. *Generosity offers value but must also be given responsibly*.

Dad would say that *charity starts at home*. If we were more responsible managing our bountiful resources, we not only would insure our own wealth and to be able to help with extended family needs, there would also be surpluses to help others in need. Dad would have shared our pride on Matthew's eighth birthday, as he decided to donate all of his presents to the children's hospital because he had more toys than needed.

My wife and I budget time and money for certain charities that demonstrate a reasonably low percentage spent on marketing and administration versus the needed cause. I also coached my son's soccer team until recently and now mentor young entrepreneurs who qualify under a government loan program similar to my first business loan.

Both of our basic cars are over 6-years old and I have never owned a new one, but my wife and I have provided family loans, mortgage down payments, education funding and honeymoon cruises. However we won't throw our hard earned money away to back a family member's bad investment decision, especially if we advised against it!

I have learned the hard way what dad meant by *the quickest way to lose a friend is to loan him money* and *don't confuse the word loan with give*. Dad would also say *don't go shopping if you are hungry* and *on-sale equals spend unless you already needed it*.

Dad would say that *most people are not wealthy because they don't practice wealthy habits!* Achieving wealth becomes easy as soon as you decide to break out of your comfort zone, put together your excel wealth plan and make reasonable adjustments! A wealthy mindset starts as you *think about and plan your wealth future!*

I may have embellished a bit in my examples, but not too far. I hope you found some thought provoking value in this book and will use my excel tools provided to develop your own wealth plan. In summary, my value perspectives are listed below.

My Value Perspectives growing up:

- ➢ waste not, want not
- ➢ large amounts of wealth start with small amounts of savings
- ➢ easy and sure opportunities should not be squandered
- ➢ every journey, no matter how long, has a starting point!
- ➢ if you take care of the pennies, the dollars take care of themselves
- ➢ if you are given everything you want, you won't learn how to get what you really need
- ➢ turn lemons into lemonade
- ➢ learning comes from doing
- ➢ persuasive negotiation and little extras add up over time
- ➢ people prefer to do business with people they like
- ➢ easier said than done
- ➢ you need to work smart!
- ➢ break the problem down, think about it while putting yourself in the other guy's shoes
- ➢ act only when you have a solution
- ➢ it's not how much you make, but how much you save that makes you wealthy
- ➢ save for a rainy day
- ➢ a penny saved is a penny earned
- ➢ if you save today, you will have what you need tomorrow
- ➢ kids just need to experience, to appreciate and develop wealthy habits

- ➤ kids need to learn about money
- ➤ money isn't everything
- ➤ if you start something, you should be prepared to finish it
- ➤ think outside the box
- ➤ giving people what they want sometimes gives you what you need
- ➤ the first offer is usually the best one
- ➤ discipline and self-control needs to overcome reckless impulses
- ➤ success is not always fair, you need to know how to play the game
- ➤ you don't know what you don't know
- ➤ I've never owned a car that has gone up in value

My Value Perspectives when starting my first business:

- ➤ a business is like a marriage
- ➤ decision makers are the most valuable customers, even more than the person paying
- ➤ banks don't lend when you need money, only when you have money
- ➤ turn weaknesses into strengths
- ➤ contracts are valuable only when both parties are reasonably happy with the terms
- ➤ the legal system is inept in enforcing business contracts
- ➤ avoid doing business with unreasonable people
- ➤ contracts are like paper money, simply a promise to pay
- ➤ the power is where the money is
- ➤ he who has the gold, makes all the rules
- ➤ businesses can build wealth value, but only if the terms are reasonable and you are totally committed!

> ➢ there is an easy and a hard way to do things
> ➢ think long and hard before acting on your impulses

My Value Perspectives from stockbroker to speculator to investor:

> ➢ dialling for dollars is the name of the game
> ➢ just smile and put some lipstick on this pig
> ➢ stockbrokers are under various pressures to produce results that may conflict with your wealth goals
> ➢ client's value brokers as personal wealth managers
> ➢ firms value them only as salesmen, asset gatherers and distributors of financial products
> ➢ brokers have to find a home for cold stock issues to have any real chance of receiving hot IPO's
> ➢ it's just a numbers game
> ➢ churn-em and burn-em
> ➢ you can shear a sheep for life, but you can only skin it once
> ➢ customer service, satisfaction and portfolio performance is irrelevant; as long as new accounts, deposits, transfers and commissions keep rolling along
> ➢ high rolling superstar brokers become unemployed liabilities in a heartbeat
> ➢ the only investment value of options is writing slightly out of the money covered-calls
> ➢ covered calls should only be done on quality stocks you would hold anyway
> ➢ futures are simply a crapshoot that investors should avoid!

- as your resources and options become limited, and future opportunities seem less predictable, anxiety and stress build
- the bond game is all about investment safety and yield!
- good and bad luck runs in threes
- you must always be prepared for the unexpected
- you need to position yourself to protect your upside just as much as your downside
- don't assume anything
- the right way doesn't work in this business
- speculations are perceived as investments when greed and fear overcome rational thinking and recognizing real business value
- for short-term profits, you should never fight the tape
- market makers love momentum traders and take opposite positions
- charts and technical trading patterns give important clues to a stocks short-term direction, but have nothing to do with the long-term intrinsic value of an investment
- insider trading affects all stocks and if you are not inside, you are outside
- current stock prices try to predict future events
- rules are broken and short-term prices are unreliable, while recognizing long-term value is the safest way to make investment decisions
- small cap stocks tend to run from January to April, hence the saying sell in May and go away
- put all these pieces of the puzzle together like a story
- small cap stock plays are attractive only when the story is still in the early stages and the promotion cycle hasn't ended

- ➢ stock prices rise with expectations of positive news, plus above average trading volume.
- ➢ however it only takes a lack of news, or low trading volume, for prices to fall!
- ➢ for small cap stocks there is no fundamental value other than the public value perception of the story
- ➢ small cap stocks are simply promotions as insiders, tout sheets and other shareholders often say buy at the same time they are selling or shorting stock to you
- ➢ small cap stocks are musical chairs that almost always get pulled from under you as the promotion cycle ends
- ➢ for low-quality high-risk small caps, analyzing the story, buying low and avoiding losses are the key values to overall and consistent trading performance
- ➢ small cap stock trading is gambling, driven by greed and fear
- ➢ buy on mystery and sell on history
- ➢ brokers operate in a fish bowl and should not be buying speculative stocks
- ➢ there is never just one cockroach when material errors surface, such as accounting irregularities or fraudulent drill results
- ➢ there are too many reasons why small cap stocks are simply not a reasonable investment
- ➢ the best way to achieve wealth is to avoid losses and compound returns safely
- ➢ almost anyone with a common sense understanding of real value can outperform most financial experts
- ➢ wealth education is as important to value as any other type of education
- ➢ know-your-client

- you can't make demands or pray with conditions
- the whole point of prayer and faith is accepting that you will receive the help you need, not necessarily what you want
- recommendations and opinions on most stocks have conflicts, both big and small caps
- it's different this time; words that investors should always be wary of
- the stock market shell game repeats with every bull market cycle!
- bull markets change investor perception, but not intrinsic values
- don't confuse brains with a bull market
- intrinsic value eventually wins and determines a stock's real worth!
- invest, don't speculate!
- after following hundreds of small cap stocks, I can count on one hand the plays that have turned into real businesses with long-term value
- small cap stocks are funding and trading vehicles, for insiders to unload worthless paper
- value need over greed, or fear
- for small cap stocks, the deal is more important than value
- when, not if, a deal blows up, if the insiders have distributed most of their stock, they usually roll back or consolidate the share structure to fund the next deal
- follow what insiders do, not what they say!
- small cap stocks are not businesses, they are simply stock deals that rarely have any real fundamental investment value

➢ everything was backwards during the dot com frenzy
➢ companies and deals were thrown together in days instead of developing over years!

My Value Perspectives on franchises:

➢ franchises usually result in surrendering control of your wealth destiny to a system designed to collect royalties and dictate rules
➢ franchises offer the illusion of safety but really just limit your upside, like buying a job
➢ fees, training and royalties are expensive and never end
➢ costs are usually higher than independent businesses receive
➢ franchisors make risk free money while franchisees take all the risks
➢ franchisors have almost total control and can change the rules if franchisees somehow start making more than a survival wage
➢ franchisees get hit when they enter, exit and every time in between
➢ the grass is not always greener on the other side
➢ franchisees borrow and pay a relative fortune for a business
➢ franchisees own the depreciating assets, while the franchisor owns the valuable assets
➢ your needs are not valued, just the system's needs
➢ be wary of things already worked out for you!
➢ make sure that all franchise costs are reasonable and know that simplicity really means loss of flexibility

My Value Perspectives in general:

- ➢ the devil is in the details
- ➢ showing your work is often more important than having the right answers
- ➢ genius is 1% inspiration and 99% perspiration
- ➢ anything worth doing is worth doing well!
- ➢ true wealth comes from value, the freedom of being in control and focusing on needs before wants
- ➢ generosity offers value but must also be given responsibly
- ➢ charity starts at home
- ➢ the quickest way to lose a friend is to loan him money
- ➢ don't confuse the word loan with give
- ➢ don't go shopping if you are hungry
- ➢ on-sale equals spend unless you already needed it
- ➢ most people are not wealthy because they don't practice wealthy habits!
- ➢ think about and plan your wealth future!

Limit of Liability / Disclaimer of Warranty

While the publisher and author have used their best efforts in preparing this book and its companion excel spreadsheets, they make no representations or warranties with respect to the accuracy or completeness of the contents of this book and its companion excel spreadsheets, and specifically disclaim any implied warranties of merchantability or fitness for a particular purpose. No warranty may be created or extended by sales representatives or written sales materials. The advice, examples and strategies contained herein may not be suitable for your situation. You should consult with a professional where appropriate. Neither the publisher nor the author shall be liable for any loss of profit or any other commercial damages, including but not limited to special, incidental, consequential, or other damages.